Fort Reno and the Indian Territory Frontier

Fort Reno
and the
Indian Territory
Frontier

STAN HOIG

The University of Arkansas Press
Fayetteville
2000

04   03   02   01   00   5   4   3   2   1

Designed by Liz Lester

☉   The paper used in this publication meets the minimum require-
ments of the American National Standard for Permanence of Paper for
Printed Library Materials Z39.48–1984.

Library of Congress Cataloging-in-Publication Data

Hoig, Stan.
       Fort Reno and the Indian Territory frontier / Stan Hoig.
           p.   cm.
       Includes bibliographical references and index.
           ISBN 1-55728-622-1 (alk. paper)
           1. Fort Reno (Okla.)—History. 2. El Reno Region (Okla.)—
       History. 3. Frontier and pioneer life—Oklahoma—El Reno
       Region. 4. Cheyenne Indians—Oklahoma—Government
       relations. 5. Arapaho Indians—Oklahoma—Government
       relations. 6. Land settlement—Oklahoma—History. I. Title.
           F704.F69 H65 2000
           976.6'39—dc21   00-010164

It is entirely fitting that this book should be dedicated to the man who epitomized the role of Fort Reno in the history of western Indian Territory, who helped bridge the societal gap between tribal Americans and the white community of the region, who performed so very many difficult and hazardous duties in behalf of the military and the Cheyenne and Arapaho Indians, and whose highly respected presence extended from beginning to end of the one-time cavalry post. This, of course, would be the noted scout, interpreter, and plainsman Benjamin Clark.

CONTENTS

PREFACE

This book is indebted to a number of people who contributed to its creation. First I wish to credit Bob Schulz, board of directors of the Oklahoma Historical Society, for suggesting a need for the book and a general scheme of approach; and Dr. Bob Blackburn, director of the Oklahoma Historical Society, who lent his personal and professional encouragement to the project.

Dr. Jack L. Whenry, whose heart and soul are intimately connected to Fort Reno, the place where he grew up and spent his Huck Finn days, provided not only a great deal of research help but also inspiration.

There are many others who were of great help in my research of Fort Reno and Darlington. These include George Wint, former Director at Darlington; Jerry Quisenberry, laboratory director, Fort Reno; Connie Hart Yellowman of the Fort Reno Visitors' Center; Carolyn Barker, who has so diligently researched El Reno newspapers; Dianne Costin and Debbie Elmenhorst of the El Reno Carnegie Library; David Williams, Nicole Willard, Equalla Brothers, and Annette Ryan of the University of Central Oklahoma Library and Oklahoma Collection; Bill Welge, director of the Oklahoma Historical Society Archives and Manuscripts Division, and his staff; Fred Standley of the Oklahoma Historical Society Library; John Lovett of the University of Oklahoma Western History Collection; Mrs. Clyde Meschberger of Calumet, Oklahoma; Towanda Spivey, director, and Ann Davies, curator, of the Fort Sill Museum; Sarah Erwin, curator of Archival Collections, Gilcrease Institute; Mary Erskin of Alva; Western history scholar Wayne Kime; and a couple of modern-day saddle mates who helped me scout out some historical sites, Alvin Alcorn and Jack Hoffman.

As always, I am immensely indebted to my wife, Patricia Corbell Hoig, for her work in reading, editing, and improving this manuscript.

PROLOGUE

A Fort for All Seasons

Possibly more than any post on the Western frontier, Fort Reno, Indian Territory, served as a regulatory force between the Indian and the white man. Originally established to protect the white man from the Indian, it also functioned as the primary arm of government for restraining land-hungry whites from invading country once solemnly promised to the Indian by treaty.

Fort Reno came into being in 1875 following the Indian outbreak of 1874, commonly known as the Red River War. Its original assignment was to exercise control over the Cheyenne and Arapaho Indians, whose agency on the opposite bank of the North Canadian River preceded the fort by four years. But Fort Reno also played other important roles. For many years its military marshaled over a large portion of the outlaw-ridden Indian Territory, including the heavily traveled Chisholm Cattle Trail. During this time, the post served as an embryonic frontier settlement around which the first trappings of Anglo-American society began to develop.

As pressure grew to settle the lands of Indian Territory, however, Fort Reno's military became the government's principal means of restraining early intruders. Then, when the great land openings took place, its troops were used to monitor successive invasions by U.S. citizens. After settlement was done, the Fort Reno military acted to resolve disputes arising between whites and resident Indians.

Most of these needs were dissolved with the formation of the new Territory of Oklahoma and introduction of civil law, forcing Fort Reno to seek a renewal of purpose. This came early in the twentieth century when the former frontier post was transformed into a cavalry remount center. As such, its horse- and mule-filled pastures presented a visual reflection of the day when the military and society in general depended so heavily upon animal transportation.

Mechanization of the military finally brought an end to the romantic old horse cavalry and the demise of Fort Reno as a military post. No more poignant finale could be found for Fort Reno than the despairing but prideful image of Ben Clark, the longtime scout who had ridden with Custer in 1868 and outlived the frontier he knew and loved, ending his own life before a mirror in 1914.

Clark, who with his wife and children is buried in the Fort Reno cemetery, is but one in the cornucopia of memories that haunt the grounds of Fort Reno. There are so many others: blue-coated troopers riding forth in double column to unknown adventures; stately, blanket-clad Indian chiefs arriving to smoke their calumets and declare, as only they could, their great love of the land; dusty herds of Texas cattle bawling their way past the fort to Kansas markets; lumbering bull trains carrying their fare between the Indian agencies and Kansas railheads; indignant but determined Oklahoma boomers being ushered into the post behind army wagons; the sounds of military drills and bugle calls that reverberated across the North Canadian valley to where the Darlington Indian agency sat quietly surrounded by shining white tepees and where dedicated missionaries taught Indian youngsters the rudiments of white society; gala Fourth of July celebrations with exciting horse races and jubilant intercompany contests; dressy Christmas and New Year social balls; and scores of other events and people that shaped the unique, colorful era of Fort Reno amid the robust American West of Indian Territory.

It is to these memories and many others that this book addresses itself.

CHAPTER 1

Agency on the North Canadian

The War Department founded Fort Reno primarily to provide military protection and enforcement for the Cheyenne and Arapaho agency, which had been established earlier on the banks of the North Canadian River. In essence, however, its existence contradicted the underlying concept of the then-Quaker-operated Indian Bureau, that of dealing with the native tribes through brotherly love. But dark events had shaped the course of Indian-white relations and challenged the view that loving friendship and mutual trust alone could solve the difficult problems that were spawned by white intrusion onto Indian lands.

Beset by rising complaints against the army's handling of Indian affairs, in 1869 newly elected President Ulysses S. Grant turned the nation's Indian problem over to the Society of Friends. Grant hoped that the Quakers could exercise the same benevolent regard that had worked so well for their illustrious predecessor, William Penn, in his dealings with the Leni-Lenape Indians of Pennsylvania during colonial times. For Grant it was a much appreciated opportunity to lay the Indian problem squarely on the shoulders of the so-called olive-branchers of the day.

Grant named Col. Ely S. Parker, a Seneca tribesman, a Quaker, and his former army aide-de-camp, as commissioner of Indian Affairs. In turn, Parker appointed members of the Society of Friends to the task of dealing directly with the various Indian tribes of the nation. Iowa Quaker Brinton Darlington was named as agent for the Cheyenne and Arapaho Indians who had been assigned a reservation in Indian Territory by the Treaty of Medicine Lodge of 1867.

The mild-mannered Darlington had reached sixty-five years of age when he arrived in Indian Territory in the summer of 1869 and was by no means in strong physical condition.[1] Further, he had under-taken a challenging new mission in life, one for which he had little qualification other than his deep religious faith as a Quaker. He was to be, by his own choosing, the government agent for the two tribes who had long been allied. Darlington had never met a Plains Indian, spoke neither the Cheyenne nor Arapaho language, and knew nothing of their culture or history.

During the spring of 1869, Darlington traveled with his son-in-law Jesse R. Townsend to Lawrence, Kansas, then the terminus of the Kansas Pacific Railroad. There the men learned that the new Cheyenne and Arapaho reservation straddled the Kansas–Indian Territory border. A site for the new agency had been selected at a wild, uninhabited location on Round Pond Creek some twenty-five miles inside Indian Territory.[2]

Gen. William B. Hazen, who had been among the tribes at Fort

Kindly Brinton Darlington quickly won the affection of his Indian charges. *Courtesy Archives/Manuscript Division, Oklahoma Historical Society.*

Cobb in the territory, held strong misgivings about the site. He pointed out that while good buffalo and mosquito grass covered the reservation, the area embraced the Salt Plains, causing streams to be very salty and offering very little fresh water anywhere that was fit to use. The Indians did not like the location of the new reservation, and Hazen did not think it would be suitable for them.[3] "I have been fearful from the first," Hazen wrote to Indian Superintendent Enoch Hoag at Lawrence, "that the Reservation assigned these people [the Cheyennes and Arapahos] will not answer. They objected to it at first, and why not give them some voice in where they shall go . . . Why not let them go on the North Fork of the Canadian where they ask to go?"[4]

Darlington, however, was anxious to get started, and he had no choice but to follow the dictates of the Medicine Lodge treaty. At Lawrence, he purchased a wagon, tools, and other supplies. The army offered to provide military escort for him into the territory, but Darlington opted in favor of godly protection and with Townsend set off bravely through the searing July heat into the still dangerous land of the Indians.

At Round Pond Creek, the two Quakers began industriously felling trees, digging a well, starting two log cabins, and breaking the virgin soil to sow a stand of corn. These things done, they waited impatiently for the Indians to arrive. Not a single tribesman appeared. When General Hazen visited the site in mid-July, he found the two men discouraged, weary of waiting, and anxious to get the agency in operation.

Capt. Seth Bonney, Camp Supply officer in charge of issuing rations to the bands that had come in to that post, seconded Hazen's estimate of the site's poor quality. "The Indians are all quite well satisfied with the arrangement here," Bonney reported, "but all the Cavalry in the Department cannot drive them to where Agent Darlington is in my opinion, for they would scatter to the four winds."[5]

Lt. Col. Anderson D. Nelson, commanding Camp Supply, ordered Lt. Silas Pepoon to conduct a reconnaissance of north-central Indian Territory for a choice site to locate the agency and possibly a new fort.[6] Pepoon's detachment of twenty-six Tenth Cavalry troops and five Arapaho guides arrived at Round Pond Creek in July. Pepoon found that Darlington and Townsend had finished their two log cabins, one of which was to serve as a warehouse for Indian annuities, and had dug a well. The few acres of corn that had been planted long out of season were badly burned and stunted.

Continuing on, Pepoon located three sites other than Round Pond Creek. One was a location on the North Canadian 105 miles downriver from Supply; one at the juncture of Hackberry and Skeleton Creek; and another on Bluff Creek. Bluff Creek, with its waterfalls and good stands of timber, was his first choice, though it would prove to be too close to the Osages for the Cheyennes and Arapahos, who feared for their families and their horses. Despite its spring, timber, and level bottomland, Pepoon ranked the North Canadian as his third choice.[7]

On July 30, Hoag forwarded Hazen's recommendation requesting that the two tribes be relocated on the North Canadian to Commissioner of Indian Affairs Parker.[8] As a result, the president issued a proclamation canceling the former reservation and creating a new one of five million acres between the Cherokee Outlet of northern Indian Territory and the Kiowa-Comanche and Wichita reservations to the south, extending from present central Oklahoma to the Texas Panhandle.[9]

During early August, Quaker commissioners John Butler, Achilles Pugh, and Thomas Stanley left Topeka for Indian Territory in a buggy and wagon. They were accompanied by a driver and by Indian trader William "Dutch Bill" Greiffenstein—soon to become the principal founder of Wichita, Kansas—whom they had hired as a guide and interpreter.[10]

At the foundling settlement of Wichita, a messenger from General Hazen met the party. Hazen requested that they go to Round Pond Creek and escort Darlington to Camp Supply, where he could begin issuing annuity goods to his charges. Upon reaching Camp Supply on August 10, the men were met by a three-man presidential commission —Felix R. Brunot, Nathan Bishop, and W. E. Dodge—that had arrived via Forts Harker and Dodge. After an interview with Cheyenne chief Medicine Arrow, both groups visited the Cheyenne camp of 270 lodges that stood along Wolf Creek seven miles above its juncture with the Beaver. The commissioners then moved on to Fort Sill for talks with the Kiowas and Comanches.[11]

During the last of August, Darlington wrote to Hoag stating his dire need for an interpreter as well as for six strong teams of horses and two wagons with which to relocate his agency. Hoag responded. He sent a man from Lawrence with a team and wagon, and Darlington hired Charles Dudley as a clerk to issue rations.[12]

At best, Darlington faced a tenuous situation at Camp Supply. The army still felt strongly that intimidation was far more effective than saintly love in controlling the tribes. But military force had its limitations, as an officer's wife noted when a band of warriors ravaged the post's gardens by dashing their ponies through them. A company of infantry rushed to the gardens, but they were ineffective against the mounted warriors. A troop of cavalry then galloped out; but because of fear of starting an Indian uprising, they were ordered not to fire. The warriors soon realized their advantage and showed little fear.[13]

Darlington complained on August 27 that there was no place he could purchase bread or flour without violating military regulations. To further complicate matters, the annuity goods previously stored at Round Pond Creek had arrived at Supply in worthless condition.[14]

For a time, because he could not pay as much as could the military, he was unable to hire an interpreter and thus was unable to converse with the Indians. He finally secured the services of half-blood Ralph Romero. Upon receiving new instructions by mail regarding the issuance of rations, Darlington wrote on September 1 that he had called to his assistance George Bent and John Simpson Smith, both of whom had been closely associated with the Cheyennes for many years, to explain the matter to the tribes.[15] Chief Little Raven of the Arapahos, he said, complained that the government treated them like animals by feeding them corn that even their horses would not eat.[16]

On September 7, accompanied by Kansas trader W. A. Rankin and a group of Cheyennes and Arapahos, Darlington headed down the North Canadian to the site that Pepoon had visited earlier.[17] On his return, the Quaker agent reported that he had found a place on the North Canadian with good arable bottomland, grass, water, wood, stone to use for buildings, and a good stand of oak timber. He felt the location could provide an eighty-acre farm for every Cheyenne and Arapaho male over eighteen years of age.[18]

Darlington wanted to move his agency from Camp Supply to the new location immediately that fall, but his request was denied. As a result, he waited out the winter at Camp Supply. During that time the

Quaker began to learn some of the unique facts of frontier life. When the army turned the beef issue over to him, he permitted the Indians to kill their own beef. The warriors found it great sport and chased the cattle on the run as they did buffalo, riddling them with arrows and bullets. As a result, the hides were worthless and could not be returned to the commissary office as required by the Military Department of Missouri.[19]

In early November, Darlington conducted a council with the Cheyennes and Arapahos at Camp Supply. It pleased him that the leader of the Cheyenne Dog Soldiers, Bull Bear, attended. Bull Bear, whose son would eventually become one of the first schooled Cheyennes and take up the name of Richard Davis, declared that with each rising of the sun the Cheyennes felt better about the white man.[20]

The agent found that the Indians in his charge were regularly victimized by white horse thieves, whiskey runners, and unprincipled traders from Kansas. Rankin was one of those he found selling ammunition to the tribes. In a letter to Lieutenant Colonel Nelson, Darlington said that Rankin had made himself obnoxious to all within the first twenty-four hours of arriving at Supply. He considered the trader unfit to be in the Indian country.[21]

Because Rankin had been sent by Hoag, however, Darlington had permitted him to visit the new site of the agency. Rankin had tried to bribe Darlington and to lure Townsend into an illegal partnership. Even though Rankin claimed he was working with Kansas congressman Sidney Clarke, Nelson issued orders for him to leave the territory.[22]

First utilization of the Cheyenne/Arapaho agency site took place on March 12 and 13, 1870, prior to construction and occupation, when a big Indian council convened there. The report of the meeting indicated the presence of several Quaker officials and agents, including Darlington, and representatives of the Cheyenne, Kiowa, Comanche, Wichita, Caddo, Keechi, Ioni, Kaw, and Absentee Shawnee tribes. Black Beaver, the famous Delaware frontiersman, attended. Quaker official Thomas Wistar opened the meeting with a prayer, asking that "the Great Spirit spread the mantle of his love over us."[23]

Wistar read a letter addressed to the tribes from Parker. It implored the Indians to remain at peace, take up the pursuit of agriculture, and accept education for their young. A similar message from

The Cheyenne/Arapaho Agency (Darlington) was founded on the North Canadian River during the spring of 1871. *Courtesy, Western History Collections, University of Oklahoma.*

General Hazen was also delivered. Enoch Hoag then made a speech, citing William Penn's ethic of all men living together in peace and the Quaker abhorrence of war.

The chiefs responded in kind. Eas-bah-bee, a young war chief of the Comanches, said that the talk of the white people was also his talk. Ale-go-wah-bu (or Sitting Floating) of the Kaws said that he had been to Washington and had put the words of the Quakers into his pocket to keep. Tinah, head chief of the Caddos, recalled that his people had been promised homes and farms; but when they settled on the Brazos, bad white men got up a war against them, and they were driven in poverty to the Washita. E-su-da-wa of the Wichitas recounted a similar fate for his tribe. "This country all belongs to us (on the Washita)," the chief noted, "but white men are building forts and agency buildings on it. What right have the white people to build houses and forts for themselves in our country, and yet to build none for me?"

Stone Calf, the lone Cheyenne chief in attendance, spoke briefly and indicated that he would agree to settle down and take up farming. Comanche chief Tosewah said that he feared he was almost too old to be a wise man, but he still remembered Texas agent Robert Neighbors, who "taught me on the Brazos when I was young and active, and could chase the buffalo. Now I am old, wrinkled and thin, and my strength has gone, and yet the promises so long made us have not come."[24]

Full-Chief, headman of the Kaws of Kansas, expressed his disappointment that more Cheyennes, with whom his tribe had often warred, were not present. But he warned: "See these old men! They have only one road—the path of peace—but there is a little road beside it—the war path!"[25]

When the council adjourned, a portion of the Quaker delegation accompanied agent Lawrie Tatum to Fort Sill while others proceeded to Camp Supply in hopes of meeting with the Cheyennes and Arapahos. There Cheyenne chief Minimic, or Eagle's Head, told them: "We, the Cheyennes, had never claimed this land. We once lived further north. We did not come here from choice, but we were compelled to come; and if it is best for us to live further down, we will do so and be at peace."[26]

On May 3, 1870, Darlington and a train of wagons loaded with equipment, materials, and supplies under escort of a detachment of cavalry began the journey down along the north bank of the North Canadian. Most of the Cheyennes and Arapahos who had been camped near Camp Supply, including the Cheyenne families of George Bent and Smith, followed along behind. The Indians pitched their camps upstream a distance from the agency site itself. Not liking a location so far away from the buffalo grounds, many of them soon returned to the prairies.[27]

Now began the business of erecting the physical structure of a new agency—houses in which to live, warehouses for the storage of annuity goods, sheds, fences, stables, blacksmith shop, commissary, and eventually a schoolhouse. Darlington very much wanted more ground to be broken as soon as possible so that the first crops could be sown on schedule.[28] He was anxious, also, to build facilities for schooling Indian children. Many of them had died of whooping cough during the winter. Darlington appealed to Hoag for clothes for children who wished to attend school.[29]

Darlington soon assembled his meager staff at his new North Canadian agency. A list of agency employees reveals that those hired in 1870 included Darlington's nephew John F. Williams as blacksmith; John Murphy, commissary helper; Ed O'Leary, chief herder; A. W. Robison, farmer; and Richard Carey, farmer. Jesse Townsend was his issue clerk, and Alfred J. Standing led construction of a schoolhouse, an unpainted cottonwood shack containing a couple of tables and benches. There was no blackboard. Here Indian children were introduced to the new world of formal instruction. Townsend's wife, Elm, who was Darlington's niece, held classes in the school until Julia Cottell, the first paid teacher, was hired in April 1871.[30]

Seeing the need to separate children of the two tribes because of their conflicting attitudes toward schooling, Standing moved the Cheyenne youngsters into one of the dirt-floored and dirt-roofed picket structures. A larger building, spacious and comfortable enough to serve as a dormitory for thirty-five children, was eventually constructed for the Arapahos.

Israel Negus, whose wife, Ruth, came to the agency also, would plow, plant, and instruct the tribesmen in the science of agriculture. Edwin F. Williams was hired as engineer. Additionally there were farmers, farmer's helpers, herders, a night watchman, a baker, a miller, and a supply clerk.[31] Dr. Adolphus Henley first served as agency physician, but Dr. Jason Holloway soon replaced him. John S. Smith was employed as the agency interpreter.[32]

Edwin Williams, then a young machinist and engineer, installed a sawmill at Darlington during the early summer of 1870, hauling the steam engine, saw, boiler, and accessories from Abilene to Darlington by mule train. The mill was first put into operation even before its shelter was built.[33] In a short time it began producing lumber for other agency buildings. As the supply of timber became depleted in the agency area, the sawmill was moved to Dead Man's Crossing near the lucrative Council Grove. The heavily timbered area was eventually set aside as a wood reserve to furnish Fort Reno with fuel and fence posts.[34]

After meeting with Cheyenne leaders in January 1871, Darlington reported their general satisfaction with their treatment, though they were concerned about the lack of trade goods they were receiving. The agent responded by permitting licensed traders to visit their camps more freely.[35] When the hungry bands under Bull Bear and Medicine Arrow returned south in March, they went to Camp Supply. New commander Lt. Col. John W. Davidson, Tenth Cavalry, issued rations

John Simpson Smith and Brinton Darlington *(standing fourth and fifth from left)* during their stay at Camp Supply. *Courtesy Archives/Manuscripts, Oklahoma Historical Society.*

but warned that the Indians would be punished if they left their assigned lands again.[36]

Darlington wrote in April 1871 that the agency was nearly out of every kind of subsistence for them. There was no coffee, but even worse was the lack of beef. Darlington called it the "darkest period" in the affairs of the agency.[37] The tribes remained peaceful, nonetheless. Following a council between the Quakers and the tribes at the Wichita agency, Darlington told Hoag that "without hesitation, I can say that never since my arrival in this Agency, has the prospect for permanent peace been more flattering."[38]

Capt. Jeremiah P. Schindel, Sixth Infantry, commanded the first detachment of U.S. troops to be posted at the new agency site preceding the establishment of Fort Reno. He worried that the Indians would attack a crew of Atlantic and Pacific Railroad surveyors who were in the field nearby.[39] A letter by a visitor to the territory during the spring of 1871 provided a glimpse of the frontier settlement and its initial military presence:

> On the north bank of this river [North Canadian] we saw the buildings of the new Cheyenne and Arapahoe Indian Agency, consisting of a saw mill, four stores or trading establishments, five or six dwelling houses and the quarters of Captain Schindle and those of a company of the Sixth U.S. Infantry. You can see, by a glance at these quarters, the huge ice house well stored with that soothing luxury, the sentinel as he treads to and fro.[40]

The original domiciles on the banks of the North Canadian were picket houses constructed of green cottonwood planks. By the time winter arrived, the boards had dried and warped badly, leaving gaps between and making them very breezy and cold. The housing situation was not improved when upon departing April 28, 1871, Captain Schindel sold the doors and windows of the buildings used by the troops to the stage station. Further, the earth roofs leaked badly and all of the buildings had dirt floors. Indeed, the first winter sorely challenged the Quaker desire to bring Christianity to the Indian.[41]

Cavalryman H. H. McConnell, traveling up the Chisholm Cattle Trail with six companies of Sixth Cavalry troops from Fort Richardson, Texas, to Fort Harker, Kansas, passed by the Cheyenne and Arapaho agency in May 1871. In his daily record of the journey, he observed that in addition to some two hundred lodges on the agency grounds, tepees dotted the North Canadian valley to the west for miles. As his company passed by the agency, the trooper could hear the voices of Indian children being led by their lady teacher in singing hymns. "Too much praise," McConnell observed, "cannot be awarded the devoted men and women who undertook to make the [Quaker] theory work."[42]

Thus far the Cheyennes and Arapahos had remained peaceful, reflecting a growing respect for the kindly, white-bearded agent whom they called Tomiseeah. On the suggestion of Arapaho chief Little Raven, who thought it would help the cause of peace, Darlington arranged for a visit of an Indian delegation from his agency to the White Father at Washington, D.C. Little Raven, Bird Chief, and Powder Face of the Arapahos; Little Robe and Stone Calf of the Cheyennes; and Buffalo Goad (or Buffalo Good) of the Wichitas made up the group. Darlington did not go, but John Simpson Smith, who had accompanied a similar delegation to Washington in 1863, went along as interpreter.[43]

The delegation visited the nation's capital and was well received in many East Coast cities as well. It had been back for only a short time when on June 29, 1871, Smith died, probably of pneumonia contracted on the trip. Agency personnel buried the longtime frontiersman, who had first come west in 1830 and had spent many years with the Cheyennes, among a grove of trees on the banks of the North Canadian a half mile west of the agency.[44]

During late November 1871, Quaker agents of the various tribes met at Hoag's office in Lawrence. Darlington was among those present at the meeting and presented a hopeful view of the situation in the territory. A Kansas newspaper reported:

> We learn that the most encouraging circumstances developed at this meeting were the peaceable conduct and apparent intentions of the Cheyennes and Arrapahoes and other tribes recently roaming over the plains, plundering and murdering settlers and travelers, and the progress made during the past year in their settlement upon reservations, and the indubitable proof of the practicability of bringing the Indians under the power and into the life of the Christian religion.[45]

This optimistic scenario still existed five months later, when, on May 1, 1872, Darlington died following a brief illness. The cause of death was said to be brain fever. A large body of Cheyennes and Arapahos attended his funeral, crowding every room of the house and gathering at the doors and windows. They stood with hushed respect during the funeral ceremony as a chief made a farewell speech. The assembly of whites and Indians alike passed by the open casket. Many of the chiefs accompanied the body to a gravesite in the sand hills a half mile west of the agency, where he was interred, Quaker fashion, without a marker. Many years later, his son William had him reburied and a marker erected on a small knoll overlooking the agency from the north.[46]

The gentle Quaker agent would long be remembered by the tribespeople who knew him. To them, his motion of taking out his false teeth had become a sign for connoting an Indian agent.[47] After his death, the Cheyenne/Arapaho agency would become known as the Darlington Agency. The great hope of peace and goodwill that he had brought to the North Canadian, however, would soon fall to the forces of frontier conflict.

CHAPTER 2

Cattle, Commerce, and Conflict

Though the Cheyennes and Arapahos had remained quiet during Darlington's three years as agent, increasing concern had risen over the government's inability to feed them as they had been promised by the Treaty of Medicine Lodge. Inadequate funding by Congress, government bureaucracy, emaciated and sickly beef supplied by Texas contractors, inferior foodstuff shipped from the East, and the difficulty of transportation on the frontier all added to the problem. A Kansan who rode down the Chisholm Trail to Texas and back during the spring of 1871 wrote:

> Through the fault of the Government, freighters, and contractors, promises made to Indians are not complied with. As we went down last January a train loaded with annuity goods [for the Kiowa/Comanche agency at Fort Sill] was camped on Kingfisher Creek, eighteen miles this side of the Cheyenne agency; stock poor and unable to move. As we came back last Saturday we met this same train, with these same annuity goods, eight miles beyond the Cheyenne agency. Twenty-six miles in three months! These annuity goods were due the Indians last October; they needed and expected them for the winter, yet they have "shivered through" without them, and they are now useless.[1]

At the same time, Texas cattle herds were flooding northward to Kansas railheads on the Chisholm Trail, many of them passing close by the Darlington agency and the soon-to-be site of Fort Reno. The 150,000 head that came up the trail in 1869 doubled to 300,000 in 1870, then doubled again in 1871 to 600,000. The year 1872 was a banner year for the cattlemen and trail drovers, but in 1873 a financial panic swept the East, causing a great disaster for the Western cattle industry. Even so, it was estimated that some 450,000 head of Texas cattle entered Kansas by way of Indian Territory that year, mostly to Wichita and Ellsworth, while another 50,000 were shipped out of Coffeyville.[2]

Many of these herds crossed the reservation lands assigned to the Cheyennes and Arapahos as well as those of other tribes. Generally the hungry Indians were willing simply to extract a passage fee of either money, beef, or horses. At times, however, they presented belligerent opposition to the Texas herds passing across their lands. An example of this took place in August 1869 when a herd owned by Charles Apitz was attacked on the Salt Fork of the Arkansas. Apitz, a citizen of Lawrence, Kansas, had gone to Texas to push his line of harnesses, saddles, and other supplies. While there he purchased a large number of cattle and hired a dozen or so Texas men to drive them to Kansas for him. While the drovers were camped on the Salt Fork, a band of Comanches and a few Kiowas made a sudden attack. The Indians were successful in running off nearly all of the drovers' horses; then they turned on the Texans, who were armed only with revolvers. The raiders were finally driven off after a fight, but two of the drovers were killed and seven more badly wounded.[3]

This ongoing conflict between drovers and Indians was inherited by Quaker John D. Miles, former agent for the Kickapoos in north central Kansas, when he succeeded Darlington as agent for the Cheyennes and Arapahos. A much younger and more energetic man than Darlington, with a good head for business, Miles also had the great advantage of a helpful wife. A likable woman of good judgment, Mrs. Miles was of great assistance to her husband in the operation of the agency. She soon became known affectionately as "Aunt Lucy" to all.[4]

Upon taking charge at Darlington on May 31, Miles found some of the Arapahos comfortably settled there with vegetable gardens under way. The Cheyennes, however, were absent, and Miles much feared that they were being goaded into warring activities by the Kiowas.[5]

During the spring of 1870, military officers at Camp Supply feared that an Indian war was about to break out. Although the Cheyennes were not overtly hostile, neither were they ready to follow the Arapaho lead in taking up farming or accepting schooling for their children. Both bands preferred to take their trade robes to Camp Supply rather than haul them the much longer distance to the new agency. Also, there was still strong dissatisfaction over the poor quality and limited amount of rations being issued. Those Cheyennes who had not gone

John D. Miles broke
Quaker tradition and
called for troops to protect
his Cheyenne/Arapaho
Agency. *Courtesy
Archives/Manuscript
Division, Oklahoma
Historical Society.*

north to join the militant Dog Soldiers mostly remained away from
both locations, holding to their camps along the streams of western
Indian Territory.

Special U.S. commissioners Capt. Henry E. Alvord and Prof.
Joseph Parish—who would die while at Fort Sill—arrived in the territory during the fall of 1872. Alvord, who had worked with the tribes
under General Hazen at Fort Cobb during 1868 and who would one
day become head of what is now Oklahoma State University, visited
Darlington on September 9.[6]

Alvord met with the Arapahos in council, but the Cheyennes were
still far afield. Neither were they represented at a council held later on
the Washita River with other Plains tribes. Alvord took a hard view,
arguing that the Cheyennes should be forced back onto their reservation and their rations issued according to their behavior.[7] During the
fall of 1872, the Cheyenne bands had gone west to Sheridan's Roost
and on to Wolf Creek to hunt buffalo. While on Wolf Creek, some of
the Cheyennes obtained some whiskey, and a drunken brawl broke

out. An Arapaho brave named Walk-a-bit was killed, as was the Cheyenne wife of scout Ben Clark.[8]

The winter of 1872–73 was relatively quiet, but events in the spring would show that the tribes were still far from being under control and that Indian Territory was still a dangerous place for whites. Particularly at hazard were railroad and government surveyors. The Indians especially resented them, having learned that these men, with their chains and equipment, were harbingers of wagon roads, railroads, and other elements of the white man's commerce.

In 1870 the U.S. Land Office had effected contracts with independent operators for the survey of Indian Territory west of the Indian Meridian, an arbitrary line running north from an initial point on the Red River to the Kansas line and dividing the territory almost equally in half. E. N. Darling had been assigned the task of surveying north-central Indian Territory and determining precisely the south boundary of Kansas. During a recent surge of settlement along the line, many white families located too far south into the territory. Darling employed more than four hundred men on the project, many of whom came from the Kansas border area. A field headquarters was established twelve miles south of Arkansas City by chief surveyor A. N. Deming. Another surveying party under Theodore H. Barrett set up its headquarters at Darlington.[9]

In December 1872 a Cheyenne war party intercepted a crew working at the eastern end of their reservation. They warned the surveyors that if they continued they might well lose their scalps.[10] This dire threat was carried out on March 18, 1873, when Cheyennes fell on Deming's camp some thirty to thirty-five miles northeast of Camp Supply near the Kansas line. They beat the camp cook with pistols and rifle butts and shot him with arrows as he ran to escape. The raiders then stole or destroyed everything in the camp. A larger group returned later to kill Deming and three of his men. Deming was found scalped and with both hands cut off. It was some time before the bodies were found, and then it was not immediately known who had committed the murders. Following this affair, the military provided escort for would-be surveying parties in the field.[11]

Another commercial intrusion took place on February 12, 1873, when T. A. Todd established a stage line and mail route between

Wichita, Kansas, and Gainesville, Texas. The route ran by way of the Darlington agency, the Wichita agency at Anadarko, and Fort Sill.[12] Todd's Southwestern Stage Line set up relay stations—these stage and drover supply points were known as "ranches"—along the route every twelve to fifteen miles and stocked them with good horses. The 240-mile trip took two days and one night of continuous stagecoach travel at a fare of twenty-five dollars.[13]

The various locations on the trail from the Kansas border to Darlington were Polecat Creek, Round Pond Creek (also known at various times as Hopkin's, Hull's, or Sewell's ranche), Skeleton station, Buffalo Springs station (also known as Bison or Mosier's ranche), Bull Foot station (established later near present Hennessey), Baker's ranche on Turkey Creek, Red Fork station on the Cimarron,[14] Kingfisher station, Raven's Spring (later known as Left Hand Springs), and Darlington.[15]

The coaches were drawn by two spans of mules, which were changed at every stop. They could carry eight passengers—six inside and two on the driver's seat. Fording the creeks and rivers during periods of flooding was a major hazard. Most stations, however, were located on the main streams and some had boats with which to transport the mail, express, and passengers across. Hotel accommodations were available at both Fort Reno and Darlington.[16]

A doctor who made the trip in mid-April described his experience in making the journey. As the stage crossed the border below Caldwell, passengers viewed a sign on the Kansas side reading "Last Chance" and on the Indian Territory side, "First Chance."[17] Stage driver Billy Brooks explained that these messages meant the last chance in Kansas and the first chance in the territory to buy a drink.

The stage entered the territory on the cattle trail, which was already very wide and well beaten. Stops were made during the night, with only brief pauses before dashing on. With daylight the occupants of the coach saw their first buffalo, hundreds of them, grazing lazily on the endless prairie. They also spotted an occasional wolf and prairie dog town. At Baker's ranche they met the northbound stage. From there, it was on to Red Fork ranche on the north bank of the Cimarron River.

The first Indians were encountered at Darlington, which was reached at nine o'clock that night. The event left the travelers a bit

The stagecoach constituted the main connection between Darlington/Fort Reno and the outside world. *Courtesy National Archives.*

shaken because of reports of attacks by the Cheyennes on surveying parties inside the territory. However, there was no trouble from the peaceful agency Indians, and the stage continued on to the Wichita agency, where horses were changed and breakfast partaken before heading on to Fort Sill.

Despite occasional flare-ups of Indian conflict, Kansas trade with occupants of Indian Territory continued unabated. This fact was visible daily on the streets of Wichita, then the main entrepôt to Indian Territory and Darlington. Long ox- and mule-drawn wagon trains could be seen headed south with their caravans of traders' merchandise, government supplies, or Indian annuities. These or similar trains came back loaded high with buffalo hides held in place with boom poles and covered over with wagon sheets to keep the rain off.[18] Others unloaded piles of buffalo and cattle bones alongside the railroad tracks for shipment to the East. Blue-clad cavalry troops, carbines slung across their backs, galloped in formation out of town, headed for adventures with the hostile tribes, while small parties of surveyors waved brave farewells from the backs of canvas-covered army ambulances.

Freighting operations up and down Chisholm's road expanded constantly. Typical was a Beard and Vance train of fourteen wagons that headed off for the Cheyenne/Arapaho and Wichita agencies in July 1873 loaded with 84,000 pounds of flour. Another was the Lafflin train of thirty-four prairie schooners that arrived back in Wichita from the territory and was reloaded with coffee, sugar, and other annuity goods for its return trip.[19]

Like many of the tribes, the Cheyennes were split between peace and warring factions, one tending the civil needs of the tribe and the other operating as martial societies. This conflict came to a head during the summer of 1873 when the Cheyennes prepared for their annual Sun Dance, an emotionally charged event when young warriors felt challenged to prove themselves. Stone Calf, holding to the pledge of peace he had made in Washington, refused to attend the Sun Dance. As a result, the Cheyenne Dog Soldiers slashed his lodges and killed some of his horses.[20]

During the fall of 1873, Miles, accompanied by Mrs. Miles and interpreter Edmund Guerrier, led a delegation of Cheyennes and Arapahos to Washington to talk with Commissioner of Indian Affairs Edward P. Smith regarding a new alignment of their reservation. Though an agreement was reached to separate the two confederated tribes, Congress failed to enact ratification. While the delegation was at rough-and-rowdy Dodge City on its return, a group of saloon wags tossed some gunpowder mixed with red pepper into the stove where the Indians were lodged. This, along with whiskey that someone slipped to the chiefs, almost excited a brawl.[21]

As the year ended, the signs for pending trouble were foreboding. Entrepreneurs along the lawless Kansas border and from New Mexico were keeping the warriors well supplied with whiskey, guns, and ammunition. The trade made such a demand on the Cheyennes' supply of robes that in protest the women of the tribe conducted an organized slowdown of preparing them.[22] Meanwhile, peace in the territory was being further threatened by white horse thieves such as Hurricane Bill Martin and Dutch Henry, whose well-organized gangs were raiding Indian herds and doing a lucrative business in Indian ponies. Cherokee Strip cowboys also regularly raided the Cheyenne and Arapaho herds. Oliver Nelson, who worked for the Texas Land and Cattle Company north of the Cimarron, described one method: "It was no trouble to find a bunch of split-eared Cheyenne ponies in the sand hills southwest of the home camp. The boys would hook a few, cross the Cimarron, and follow with a bunch of cattle to blot out the trail. If the Indians followed, some of the boys would be laying on the trail to shoot at them."[23]

Indian Territory abounded in hard men who lived beyond the pale of the law. Many of these outlaws preyed upon the Indians through whiskey dealing, horse thievery, and other illegal acts. Whenever one of them was arrested either by troops or Indian police, it was necessary to take him to Judge Isaac Parker's federal court at Fort Smith. In 1873 Ben Williams, a Civil War veteran and one-time prisoner at the infamous Confederate prison at Andersonville, was appointed as a deputy U.S. marshal not only to make arrests but also to transport offenders by horseback to Arkansas. As such on a $100-a-month salary, he became the first civil law enforcement officer in the region. Williams, a disaffected Quaker, was one of the interesting characters of the frontier who had no reluctance to shoot it out with outlaws. In his work, he spent a great deal of time among the Indian camps on the prairie and became a good friend to many of the Arapaho and Cheyenne leaders.[24]

A long drought that had ruined crops for white settlers on the Plains caused many Kansas men to take up buffalo hunting as a means of sustaining their families. These men, along with professional hunters, constituted an estimated two thousand or more non-tribesmen who were active in slaughtering buffalo on the western Plains of Kansas, Indian Territory, and the Texas Panhandle. Eastern markets paid from two to three dollars each for buffalo hides, and choice buffalo steaks cost one and a half cents a pound in Kansas stores. It is believed that some 7.5 million buffalo were killed during the period of 1872–74.[25]

All of these factors pointed to the potential of an Indian outbreak, and danger loomed large for Miles, whose agency on the North Canadian River was an isolated outpost a far distance from all points. Its remoteness and vulnerability would be made abundantly clear by events in 1874.

CHAPTER 3

Birth of Fort Reno

A visitor to the Darlington agency during the fall of 1873 wrote back to Kansas saying that it was quite a place, having two stores, a blacksmith shop, and a good number of dwelling houses—"a lively little town."[1] Still, the agency stood separated some seventy-five miles—a three-day march even for cavalry—from U.S. troops at Fort Sill and more than 130 miles from those at Camp Supply. There were also a few troops stationed only some forty miles away at the Wichita agency. In the event of an Indian uprising, however, those troops could hardly be spared; and Darlington's small detachment of infantry would provide scant protection against an attack of any size.

The military's situation was further complicated by its organization at the time, which essentially divided protection responsibility for western Indian Territory north-south along the Canadian River. Fort Sill, the Wichita agency, and the Kiowa/Comanche reservation were included under the military Department of Texas, commanded by Brig. Gen. Christopher C. Augur with headquarters at San Antonio. Camp Supply, Darlington, and the Cheyenne/Arapaho reservation were under Brig. Gen. John Pope, commanding the Department of the Missouri with headquarters at Fort Leavenworth.[2]

Though by no means committed to any form of consolidated fighting body, the tribes were nonetheless united by situation and by resentment against the whites who ruled over them. The wholesale slaughter of buffalo by white hunters exacerbated the hunger that the inadequate and poor quality of beef left in their camps. It had long been U.S. policy to consider Indian annuities as merely supplemental to the Indians' supplying themselves through the hunt. At the same time, the government did absolutely nothing to stop the decimation of the buffalo by U.S. citizens. There were those, in fact, who felt that extinction of the buffalo—which meant the starvation of Indians—was the most practical and less costly means of solving the nation's Indian problem.

The Darlington agency saw its first Indian-white violence on
May 21, 1874, when Frank Holloway, the teenage son of agency physician Dr. Jason Holloway, was shot and killed. By one account, the boy,
who worked at the sawmill, tripped and fell into a young Indian male.
In reaction, he scowled at the tribesman, then cursed and shoved him
through a doorway. It was the next day, according to a letter by Dr.
Holloway, that two Indians carrying carbines across their saddles rode
up to the Holloway house. One of them shot Frank through a window. The boy grabbed his gun and started for the door to return the
fire, but after a few steps he collapsed in his father's arms. He lingered
in great agony until the night of May 25, when he died.[3]

The killing aroused great trepidation among the agency personnel, who feared that this was the start of a general attack by the
Cheyennes. With only a company or two of soldiers to provide protection, everyone armed himself as quickly as possible. A band of
peaceful Arapahos who were camped some four miles up the river
under Chief Little Raven moved to the agency to guard it until a troop
of cavalry from Fort Sill arrived.

It was later discovered that it was not a Cheyenne but a young
Arapaho who had killed Frank Holloway. When efforts to capture the
perpetrator failed, Miles had several Arapaho chiefs arrested and placed
in the guardhouse. Some of the young Arapaho hostiles mounted their
horses and tried to persuade the Cheyennes to help them clean out the
agency. The Cheyennes refused. Eventually the offender was brought
in, and the chiefs were released.[4]

Following a joint Sun Dance held by the Kiowas, Comanches,
Cheyennes, Arapahos, and Plains Apaches in June 1874, a series of
events would severely shake Miles's Quaker faith in heavenly protection. The first of these took place at sunrise on the morning of the
twenty-seventh, when a consolidated party of warriors launched an
attack on a buffalo hunter settlement at Adobe Walls in the Texas
Panhandle. The long guns of the buffalo hunters, however, held the
attackers at bay and killed a number of them and their horses.[5]

Miles learned of the Adobe Walls affair five days later when a participant reached the peaceful Cheyenne camps at the agency. This
indication of an uprising being under way was borne out when Chief
Whirlwind told Miles that three Cheyenne men and a woman had

Agent John D. Miles, his son Whit, Ben Clark, and Cheyenne chief Little Robe were photographed while on a visit to New York City. *Courtesy Archives/Manuscripts Division, Oklahoma Historical Society.*

murdered and scalped William Watkins on the road thirty miles north of the agency between Kingfisher Station and the Cimarron River. On July 2, scouts reported that the tracks of five war parties had been discovered north of the agency.[6]

The worst fears of the agency were confirmed when two young agency employees, C. M. Monahan and Edward O'Leary, went out to look for stray cattle. When they did not return, a search was made. Monahan was discovered dead, his head riddled with bullets. O'Leary's body was not found.

Miles sent a courier galloping to Fort Sill for troops. Even though Darlington was not included in his military jurisdiction, Lieutenant Colonel Davidson immediately dispatched a troop of cavalry to the agency. Miles soon decided, however, that this was not protection enough. Taking a small party of agency employees as an escort, on the morning of July 6 the agent set off to make a dash up the danger-ridden trail to safety in Kansas.[7]

Employees at Kingfisher station reported that Indians had been seen there heading north. Gathering all the men and stock there, Miles proceeded on to Baker's ranche on Turkey Creek, where it was reported that the Indians had attacked that place on July 2 but had been repulsed with only the loss of some harness. It was only four miles up the road that Miles's party came onto a gruesome scene.[8]

Scattered about the rutted trail were the charred remains of three freight wagons. Near them, lying in the road, were the corpses of three teamsters, all of them scalped. Tied to the wheel of one still-smoldering wagon was the body of head freighter Pat Hennessey. Hennessey had departed Wichita on June 30 for Fort Sill with three wagon loads of sugar and coffee. Driving the wagons were teamsters George Fand, Thomas Calloway, and Ed Cook. On July 3, Hennessey camped his wagons at Burr Mosier's ranche at Buffalo Springs. Though cautioned against it, on the morning of July 4 Hennessey had continued on south.[9]

Upon arriving at the scene, Miles gave the men a hasty burial before hurrying on to Buffalo Springs. There his party was met by an assortment of teamsters, cattlemen, stage drivers, passengers, and others who had taken refuge at the station. It was reported that a war party of a hundred or more Indians had recently passed by. Miles and his men galloped on north, taking with them the women who were at the ranche.

Night had fallen when the fleeing entourage reached the next station at Skeleton Creek. The Indians had reportedly gone into camp on the creek four miles to the east. On Miles's advice, all those at the stations joined him in making a final retreat through the night to Caldwell. Miles reached Osage City, Kansas, before he wrote to Commissioner E. P. Smith, giving the details of his exodus from the territory. He concluded the letter with a plea that would cause his Quaker superiors monumental concern. He wrote:

> I have offered my life in passing through their [the Indians'] line to save others, and I now ask and expect to receive at once two or three companies of cavalry, one to be stationed at Baker's Ranche, to protect government interests on this road, and one at the Agency. These troops should be transported as quickly as

possible to Wichita, by rail. No hostile Indians shall be quartered at the Agency, and I must have troops to back it up. Let the hostile bands be struck and with as much power as shall make the work quick and effectual.[10]

General Pope immediately ordered three companies of cavalry from Fort Leavenworth to open and secure the road to the Darlington agency.[11] After reconnoitering along Kingfisher Creek, Company E, Sixth Cavalry, went into camp near the Darlington agency on August 1. It left again on the fourth on a scout to Bluff Creek, returning to Darlington again on the fifteenth. In the meantime, Company B, Fifth Infantry, arrived from the Creek agency, as did Company G, Fifth Infantry, from near Caldwell. These units constituted the first garrison for the military camp soon to be identified in official reports as "Camp Near Cheyenne Agency."[12]

Still more depredations surfaced in the coming weeks. Seven buffalo hunters were said to have been killed on July 9 by a party of seventy-five Cheyennes, possibly by the same war party that Miles reported.[13] Within the month, a committee of Friends at Lawrence met behind closed doors for two or three days regarding Miles's action. They emerged to "kindly request" that Miles resign his post. He had, they determined, "allowed his inner nature to gain the ascendancy of his non-combative exterior."[14]

Miles, however, refused to step down, and he was supported by Commissioner Smith.[15] Moreover, the plea from a Quaker for use of military troops in quelling the Plains tribes, bolstering as it did the military's reentry into Indian affairs, was well received by the War Department in Washington.

The Indian Bureau agreed to the punishment of Indians who committed depredations, but it wanted troops kept off the reservations.[16] Smith felt the necessity of making a personal visit to the Cheyenne/Arapaho agency in September. He left Arkansas City with a strong escort of troops that had orders to fire on any and all Indians discovered off their reservation.[17] At Darlington he found that Lt. Col. Thomas H. Neill had arrived in mid-July to establish a temporary military camp. Neill's forces included four companies of Fifth Infantry and one troop of Sixth Cavalry, a complement of 164 men and officers.[18]

Other tribal depredations throughout the region followed the Adobe Walls fight and Hennessey massacre, spreading alarm that a

general Indian uprising was under way. A cattleman reported that the
Cheyennes and Arapahos had raided his herd on the Arkansas in Bent
County, Colorado.

"On the Fourth of July," he claimed, "a band of Indians came
rushing down upon them from the sand hills, whooping and yelling
like demons and shooting at the cattle and herders. The cattle stampeded and the herders only escaped by having more fleet horses than
the Indians had."[19] The Indians took possession of their camp, pil-
laged it, burned what they could not carry away, and stole nine horses.
A woodcutter was found axed to death a mile away.

An eruption between U.S. troops and the Kiowas and Comanches
took place at the Wichita agency at Anadarko on August 12. Bands of
those two tribes had gone there to join in the disbursement of food
to the Wichitas, Caddos, and other tribes of that agency. The fracas
began when troops attempted to disarm a Comanche chief named
Red Food. Red Food rebelled at giving up his bow and arrows and
with a whoop jumped on his pony and fled. When the soldiers fired
after him, some of the Indians, mainly Kiowas, began firing back at
the soldiers. A general melee resulted, with the tribesmen burning
houses and fields and killing several men who worked for the agency.[20]

The Cheyennes were not involved in the Wichita agency fight,
but on the twenty-fourth of the month, a Cheyenne war party under
Medicine Water massacred six surveyors under Oliver F. Short some
forty-five miles southwest of Fort Dodge. Three days later the abandoned equipment wagon was spotted by another surveying team.
Upon approaching it, the men found the six corpses, two of which
had been scalped. The draft oxen had been killed in their traces, and
the carcass of the camp dog lay nearby.[21]

Cheyenne chiefs Little Robe, Pawnee, and White Shield brought
some 130 of their people into the agency.[22] They acknowledged that
the Cheyennes were on the warpath. Numerous other incidents of
Indian infractions were reported throughout the region, strengthen-
ing the determination of Gen. Phil Sheridan to conduct a punitive
campaign against the tribes. Under Sheridan's orders a multipronged
invasion of the Indian country was set into motion in September. A
command under Col. Nelson A. Miles moved southwest from Camp
Supply into the Texas Panhandle; Maj. William R. Price east from
Fort Union, New Mexico; Col. Ranald S. Mackenzie north from Fort

Concho, Texas; and Davidson west from Fort Sill. Still another strike force under Lt. Col. George P. Buell from Fort Richardson, Texas, would scour north Texas and southwest Indian Territory.[23] The operation would become known as the Red River War.

On September 9, a train of thirty-six wagons commanded by Capt. Wyllys Lyman was hauling supplies from Camp Supply to Colonel Miles's command in the Texas Panhandle when it was attacked by a large force of Kiowa warriors. Unable to overrun it, the Kiowas laid siege to the train for four days before withdrawing. A sergeant and a wagon master were killed, and Lt. Granville Lewis, Fifth Infantry, was severely wounded in the knee. After spending three days without medical attention, he was taken to Camp Supply, where it was thought he would die. He did recover, however.[24]

Even as this confrontation was taking place, another smaller but similar battle occurred several miles to the north. Four soldiers, accompanied by scouts Amos Chapman and Billy Dixon, were carrying dispatches from Miles's command on McClellan Creek to Camp Supply. They were nearing the Washita River at sunrise on the morning of September 12 when they were attacked by 125 Kiowa and Comanche warriors. Taking shelter in a buffalo wallow, the men managed to hold off their attackers into the afternoon when a cold, bone-chilling rain, aided by the accurate fire of the six men, chilled the warrior party's desire for battle and caused them to withdraw during the night.

Three of the soldiers were badly wounded, one of them dying. Both Chapman and Dixon had also been wounded in the leg, Chapman severely enough that when he finally reached Camp Supply the post surgeon amputated his foot above the ankle. Chapman recovered and continued to be deeply involved in events related to the Cheyennes and western Indian Territory.[25]

With Sheridan's armies in the field, the hostile elements of the Kiowas along with some Comanches, Cheyennes, and Arapahos retreated to the supposed safety of Palo Duro Canyon in the Texas Panhandle. On September 26, however, advance scouts of Mackenzie's Fort Concho column discovered the Indian encampment on the floor of the canyon. Mackenzie's cavalry attacked and burned the camp, afterward destroying some fourteen hundred Indian ponies whose bones would litter the canyon basin for years to come.[26]

Even as U.S. troops were scouring western Indian Territory and

the Texas Panhandle and striking the tribes wherever found, a
Cheyenne party led by Medicine Water attacked the night camp of a
migrating family named Germain (often referred to as German) on
September 11. Originally of Georgia, the Germains had lived in Missouri
for three years before moving on to the vicinity of Elgin, Kansas. They
were on their way to make a new home in Colorado when they were
fallen upon early in the morning while breakfasting on the Smoky
Hill River near the Kansas-Colorado border. John Germain; his wife,
Lydia; twenty-one-year-old daughter Rebecca Jane; nineteen-year-
old Stephen; and fifteen-year-old James were brutally murdered.
Catherine Elizabeth, eighteen; Sophia Louise, twelve; Julia Amanda,
seven; and Nancy Adeline, five, were taken captive.

The saga of the Germain massacre and the four girls' captivity
would play an important role in the anti-Indian fever that excited the
frontier and fostered military action during the weeks ahead. Kansas
newspapers would print the horrific story of how the girls saw their
parents, brothers, and older sister shot and axed to death by a band
of Cheyennes that included two Cheyenne women.[27]

Upon her release from captivity at Darlington, Sophia recounted
how the two younger girls had been abandoned on the prairie and
lived on hackberries until finally they were picked up by other Indians.
In the face of the brutality of the war party, little newspaper attention
was paid to the statement of the girls that one of the two Cheyenne
women with the attacking party had saved the lives of the two younger
girls. A report from Darlington after the final release stated:

> The youngest of the two women showed great kindness in
> the bereaved children. After weeping bitterly over their wrongs,
> she also saved the life of the youngest sister, only five years old.
> An Indian had taken aim on the little one, when this brave and
> noble red woman snatched the gun away and sprang between
> the murderer and the little innocent.[28]

Further, chiefs Stone Calf, Big Horse, and Whirlwind had
attempted unsuccessfully to secure the release of the girls by offering
their own ponies in exchange.

Kiowa war chief Satanta had been present during the fight at the
Wichita agency. Earlier the Kiowa leader had been sent to prison at
Huntsville, Texas, for raids in that state, then released on the promise

of good behavior by himself and the Kiowas in general. There is no evidence that he took part in the Wichita agency disturbance, but afterward he and his band took refuge in the Red Hills along the Canadian River west of Darlington. Fearing to return to his agency at Fort Sill, on October 1 Satanta sent Big Tree and others in to Darlington to say that he wished to surrender there.[29]

Miles talked to Big Tree, declaring that the friendly Indians belonged to him, but those that wished to fight belonged to the soldiers. Neill then addressed the delegation. He promised that Satanta and other Indians would be treated kindly if they gave up their arms and submitted to arrest. Two days later, Arapaho chief Left Hand escorted Satanta with twenty-four lodges and 145 men, women, and children in to the post. The Kiowa chief was immediately placed in irons and sent by wagon to Fort Sill under heavy guard. From there, Satanta was returned to prison at Huntsville, Texas.[30]

On October 27, Miles reported that two companies of cavalry and one of infantry under Maj. Adna R. Chaffee of Miles's command had attacked an Indian village at Raven's Spring on the North Fork twenty miles to the west, the Indians escaping. Chaffee had come on to the agency to confer with Sheridan.[31]

Evidently hoping to take advantage of the military's distraction with the Indian war, three white horse thieves raided a horse herd of Powder Face on Kingfisher Creek.[32] Some of the horses belonged to frontiersman J. S. Morrison, who followed the thieves to Fort Dodge. There General Sheridan, who had just arrived from Camp Supply, ordered a detachment of cavalry out in hot pursuit with orders to catch the robbers and "plant them on the prairie." The troops followed the stolen herd to Pawnee Fork in western Kansas, where a galloping chase ensued with the thieves driving the herd at a breakneck pace before them. The race continued for some fifteen miles, with the soldiers steadily gaining on the horse thieves. Finally the three desperados dismounted and put up an intense standoff fight until the troops finally killed two of them, one man making an escape.[33]

Like Satanta, war-weary Cheyennes looked to the Darlington agency as a place to take their bands to surrender. On October 20, Cheyenne chief White Horse, who had escaped from Mackenzie at Palo Duro, brought in a small party.[34]

One critical engagement of the so-called Red River War occurred on November 8 in the Texas Panhandle, where an expedition under Colonel Miles was searching for Indians. Lt. Frank D. Baldwin was sent north with a cavalry troop to escort a convoy of twenty-three wagons to a supply camp on the Washita. A company of infantry was riding in the unloaded wagons. When his scouts sighted a large Cheyenne camp under Grey Beard on McClellan's Creek, Baldwin launched a war-whooping charge on the village with his cavalry and infantry firing from the sides of their mule-drawn wagons. The surprised Cheyennes fled, leaving behind the two youngest Germain girls, Julia Amanda and Nancy Adeline. Baldwin was later awarded one of his two Medals of Honor for his decisive action.

The girls were taken to Fort Sill and from there escorted to the Polly Hotel, a stage station located just south of present Shattuck, Oklahoma, en route to Camp Supply and Fort Leavenworth. Mrs. Polly described the girls as being in such a demented condition from their captivity that they cowered in a corner of the cabin with a blanket over their heads, seemingly unable to communicate.[35]

On December 20, eight warriors and thirty-nine women and children belonging to Medicine Water's band surrendered themselves at Darlington.[36] This was followed on February 25, 1875, by Stone Calf's arrival at the agency under escort of Marshal Ben Williams. Neill described the event:

> This surrender of the last of the Cheyennes presented a very grand, imposing and picturesque sight which words are inadequate to depict, and justice could only be done to the view by an artist or photographer. The Indian warriors with their bronzed and scarred countenances, silent, respectful, and thoughtful;— the young men and boys with an expression between fear and shame; the women with their babes in their arms, hiding the heads of the children under their blankets to prevent them from seeing the white man, who they had been taught to fear as their worst enemy; the parti-colored blankets and leggings; the tepis or lodges behind them, and the trees in rear of all, presented a scene at once grand, important and unequalled, and which we shall never see again.[37]

Stone Calf agreed to the surrender of some sixteen hundred Cheyennes along with the two older Germain girls. An ambulance that had been sent to bring in the girls returned to Darlington with them on March 1.[38] The military officers, troops, and agency employees contributed generously to the welfare of the girls before they were taken off to Fort Sill, where they could receive medical examination and better care. Eventually they would be sent via Dodge City to Fort Leavenworth to join their younger sisters. General Pope later took the four parentless and destitute girls to Lawrence, where they were placed in the care of a farm family named Wilson.[39]

At Fort Sill, hostile bands of the Kiowas and Comanches were surrendering also, and by the last of May 1875 the Red River War had essentially ended. It had been determined by the government that the worst of these belligerents would be punished by sending them off to Fort Marion, Florida. There they would be imprisoned in the ancient Spanish fort of St. Augustine, where the Seminole chief Osceola had once been held.

Cheyenne chief Stone Calf, shown with his wife, was a strong defender of tribal interests. *Courtesy National Museum of Natural History.*

In the early afternoon of April 6, a guard detail was making preparations for the transfer by placing leg irons on the selected prisoners
at a makeshift prison camp two miles north of the agency. A young
Cheyenne named Black Horse, noted for his independent nature, was
chosen as the first subject for ironing. As the post blacksmith prepared to do his work, however, Black Horse was being taunted by
Cheyenne women. Suddenly he bolted for the Cheyenne camp. He
was pursued by Capt. Andrew S. Bennett and six men. Black Horse
was shot and killed, and at the same time a Cheyenne woman was
killed by a stray bullet.[40]

Cheyennes in the camp began shooting at the soldiers with rifles
and arrows. The soldiers fired back, causing the entire village of more
than three hundred tribespeople to flee as they commonly would
when their camp came under attack. When advised of these events,
Colonel Neill ordered forth a troop of Sixth Cavalry under Capt.
William A. Rafferty and two troops of Tenth Cavalry under Capt.
Stevens T. Norvell and Capt. Alexander S. B. Keyes.

Rafferty found that some 100 to 150 Cheyenne men had occupied
a strong position on an elevated sandy knoll topped by a small growth
of saplings. It is generally believed that the Cheyennes had stashed
their weapons in the sand hills before surrendering. From his headquarters, Neill ordered his mounted troops not to fire on the Indians
as they advanced. But when the cavalry halted to dismount, the
Indians began firing, driving the troops to cover.

When Neill arrived on the scene, he found Rafferty entrenched
to the east of the sand hill with Norvell and Keyes on the southwest.
Neill ordered a charge on the Indians, but Norvell persuaded him that
it was impracticable. Neill then had a Gatling gun brought forth and,
with Lt. Frank S. Hinkle, Fifth Infantry, firing it, made a charge on
the entrenchments. This and two other charges were unsuccessful,
and firing continued throughout the day.

"At the first charge on foot," Neill later reported, "I sent in the
last men I have under Lieutenant [Edward P.] Turner with orders to
continue mounted and pursue, if the charge was successful; he could
not cross a slough, so he instantly dismounted and charged with his
men on foot ahead and past Captains Norvell and Keyes' companies
in a very gallant manner, but he could not get into the work."[41]

Believing that Capt. Clarence Mauck was then en route from Fort

Sill with Kiowa and Comanche prisoners destined for Fort Marion, at 5:00 P.M. Neill dispatched a courier requesting help. The battle lasted from 2:30 in the afternoon until 10:00 at night. At that time a severe thunder storm blew in and, along with darkness, caused the shooting to cease.

The next morning Neill ordered out trenching tools, food, and a fresh supply of ammunition for a siege of the Cheyennes' position. A company of infantry under Lt. Charles E. Hargous was added to the force, leaving only a citizen guard of fifty men to guard the agency. When morning came, the military prepared for another assault on the rifle pits. It was discovered, however, that the Cheyennes had slipped away during the night. Neill had believed that he had the sand hills redoubt surrounded by his troops. But on one side was a pond that prevented any posting of guards. Agency employee John H. Seger told how the Cheyennes took advantage of this fact and the heavy rain to make their escape. According to Seger, the old men of the tribe told the others to wade out into the pond during the darkness of the storm and to drop down when lightening flashed. When they were past the soldiers, the Indians scattered "like a flock of quail."[42] After several days, they all came back together. Some of them went north and joined the Northern Cheyennes.

Six Cheyenne men and one woman were found dead on the field of battle; others were thought to have been killed and carried away with those wounded. Nineteen soldiers were wounded, three of them seriously. As soon as two troops of Tenth Cavalry could be fed and their ammunition replaced, they were ordered in pursuit up the North Canadian.[43] Pvt. Clark Young, Troop H, Tenth Cavalry, was one of the nineteen U.S. troops wounded in the fight. Having taken a shot in the abdomen, Young lingered for six days before dying on April 12, 1875. He became the second person to be buried in the Fort Reno cemetery.[44]

Agent Miles was away at the time of the fight, and acting agent J. A. Covington made the official report to the commissioner of Indian Affairs. The killing of Black Horse and the Cheyenne woman, he said, had acted like a match placed to a powder keg. In an instant, the whole camp had panicked, thinking their camp was being attacked. The women and children quickly fled to take refuge in the camp of some friendly Indians while the warriors held the troops at bay in the sand hills. The sand pits had provided excellent cover for the Cheyennes

so long as they kept their heads down.[45] "Their only hope was in digging holes in the sand and keeping as much covered as possible," Seger
later wrote. "To stand up was sure death. Some of the women were
so excited that they had to be held or tied out of the bullet range."[46]

The troops who were sent up the Cimarron River in pursuit were
unsuccessful in recapturing the Cheyennes. Rumors were heard that
a large number of Cheyennes had passed by Fort Larned, Kansas.
Elements of this group may well have been among those involved in
an engagement on the Sappa River on April 23. Lt. Austin Henley,
Sixth Cavalry, operating out of Fort Wallace, attacked a camp of sixty
Cheyennes, killing nineteen warriors, two chiefs, and a medicine man
and capturing 125 ponies. He lost two troopers in the fight.[47]

On his return after an absence of five weeks, Miles concluded that
some of the Indians were hiding in the blackjack woods west of
Turkey Creek. He was scornful of the military (Neill, by inference),
charging it was either willful stupidity or gross ignorance that permitted the Cheyennes to retain their weapons and ponies.[48] There
had, in fact, been concern expressed about the matter prior to the outbreak in a letter from the Darlington agency to the *Leavenworth Times*.
Where were all the improved breech-loading rifles, the letter asked,
that were often seen in the Cheyennes' possession before they went
on the warpath? Or all those other guns that they had traded for from
the Comanches and Mexicans? When warmer weather came, the
writer suggested, the Indians could dig up their buried arms and
return to the warpath. Neill would be severely criticized in the Kansas
press over the matter.[49]

Eventually most the bands accepted a promise of no reprisal from
General Pope and returned to the agency. Meanwhile, the preparation for sending the prisoners to Florida continued. On April 23,
thirty-three Cheyennes and two Arapahos were chained in place
aboard army ambulances and taken off to Fort Sill. Among them were
Medicine Water, leader of both the Germain and Short war parties,
and Mochi (or Buffalo Calf), the woman who put an axe in the head
of John Germain. Chiefs Minimic and Grey Beard were also included
on the general charge of being ringleaders. One Arapaho, Packer, had
killed a herder at Darlington; another, White Bear, had attempted to
kill the son of Marshal Williams. At Fort Sill they were joined by

twenty-seven Kiowas, nine Comanches, and one Caddo for their long journey by wagon to the Missouri, Kansas, and Texas Railroad (MKT) at Caddo, Indian Territory, thence by train to Fort Leavenworth, Kansas, and from there to Fort Marion, Florida.[50]

The Indian uprising gave support to agent Miles's request that the army establish a permanent military post at his agency. Secretary of War William W. Belknap had earlier authorized the creation of a new post with six companies of cavalry at Beaver Creek, Texas. On the recommendation of Sheridan and division and department commanders, Belknap redirected his orders for the new post from Texas to the Cheyenne/Arapaho agency. In turn, the Department of the Missouri issued the appropriate authorization on July 15, 1875, and the post in Indian Territory that would soon become known as Fort Reno—named by Sheridan for Gen. Jesse L. Reno, who was killed by friendly fire during the Civil War battle of South Mountain Maryland —came into being.

Maj. Gen. Jesse Reno, namesake of Fort Reno, was accidentally killed by friendly fire during the Civil War. *Battles and War Leaders of the Civil War.*

CHAPTER 4

An Interim of Tranquility

Lieutenant Colonel Neill remained at Darlington until May 1875. At that time he was replaced by Capt. Wirt Davis, Fourth Cavalry. Thus far the troops had been quartered in tents and buildings at the agency, but now they were moved south across the North Canadian to a temporary new site. A board of officers headed by Capt. Theodore J. Wint was assigned the task of selecting a permanent location for the new, Indian-surrounded post-to-be. This was done with the help of agent Miles.[1] Together the men selected a site on the high ground overlooking the river and agency from the river's south bank.

Because of funding problems, it was the spring of 1876 before daily drill was put aside and troops of the Fifth Cavalry and Fifth Infantry began construction on the fort. These initial buildings were "built of small logs, set vertically in rows, in trenches, which were filled and tamped, the interstices between the logs being plastered with clay."[2] According to Miles, one of the first buildings to be built was a stockade type structure erected by the Evans brothers for a post trading store.

"In company with my brother, Jack," Neal Evans later wrote, "we had a little log house that we used as a store and all the soldiers, Indians, cowboys and mule skinners used to congregate there to hear the latest news and gossip of the day, and incidentally spend a dollar or two for tobacco and ammunition."[3]

The log hut was later replaced by a large, forty-three-room building constructed of brick and lumber that had been hauled down from Wichita.[4] Quite often it was some time between pay days for the Fort Reno soldiers, and the military would issue post trader checks that were good for merchandise only. The Evans brothers honored these against the soldiers' pay, making change with small octagon metal coins, on one side of which the values from a quarter to a dollar were stamped. The other side of the coin read, "Evans Bros., Traders for Indians, Good for Mdse. Only, Fort Reno, I.T."[5]

A Department of the Missouri description of the post could soon list living quarters for three companies, an adjutant's office, and quartermaster's and commissary warehouses as being frame buildings with shingle roofs. One such structure served as a provisional hospital, and other buildings were under construction. Both the cavalry and quartermaster horses were corralled in a stockade of oak pickets.[6]

In February 1876, Capt. Clarence Mauck, Fourth Cavalry, became commander at Fort Reno over a garrison that consisted of Fourth Cavalry and Fifth Infantry units. Civilian employees included a commissary clerk, quartermaster clerk, blacksmith, mechanic, scout, trainmaster, ten teamsters, and five carpenters.[7]

In addition to their ultimate goal of engaging in battle, troopers at Fort Reno tended stock, provided escort details, searched for strayed horses, investigated mishaps and troubles on the trail, constructed buildings at the fort, cut timber for poles, made bricks, fought prairie fires, and, on occasion, accompanied the Cheyennes and Arapahos on their buffalo hunts. All these things were done within the post framework of reveille at 5:00 A.M., stable call, drill, noontime mess, fatigue duty, and evening mess. At 6:30 P.M. came roll call and the bugler's sounding of retreat as the post flag was lowered. Tattoo sounded at 8:30 and taps at 9:00.[8]

The garrison found recreation in horse racing, intercompany baseball and football contests, hunting excursions, performances of the Fort Reno drama club, and individual sporting contests such as target shooting, broad and high jumping, and races by foot, wheelbarrow, or gunnysack. Whiskey drinking was a standard outlet for personal frustrations for enlisted men and officers alike. Womanhood being a limited item on the frontier, the men exercised their biological inclinations whenever possible with laundresses, Indian women, or frontier prostitutes. Venereal diseases were commonly a major problem at frontier posts such as Reno.[9] The post drama club revealed the talents of the garrison's enlisted men. A correspondent to the *Army and Navy Journal* reported:

> Having consolidated the principal characters of the two troupes (the Fort Reno and Excelsiors), we now claim to be the best amateur minstrel troupe in the West . . . A fine string band is an additional attraction . . . We heartily commend this sort of

thing as a means of recreation and indirectly a promotion of health, discipline and morality.[10]

The water supply for the fort was obtained from the river, and wood for fuel was supplied by contractors. Quartermaster and subsistence stores were shipped down the Chisholm Trail by wagon from Wichita, which also offered the closest telegraph at that date. Darlington agency, a mile away across the river, served as the fort's post office.

"You can scarcely imagine," a Darlington resident wrote to a friend," the inconvenience of living in a country so far remote from railroads and telegraph lines. We have communication with Wichita by a tri-weekly stage line; but as the distance is 180 miles, the streams unbridged and the road insufficiently stocked, you may readily imagine that bad roads seriously affect our intercourse with the outside world."[11]

The surrounding countryside was reported to have exceedingly fertile soil for producing grain and vegetables, and farming was already under way in the area, presumably by the agency and Indian farmers. There were more than 3,300 Cheyennes and Arapahos and a few Kiowa-Apaches at the agency. Grass was abundant and of excellent quality for grazing the post's stock.

During the wintry days of January 1876, German emigrant Ado Hunnius made a scientific trek down the Chisholm Trail from Kansas to Darlington as a civilian employee of the U.S. Army. Traveling in a hack driven by a young Westerner called Billy, the two walked at times to keep warm. Hunnius measured distances from place to place with an odometer fastened to a wheel of the vehicle, took copious notes in sometimes faltering prose, and made revealing sketches of sites along the trail.

Twelve miles from Caldwell, the pair reached Hopkins ranche on Round Pond Creek, a large stage station with a stockade, where they enjoyed a good supper of beans and coffee. Hunnius slept that night in a loft between a horse blanket and a buffalo robe with six other men, including Hopkins himself. After being supplied the next morning with a mess chest by the two women at the station, Hunnius and Billy moved on twenty miles south to the Skeleton Creek ranche, "a very clean inviting place."[12] Here they enjoyed the luxury of a feather bed and pillows.

This log cabin homestead near Fort Reno typified the structures of presettlement Indian Territory. *Courtesy Western History Collections, University of Oklahoma.*

Hunnius found Buffalo Springs ranche to be a cabin with mud floor and walls and ceiling draped with muslin. The travelers were treated to beans, bacon, biscuits, and coffee by Mrs. Needham, wife of the agent. The next morning, Hunnius was witness to evidence of the 1874 outbreak—a grave mound marked with a board that read (incorrectly): "T. Caliway, G. Pond, B. Cook, Killed By Indians, July 3rd, 1874." Seven miles down the road, they found the burial site of Pat Hennessey, whose body had been buried on the spot. Hunnius noted: "on the east side of the road, just on the edge of it on West side there is a little Knoll of a hill the Headboard says P. Henessey, Killed by Indians July 3d 1874."[13]

The men reached Baker's ranche to find that it had been burned down by the Indians during the summer of 1874, and only a lone chimney was now standing. Red Fork ranche had likewise been destroyed, but it had been rebuilt as a stage station, a large building with a dirt but neat floor, and kept by an agent named Daniel Webster Jones. The roof was supported by posts onto which had been nailed pictures clipped from illustrated newspapers of the day. There being no extra beds, Hunnius and Billy slept on the ground.

Moving in a heavy rain on past Kingfisher station, which was a dugout on the bank of Kingfisher Creek, and Caddo Springs (named for the Caddo Indians who had once camped there), the travelers reached a rise from which "we had a beautiful view as [a] large plain opened and there was the Agency with the Mission House and behind this the new post."[14]

After camping there in 1871, trooper McConnell had described the Caddo Springs site as a wonderful one with water "pouring out of a circular opening about six inches in diameter in the face of a vertical rock, and having a temperature of about forty-five degrees all the year around."[15]

Though Hunnius drew sketches of the agency buildings and the house in which Miles resided, he provided little narrative description of the "new fort" except for a few hints of its physical capacity. He and his friend were provided a double tent with two beds, three blankets, and a stove. Hot coffee and bread were provided at the cavalry company mess.

Hunnius made note of two stores at Darlington, one operated by A. E. Reynolds and another by a man named Hoppel. These trading

stores were undoubtedly the reason why Hunnius referred to an officer at the fort as having "gone to town" where none existed. Hunnius
also told of a visit to the "old camp," where the post hospital was still
located. Dr. William R. Steinmetz, formerly assistant surgeon at Fort
Wallace, was much concerned that the portended new hospital be
situated at the northeast corner of the post away from the dusty stables
to the northwest and the main road to the ferry that connected the
post and agency.[16]

Hunnius was more descriptive of the Darlington agency and
operation of the mission school, which had been opened a short time
earlier on January 1. He told of Miles taking him to the school, its new
addition having big rooms with high ceilings. There were also wash-
rooms for the girls and boys and room for playing during unfavor-
able weather. The kitchen and dining rooms were both large and
roomy. The boys and girls slept upstairs.

But the students were the most interesting to Hunnius. He
admired the Indian children sitting at their rows of desks, girls on one
side and boys on the other. The girls were clothed neatly in dresses,
while the boys wore dark blue pants, vests, and jackets. Their teacher,
Lena Miles, called out the boys' names in English, "each one having
now lost their Indian name and being christianed."[17]

The girls learned to sew, iron, cook, preserve food, and other
household skills. It being wintertime, Hunnius evidently did not
become aware of John H. Seger's industrial training program whereby
Indian boys cultivated more than a hundred acres of land in garden
and corn crops. The boys also managed a herd of agency cattle and
handled chores such as cutting and hauling wood and eventually
learning work activities such as milking cows, butchering, baking
bread, and mending items such as shoes and harness.[18]

By preference of the two tribes, a separate agency school was constructed a mile north of Darlington at Caddo Springs. W. J. Hadley
was its first superintendent. Misses E. E. Starr, Jo Miles, and Anna
Hamilton, who was also the matron, were the first teachers. The
school was later renamed Concho, which in Spanish honored its second superintendent, Charles E. Shell, and the location eventually
became known as such.[19] Concho became the Cheyenne school, and
that at Darlington, the Arapaho school. Older Cheyenne and Arapaho

Arapaho children at Darlington attended the Mennonite's Arapaho boarding school on the far left. *Courtesy Mr. and Mrs. Clyde Meschberger.*

children were sent to Carlisle Institute in Pennsylvania or Hampton Institute in Virginia.

A springtime view of the trail and its cattle and buffalo-hide commerce was provided by accounts that appeared in the Kansas border papers. In April, it was reported from Red Fork ranche that the woods and prairies of the territory were green and millions of wildflowers were in bloom. A herd of some 6,100 head of longhorns owned by Texas cattlemen Mayberry, Driskill, and Lockeridge that had wintered there had left recently for Kansas, the first cattle to go up the trail in 1876.[20]

Some 20,500 pounds of dressed buffalo robes from Indian Territory had already reached Wichita that year.[21] A train of fifteen wagons arrived at Arkansas City from Fort Reno during July. Five of the wagons were loaded with hides and ten with buffalo robes that had been dressed and tanned by Cheyenne and Arapaho women.[22]

The Cheyennes and Arapahos had conducted their fall 1875 hunt on Wolf Creek, twenty-five miles southwest of Camp Supply and on Beaver Creek.[23] A correspondent to the *Arkansas City Traveler* wrote in January that the Osages, who camped all winter at Pond Creek, had sent out hunting parties fifty miles beyond Supply with little success. When the Osages turned to killing cattle, troops came out and attacked their camp.[24]

The buffalo were back during the spring of 1876. A man who journeyed from the Wichita agency to Arkansas City in June said that buffalo were numerous on the prairie and could be found as near as twenty-five miles west of Salt Fork grazing to the southwest. Unable to find buffalo on their own hunting ranges, the hungry Pawnees of Nebraska's Platte River had come south and killed a large number of the animals.[25]

The plight of the Indians in competing for what was left of the great buffalo herds on the prairie was well illustrated by a report that some five hundred professional buffalo hunters were active in the Texas Panhandle. Other entrepreneurs were busy gathering up buffalo bones from northwestern Indian Territory for sale at Dodge City and Wichita.[26]

In June 1876, a number of Cheyennes who had fled north during the 1874 uprising returned to Darlington. These included the bands of chiefs White Antelope and Sand Hill. On orders from General

Pope, Maj. John K. Mizner, commanding at Fort Reno, and Colonel Mackenzie, commanding at Fort Sill, disarmed and dismounted the Cheyennes before turning them over to Miles. Mackenzie, who would soon be called north to campaign against the Lakotas and Northern Cheyennes, expressed satisfaction with the peaceful attitude of the Darlington Indians.[27]

With 1876 being the Centennial year of the American Revolution, the Fourth of July was a special event around the nation. This was no less so for Fort Reno, which featured horse races, some involving Indian contestants, the makeshift firing of a salute from an anvil in the absence of artillery, and a ball for the officers and their ladies. The officers had contributed fifty dollars to purchase fireworks, but these failed to arrive.[28]

Darlington was visited during November by a large delegation of Lakota chiefs, representing some ten to fifteen thousand Indians whom the government was attempting to persuade to move south. Headed by Chief Spotted Tail and escorted by Indian agent A. G. Boone, the group was on an inspection tour of Indian Territory as a potential new homeland. In all, the Sioux numbered ninety-six and included chiefs American Horse, Man-Afraid-of-His-Horses, and Red Dog—"none of them less than six foot," the *Wichita Eagle* reported, "and all muscular and robust."[29]

Arriving at Wichita by train, the party traveled south through Arkansas City in a sixteen-wagon caravan to the Cheyenne and Arapaho agency. From there, they rode down the North Canadian River to inspect the land east of Fort Reno and Darlington before continuing on to the Sac and Fox agency. They boarded a M.K.T. train at Muskogee for their return north. The Sioux were not impressed with the country and, like the Northern Cheyennes, had no desire to give up their native homeland.[30]

When Supt. Enoch Hoag and Quaker official Stanley Pemphrey visited Darlington during the fall of 1876, Arapaho chief Big Mouth said he wished the Sioux would come and live peacefully in Indian Territory. He also wondered why the Great Father had not sent, as had been promised, the agricultural implements depicted on his silver peace medal. Cheyenne chief Big Horse, who was present with his wife and baby, echoed the sentiment, saying that his people had no wagons or ploughs and were constantly out of sugar and coffee. He also pleaded for ammunition with which to kill their beef.[31]

A new commodious school at Darlington now housed over a hundred children. Indian boys were employed in tending a field of corn, caring for livestock, chopping wood, and other chores. The girls performed domestic duties such as kitchen and laundry work, sewing, and tending to the bedrooms. These activities were in addition to class and calisthenic exercises.

Even as the soldiers across the river were doing, the residents of Darlington entertained themselves with social activities. Physician L. A. E. Hodge described one such effort:

> Under this head comes our Musical Society, which meets every Wednesday evening. The Society is ably conducted by Mrs. Miles and the membership comprises all the musical talent in the agency. The book in use is "Palmer's" latest; we have a good organ and organist, and expect to make good progress during the winter in the useful and elevating sciences of music.[32]

The doctor also told of a turkey-hunting excursion that was made shortly before Christmas. He and two others rode twenty-five miles by carriage to the ranch of Bill Williams at the Canadian crossing of the Chisholm Trail. Williams, a former Kentuckian who owned nearly a thousand head of cattle and some three hundred head of horses, was noted for making his substantial ranch house available to travelers and other guests. Williams had taken up the social courtesy of the deceased Jesse Chisholm, who, it was said, had never let a man leave his camp hungry.

Williams escorted the hunters by horseback to a turkey roost, where they had no trouble bagging twenty turkeys before dark. They returned to the roost before sunrise the next morning and added twelve more to their kill. After a breakfast of biscuits, beefsteak, and hot coffee, the agency trio nestled themselves comfortably in their carriage beneath the warmth of buffalo robes and "were soon whirling along towards home" with more than enough turkey for the agency and mission school Christmas dinners.[33]

Christmas Eve was celebrated at the mission school with a tree for the Indian children. Through private donations, the tree was well stocked with presents, every child receiving a gift. "If any argument is necessary," Hodge wrote, "to prove the humanity of the Indians, it is found in the fact that the average little Indian girl loves a doll baby just as much as the little white girl does."[34]

Further indication of this was evidenced later that year when a party of Cheyenne and Arapaho families headed by Chief Little Robe visited Wichita. They were made welcome at the spacious home of their old friend Dutch Bill Greiffenstein, now the mayor of Wichita. They pitched their lodges in his yard and presented him with gifts that included buffalo robes and a large bear robe. Later they went shopping about the town, making many purchases. These items included a number of baby dolls. The Indians would have none that was not ornamented with human hair.[35]

Two Kansas visitors to Darlington in January 1877 were witness to the growing interassociation of Indians and whites. When the men indicated their desire to witness an Indian dance, they were taken to the lodge of Chief Bull Bear and Big Horse, another soldier chief. Bull Bear, whose left arm had been slashed twenty-eight times to represent the men he had killed in battle, had recently rejected a Sioux and Northern Cheyenne entreaty to come north and fight the whites. The chief led the two visitors to a lodge where a dance was under way. Among those performing was an attractive Cheyenne girl, the daughter of a chief. During the previous fall, she had participated in a horseback riding contest at the Muskogee Fair and had taken first prize.[36]

This new social relationship, however, did not reflect the continued plight of the agency population. Physician Hodge reported that there had been a number of deaths among the Cheyennes and Arapahos due to an epidemic of measles. Miles noted that while many children had died in the camps, none of the seventy-two children enrolled in the agency school had succumbed.[37]

John Seger had begun his employment at Darlington as the agency farmer during 1876, overseeing the cultivation of a hundred acres of corn and ten acres of garden vegetables by Indians boys. He was soon placed in charge of the agency's Manual Training and Labor School and began to instruct the Indian boys in animal husbandry. His students developed a sizable herd of cattle and pigs.[38]

The improving harmony between whites and Indians at

Darlington was soon to be interrupted by the government's action of relocating nearly a thousand Northern Cheyennes from the Red Cloud agency in Nebraska to Darlington. As a result, the Fort Reno military would become involved in its most difficult and dangerous exercise of duty, one that narrowly avoided becoming another Custer massacre.

CHAPTER 5

Cousins from the North

During 1876 and 1877, the destinies of Fort Reno and Darlington were directly affected by forces extending from far beyond the confines of Indian Territory. On June 25, 1876, Lt. Col. George Armstrong Custer and his Seventh Cavalry suffered their disastrous defeat at the hands of the Sioux and Cheyennes on the Little Bighorn River. Following this, the Plains Indians' greatest military victory, many of the Cheyennes who had fled north after the Sand Hills fight of 1875 straggled back in small groups to the Darlington agency.[1] From them, agent Miles heard accounts of the Custer affair. He claimed that many of his Southern Cheyennes had been involved in the fight. The Cheyennes felt that Custer's fate was just revenge for his earlier attack on them at the Washita.[2]

A punitive campaign was launched against the northern tribes in November 1876. Many of the officers and troops involved were men who had seen service at Fort Reno, Fort Sill, and Camp Supply in Indian Territory. One arm of the campaign was led by Mackenzie, who marched north from Fort Fetterman to old Fort Reno, Wyoming. Lt. Henry W. Lawton, namesake of Lawton, Oklahoma, led the advance party that prepared the stream and ravine crossings. Pushing on to Crazy Woman's Fork of the Powder River, Mackenzie learned that a large Northern Cheyenne village was camped ahead in a valley of the Bighorn Mountains.

Mackenzie reached the village without being discovered, and early on the frozen morning of the twenty-sixth he launched his attack. Among those charging into the village was 1st Lt. John A. McKinney, who was on detached duty from Fort Reno with the Fourth Cavalry. While trying to dislodge a party of Cheyennes who had taken refuge in a ravine, McKinney was shot and killed. Former Fort Reno commander Wirt Davis may well have suffered a similar fate had not a band of Shoshoni scouts come to the rescue of him and his unit.[3]

The village was that of Northern Cheyenne chief Dull Knife, who would soon play a major role in the drama of Fort Reno. Mackenzie took captives, but most of Dull Knife's people escaped into the hills and took refuge with the Sioux. Ravaged and destitute, they suffered through the winter; but when spring came they assented to Mackenzie's summon to surrender, doing so at Fort Robinson in April 1877. There, in council with Gen. George Crook and Mackenzie, the Cheyennes reluctantly acceded to being sent to Indian Territory to join their southern cousins.

The Northern chiefs, however, looked upon this entirely as a trial move, believing that they had been promised they could return north if Indian Territory did not suit them. Early in May, the Cheyennes gathered together their scant belongings and fell in line behind Lieutenant Lawton and a small escort of Fourth Cavalry for a long, wearing journey that would continue through May, June, and July. They arrived at Fort Reno on August 5, 1877.[4]

Colonel Mizner immediately ordered an enrollment of the newcomers, finding some 937 persons of all ages. Mackenzie, who had come south ahead of them, met with the Northern chiefs, taking from them all of their horses except for one pony to a lodge. The confiscated horses were later driven to Wichita, Kansas, and sold at auction, the proceeds being used to purchase breed cows for the Indians as an experiment in adapting them to the practice of husbandry.[5]

The Northerners were turned over to the agency on August 6. Almost immediately the promises made to them at Red Cloud were abrogated. Their addition to the responsibilities at Darlington created much difficulty for the agency. The Indians had arrived exhausted and in poor health after their long ordeal on the trail, many having had to walk the entire distance. Unaccustomed to the heat and humid air of the south, a good number became ill with malaria. Miles characterized it as an especially sickly season, even among agency employees and other Indians, but admitted that the death rate was higher among the new arrivals. With only one physician and scant medical supplies —Miles's request for a hospital had been denied—the agency was ill equipped to provide adequate treatment, especially when the Indians were struck by an epidemic of measles and dysentery the following spring.

Further, annuities supplies for the Darlington agency had been restricted by a parsimonious Congress, causing a limitation of flour, coffee, and other supplies but especially of fresh meat upon which the Northern people had long thrived. Complaints by their chiefs that their children were dying of hunger and sickness went unattended. During their two-year stay at Darlington, some ninety-four Northern Cheyenne deaths occurred.[6]

A serious problem regarding the issuance of annuity goods to the Northerners also arose. Miles had made his usual trip to the beef pens one morning to monitor the allotment there. When he returned to the agency, he found that the Northern Cheyennes were not being issued their other rations by the method that he intended—that is, by individual families. Instead, a group of young men had rounded up all of the ration tickets that had been issued to the tribespeople, taken them to Miles's clerk, and demanded the goods be issued in bulk. As a result, the goods had been piled in the agency plaza, allowing the Northern chiefs to help themselves first to all they wanted and then distribute what was left to the tribe in general.[7]

The distribution was almost completed by the time Miles arrived, but through George Bent he made a strong protest and declared that hereafter they would follow the method whereby the women would present their family ticket and take the articles needed for their family lodges. The Northern chiefs insisted that, no, they would do it their old way. What was the use of having chiefs, they said, "What is there left for us to do?"[8]

Miles was adamant that each family would get its fair share, and his wishes prevailed. Still this was a discontentment added to many other disappointments, as Miles pointed out to Mizner:

> They were promised as a daily ration ¹/₂ lbs. beef net, ¹/₂ lbs. flour or ¹/₂ lb. of corn, and 4 lbs. coffee, 8 lbs. sugar and 3 lbs. of beans to each 100 rations, which promised has only been carried out in part, the supplies received being insufficient.
>
> They were also promised houses for the chiefs and assistance to build houses for others, cattle, hogs, &c., none of which have been carried out.[9]

In July, prior to the arrival of the Northern Cheyennes, the Southern Cheyennes and Arapahos had staged a very successful buffalo hunt that permitted the Indians to sustain themselves for five months. A large number of animals were killed during that hunting season, and the Indians of the Darlington agency tanned some fifteen thousand buffalo skins for traders.[10]

A joint expedition of the Darlington bands to the buffalo grounds in far western Oklahoma in November and December, however, proved to be a total disaster. Escorted by Capt. Sebastian Gunther and Troop A, Fourth Cavalry, the Cheyenne and Arapaho hunters moved slowly up the North Canadian toward Camp Supply. They soon discovered that the expected buffalo were not there. Being away from the agency and their annuity goods, the hunting expedition began to experience severe hunger.

Additionally, they found that they had been preceded by a large band of Pawnees from the Loup River in Nebraska, who had invaded their hunting grounds. The Pawnees likewise had found few buffalo and were as desperate for food as the Darlington Indians. They had applied to Maj. Henry A. Hambright, commanding Camp Supply, for subsistence and had been denied. A clash between the Darlington Indians and their longtime enemies was greatly feared.[11]

To avoid such a calamity, a compromise was reached where the Pawnees would work the country west of Camp Supply, the Arapahos would go north up the Beaver, and the Cheyennes would hunt to the south along Wolf Creek. Still finding nothing but an inadequate offering of small game, some Cheyennes went on south to the Canadian, Washita, and Red Rivers. Others pushed on to the head of Wolf Creek in the Texas Panhandle. Only a few buffalo were to be found, and the tribes were in dire condition.[12] "They soon destroyed all the small game that could be found," Mizner reported; "they lived for a time on dogs, coyotes, and horse flesh, until beef could be issued to them at Camp Supply to keep them from starving until they could reach the agency."[13]

In January, the Darlington Indians were recalled from the field to Camp Supply and, on Miles's request, issued beef by the trading firm of Lee and Reynolds. They were then ordered to return to the agency. The Indians did so, but very reluctantly because of their dissatisfaction with the food issue and treatment there.

Despite the hope that the Southern and Northern Cheyennes would mix together well, a growing breach developed between the two divisions of the tribe. The Northerners began camping well apart from the Southern bands, who called them "Sioux Cheyennes." As reports of increasing discontent among the Northern Cheyenne ranks were heard, army officials became concerned that an uprising might result.

Lieutenant Lawton was called upon to investigate the situation at Darlington. In late September, he visited the Northern Cheyenne camps and talked with Dull Knife, Wild Hog, Standing Elk, and other leaders. The chiefs assured him they would keep their promise to be peaceful. But they complained that Miles was not issuing them fair rations. Many of the beef cows, they said, were lame or starved and provided little nourishment. Further, because their village was nine miles from the agency and apart from the other bands, the post doctor failed to visit them.[14]

The Northern Cheyennes found the humidity and heat of the territory much to their dislike, and wood ticks were plentiful and painful. Many of the immigrants suffered from the white man's diseases. They did not like a place, the Northerners said, where they were always sick. They had been happy and well in Montana, but here their people were dying around them. Nor did they like Miles, who during the summer of 1878 refused to issue them coffee and sugar because they would not involve themselves in any kind of work activity.[15]

Miles rejected most of the charges made by Lawton's report, claiming that he had indeed issued sufficient rations. "I have been able to find but very few Indians," he told a Senate committee with little sympathy, "who would not say they could eat more beef."[16]

When the Northern chiefs resisted sending their children to school, Miles threatened to cut off their rations entirely. Philip McCusker, a frontiersman who had been deeply involved with the Plains tribes since the Civil War, charged Miles with cheating the Indians through his silent partnership in a Darlington trading firm and with preferential treatment to agency interpreter George Bent.[17]

However much truth there was to these indictments, there is no question that Miles was working to improve the lot of his Southern Cheyennes and Arapahos. In an effort to enhance their labor and income potential, he instituted a program whereby the Indians themselves would haul their annuity goods from Wichita and other Kansas towns to the agency. The Cheyenne and Arapaho Transportation

Company was formed under the direction of J. A. Covington, agency
superintendent of farming, and William E. Malaley. Forty wagons and
eighty sets of harness were purchased and assigned to individual tribal
members, who would pay for them from their freighting profits. The
first trip made by the Indian teamsters to Wichita occurred during
September 1877. Soon Indian freighters on the Chisholm Trail
between Darlington and the Kansas border towns were a common
sight.[18] "For the first time since my connection with this agency, now
nearly seven years," Miles wrote, "I can report the receipt of annuities before the departure of the Indians on the winter hunt."[19]

Fort Reno received a brief visit from some high brass during
February 1878. These guests were Generals Phil Sheridan and George
Crook, who came down from Wichita with their entourage supposedly to inspect posts in the territory. The officers were much more
interested in getting in some hunting. A correspondent to the *Dodge
City Times* noted: "They were received with befitting honors; salutes
fired, &c. They were expected to remain a day or two at least, but they
left the same evening for Supply or Elliott, and I didn't even get a
glimpse of the great Generals, except from a distance."[20]

Sheridan and Crook were provided an escort of twenty-two
Fourth Cavalry troops under Lt. Henry Sweeney and Lt. Wilber E.
Wilder. With this brief interruption having passed, the post returned
to its normal routine, and the garrison looked hopefully to something
more exciting than baseball contests between cavalry and infantry
nines, performances of the Fort Reno Dramatic Club, and holding a
post charity ball. The *Dodge City Times* provided a description of the
fort as it stood in early 1878:

> Fort Reno is a very neat and pretty post, situated on the south
> side of the north fork of the Canadian, 75 miles from Ft. Sill, 125
> miles from Camp Supply and 180 miles from Wichita, Kansas,
> the nearest railroad point. It is garrisoned by Cos. E and I 16th
> Inf. and H and G 4th Cavalry. The commanding officer is Col.
> J. K. Mizner, Major 4th Cavalry. The other officers are Capts.
> Gunther and Rendlebrock, Lieuts. Sweeney and Wilder of the
> 4th Cav. and Capts. Fletcher and [William H.] Clapp and Lieuts.
> Morrison, McFarland and Woodbury of the 16th Inf. Surgeon
> DeLoffe, A. A. Surg. Chase and Steward W. C. Freeman form

the medical staff, while Comy. Sergt. Fred A. McNeill presides with characteristic grace and dignity over the commissary department.[21]

In April the camps of the Southern Cheyennes and Arapahos celebrated the return of their Fort Marion prisoners, whom the government had released. The thirty-nine Cheyennes, Arapahos, Kiowas, and Comanches, all wearing U.S. military uniforms, had arrived in Wichita by train. Most of them now spoke English very well. Prominent among the Cheyennes were chiefs Minimic, the leading peace advocate of the group, and Medicine Water, who had led the Germain massacre. The Indians were greeted at the railway station by Mayor Greiffenstein, whom they hugged and shook with great affection. Agent Miles was there, also, to receive the tribesmen from their military escort and take them by wagon to the territory. Excited relatives and members of their tribes met the former prisoners at the Kansas-Indian Territory border.[22]

At Fort Marion the Indian prisoners had undergone daily military drills. As instructed by the Indian Bureau, on their return Miles organized some of them into an agency police force. The unit consisted of one captain, one lieutenant, three sergeants, and twelve privates. Fourteen of the Northern Cheyennes likewise had been enlisted as military scouts.[23]

Troops at Fort Reno, meanwhile, were breaking the routine of garrison life by forming social, literary, and sporting clubs. The enlisted men of Company H organized a drama club and presented shows featuring farces with song and dance. They also had a library association and a baseball club.[24]

To the soldiers at Fort Reno, affairs with the Indians appeared to be relaxed and calm. The discontent among the Northern Cheyennes camped west of Darlington, however, had continued to grow, approaching the point of rebellion. Some of the Northerners—Living Bear, Standing Elk, Turkey Leg, American Horse, and others—had become affiliated to the point of sending their children to school. But other chiefs—namely Dull Knife, Wild Hog, Little Wolf, and Old Crow—separated to themselves and insisted that they desired to return north.[25] Their young men were particularly discontent. "We are sickly here," they said, "and no one will speak our names when we are gone. We will go north at all hazards and if we die in battle,

During its heyday, Fort Reno featured a neat arrangement of quarters and offices around its parade grounds quadrangle. *Courtesy National Archives.*

our names will be remembered and cherished by all our people."[26]

Miles failed to read the potential threat when during the summer of 1878 a group of Southern Cheyennes came to him. Some of their best horses were being stolen, they said, and they thought the Northern Cheyennes were the guilty parties. White thieves, they said, would just round up a bunch of horses and run them all off, while these culprits took only a few choice animals from each herd. But when Miles called in chiefs Dull Knife, Wild Hog, Old Crow, and Little Wolf and questioned them on the matter, they assured him they had no intention of leaving, that the horse stealing was all a Southern Cheyenne and Arapaho lie.[27]

During early September, the Southern Cheyennes again came to Miles to insist that young men among the Northern Cheyennes were indeed stealing their horses. The warriors, the Southern Cheyennes declared, had established a camp on the Cimarron and were accumulating a herd of good mounts there to be used when they started north. On September 5, Miles sent his clerk to Mizner at Fort Reno informing him that many of the Northern Cheyennes had attempted to withdraw rations for two weeks rather than the usual one and that they had broken camp to remove to the Cimarron River. In response Mizner ordered Capt. Joseph Rendlebrock, a Civil War veteran who still spoke with a German accent despite his service of twenty-seven years in the U.S. Army, to establish a camp with Companies F and G of the Fourth Cavalry near the Cheyennes' village and keep a watch on them. Rendlebrock's scouts watched the Cheyennes with binoculars from a distance, concluding that the Indians were still in camp and none were absent.[28]

Still, a great many well-armed Indians were coming into the detachment's camp, some strapped with as much as two belts of ammunition. Lieutenant Wilder was sent back to Fort Reno to report that the Indians were fortifying their camp and digging rifle pits. Rendlebrock asked that the post's two twelve-pound Napoleon cannon be sent out in case it became necessary to shell the Indians. However, Mizner did not wish to do anything to provoke hostilities and rejected the request.[29]

In an attempt to resolve the matter, Miles called the Northern leaders to his office for a council. He instructed them to bring their

Northern
Cheyenne chiefs
Little Wolf and
Dull Knife led the
famous retreat
northward from
Fort Reno in 1878.
*Courtesy National
Museum of Natural
History.*

young men to his office for a count. Upon returning to their camps,
the chiefs sent back word that they could not come in because some
of their young men were too sick. Miles directed head farmer J. A.
Covington and Dr. Hodge to go to the Northern camp and investigate. The two men did so on September 8, a Sunday, riding out in a
buggy. They found the village all packed up as if to move. As the doctor was tending to the ill of the village, Covington talked with Wild
Hog, Old Crow, and Dull Knife.

The chiefs admitted that they did, indeed, wish to leave. They felt
that if they stayed in the south, they would all die. They had not come
to this country to live permanently—merely to see if they liked it. But
for now their people were preparing to move away from Rendlebrock's
troops because their women were too frightened to put up their camp

around the soldiers. Covington was convinced that they were not fleeing north and reported as much to Miles and Mizner.[30]

On the evening of September 9, Wild Hog, Old Crow, and Little
Wolf came to the agency once more for talks with Miles and Mizner.
Through interpreter Edmund Guerrier, Miles assured them that all
that was wanted of them was a count of their young men. If they were
only ten or fifteen short, it would not matter. Rendlebrock's troops
would then be withdrawn.[31]

"Great pains were taken to explain to these Indians," Mizner
reported, "that what the agent required could be easily complied with,
and they were informed that until his orders were obeyed, the troops
would continue to guard their camp, and that no further supplies
would be issued to them."[32]

Mizner and Miles both believed that the talk had convinced the
chiefs to be compliant, even though the chiefs refused to provide the
ten hostages requested as guarantee against their leaving. In truth,
however, both Mizner and Miles were dead wrong, for neither really
understood the desperation of the Northern Cheyennes. "We were
starving and dying off from disease," Old Crow said later. "Our children could not live on corn meal and mush alone."[33]

A loud banging on his door at three o'clock on the morning of
September 10, 1878, woke Miles from his sleep. He opened the door
to find Northern Cheyenne chief American Horse and a captain in
the Indian police. They told the agent that sometime prior to mid-
night a segment of the Northern Cheyennes had packed their lodges
and headed north, leaving their lodge frames standing and campfires
burning to mislead Rendlebrock's soldiers. Pack animals had been
used to avoid the slower and more trackable method of transporting
camp goods by travois.[34]

American Horse declared that he had been trying to get away from
them for several days, but others had threatened to kill his only horse
if he did so. Miles dashed off a note to Colonel Mizner, advising him
of the situation. In turn, Mizner immediately sent Lt. Abram E. Wood
out to join Rendlebrock with a wagon and five days' rations for the
entire command. Wood also carried orders for Rendlebrock to pursue and "spare no effort to bring the Indians back."[35]

Miles estimated the number of disaffected Cheyennes at over three hundred, with some eighty-five of them being males of warrior age. The remainder included nearly two hundred women, girls, and young boys. Dull Knife and Little Wolf would prove to be the two dominant leaders of the group. Other chiefs included Old Crow, Porcupine, Wild Hog, Tangled Hair, Blacksmith, and Left Hand. Early reports from Fort Reno indicated that the Indians were poorly provided and had few arms. No danger was to be feared as to their warlike intentions, it was believed, and they would be easily captured.[36]

In testimony given later, Mizner would acknowledge that he had merely assumed that the Cheyennes had been disarmed. But in truth, an agreement had been made at the time of their surrender that they would keep their arms in moving south. Ben Clark, who had been sent out from Fort Reno to meet the Northern Cheyennes near the Cimarron upon their arrival, would later testify that the newcomers had Sharpes and Winchester rifles in addition to muzzleloaders, pistols, and revolvers. The troops were armed with carbines, six-shot pistols, Schofield rifles, and Smith and Wessons.[37]

As had happened with Custer and the Seventh Cavalry at the Little Bighorn, Rendlebrock and his men would catch more Indians than they really wanted.

CHAPTER 6

Pursuit of the Northern Cheyennes

The stage was now set for the dramatic episode of Indian history that would become the subject of Mari Sandoz's classic book, *Cheyenne Autumn*. It would be Fort Reno's greatest challenge and most trying military venture.

Upon being made aware of the Northern Cheyennes' departure, Mizner immediately sent couriers galloping to Camp Supply and Fort Sill, the latter having a telegraph by which a message could be relayed to department headquarters at Fort Leavenworth.[1] A company of the Fourth Cavalry was dispatched from Fort Sill to reinforce Fort Reno.

The frontier expertise of Ben Clark was sought regarding the potential objective and route of the Northern Cheyennes. Their favorite camping grounds, Clark said, were east of the Black Hills along the South Fork of the Cheyenne, the Belle Fourche, and the White Rivers. They would likely follow a much-used trail that crossed the Arkansas at the head of Crooked Creek, thence across Pawnee Fork, the Smoky Hill, and Beaver Fork of the Republican to the Rickaree near the junction of Pork and Black Tail Deer Creeks. From there the trail diverged, the main branch heading in the direction of Sidney Barracks, Nebraska.[2]

The telegraph lines interconnecting the various military posts in Indian Territory, Kansas, Colorado, and the Texas Panhandle were soon tapping out the news of the Northern Cheyenne escape from Darlington, and troops in Kansas began boarding trains to key points of interception. These points were on the Kansas Pacific Railroad near Fort Wallace and two Indian trail crossings between Wallace and Fort Hays.[3]

Rendlebrock's force consisted of Company H with thirty-nine enlisted men and Company G with forty-one, for a total of eighty men. Officers with Rendlebrock's detachment were Capt. Sebastian Gunther and lieutenants David N. McDonald, Wilder, and Wood.

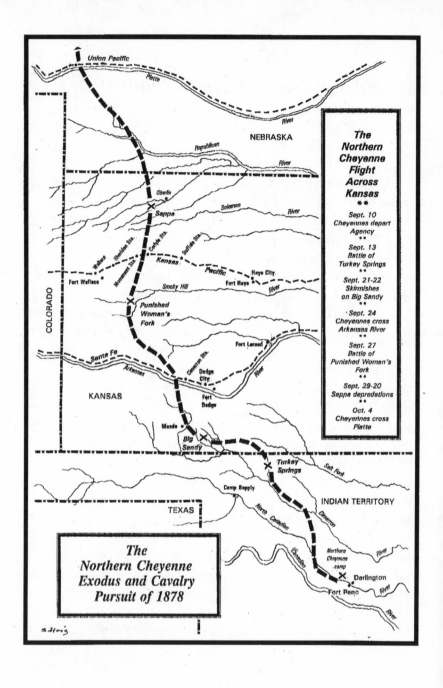

The Northern Cheyenne Flight Across Kansas

✱ ✱

Sept. 10
Cheyennes depart Agency

✱✱

Sept. 13
Battle of Turkey Springs

✱✱

Sept. 21-22
Skirmishes on Big Sandy

✱✱

Sept. 24
Cheyennes cross Arkansas River

✱✱

Sept. 27
Battle of Punished Woman's Fork

✱✱

Sept. 29-20
Sappa depredations

✱✱

Oct. 4
Cheyennes cross Platte

The Northern Cheyenne Exodus and Cavalry Pursuit of 1878

The troops were supported by fifteen Arapaho scouts who had been dispatched by Miles.[4]

The rations were divided and placed on twenty pack mules. It took about an hour to pick up the Cheyennes' trail, a dim one with only one travois cut leading through the ragged sand hills. The trail followed along the south bank of the North Canadian River, then crossed the river on a northerly course through the thick brakes of Kingfisher Creek. Rendlebrock pushed his Fort Reno command fifty-two miles that day, remaining on the trail until ten o'clock on the night of the tenth.[5]

While the command was camped at the Cimarron River, the Arapaho scouts refused to help find a trooper who had become lost. Rendlebrock angrily expelled most of the scouts from his camp. However, two Arapahos—Chalk (or Ghost Man) and Little Sitting Bull—continued on ahead the next day, leading the troops along the dividing ridge between the Cimarron and the Salt Fork of the Arkansas to a water hole—unfortunately, spoiled—where they went into camp at eight o'clock that evening after a hard march of forty-five miles over rough terrain.

The countryside now lay in rolling hills with cedar trees and brush growing in the rivulet valleys between. The region was so badly cut by ravines and stone-rimmed escarpments that at times the cavalrymen were forced to ride single file. They had moved ahead only a few miles on the morning of the thirteenth when a large body of mounted warriors was spotted some eight hundred yards ahead. The women, children, and packhorses could be seen disappearing into the barren hills beyond. The Cheyennes, who had likewise spotted the troops, were drawn up in a battle line before a grove of timber that marked Turkey Springs, a spring-fed watering hole some twenty-three miles west of present Alva, Oklahoma, and thirty-six northeast of Camp Supply. In his official report on the affair, Rendlebrock estimated the Cheyenne strength at 150 warriors.[6]

On the day before the Fourth Cavalry detachment caught up with them, advance scouts of the Northern Cheyennes had encountered a wagon driven by two young cowboys, Reuben Bristow and Fred Clark of the Comanche Pool spread that then encompassed a large area between the Cimarron and Salt Fork, extending into Kansas. The two men had been on their way to the saline just west of present Freedom, Oklahoma, to gather rock salt for the ranch's cattle.[7]

Charles Colcord, then a young cowboy and later a prominent citizen of Oklahoma City, arrived at the scene later. By his reckoning of the hoof marks and wheel ruts, the Cheyennes had surrounded the wagon and, when the mules stampeded, galloped alongside and poured arrows into the two cowboys in buffalo-killing fashion. Colcord found the bodies still in the wagon, each with three or four arrows protruding from his torso. The mules had been cut loose from their traces and driven off.[8]

This event was yet unreported when Rendlebrock's command caught up with the Darlington refugees at ten o'clock on the morning of September 13. Captain Gunther described the meeting:

> When we approached the rough country, where the Indians were supposed to be, we heard a loud voice in the cedar brake. It was the voice of an Indian. Then we were sure that the Indians were near there. As soon as we got over a very high knoll, over the broken country we could see the Indians, about a mile the other side of the ridge. We approached to within half a mile of them, when we were in between two canons. After we got in, we found ourselves surrounded by the Indians. They were already lying in the canons, waiting for us, although a majority of the Indians showed themselves a quarter of a mile further up, on rising ground. Some few Indians then rode within two hundred yards, backward and forward, as all Indians do before a battle.[9]

The initial contact was made when Rendlebrock sent Chalk forward to urge the Cheyennes to return to the agency with the troops.[10] According to Gunther, Chalk threw up his blankets and made different signs for them to come in. Finally a parley was held, the Cheyennes declaring firmly that they would never return to Darlington to be starved again. They did not wish to fight, but they would do so before they would return.[11]

It was the troops who initiated the fight at Turkey Springs when Lieutenant Wood ordered his Company G to commence firing. The Cheyennes responded instantly, returning fire as they surrounded the troops and poured lead at the detachment from the front as well as from the canyons on the right, left, and rear. Lieutenants McDonald,

Wilder, and Wood attempted a countercharge, but the troops were quickly driven back.

Along with the men, the cavalry horses and pack animals took much of the Cheyennes' fire, and Rendlebrock was forced to dismount his command. The horses were secured in a deep ravine; but with some thirty troopers required to hold the animals, the command was left with only fifty-some effectives for battle. These remaining soldiers dug rifle pits to form a firing-line defense. Rendlebrock held a position on a knoll that the Indians attacked three times but each time were driven back.

During the first day of action, Cpl. Patrick Lynch and Pvt. Frank Struad (Strnad) were killed and three others wounded. The two dead troopers were buried in a ravine during the fight at Turkey Springs on September 13.[12] Pinned down and unable to advance on the Indians, the cavalry troops were held to their positions the rest of the day and through the night. On one occasion the Indians fired the prairie, but the wind did not carry it to the troops. Having been unable to fill their canteens at the last watering hole, the men were suffering badly from thirst, as were their horses. A few troopers tried to go in search of water but were driven back.

With no medical help for the wounded, ammunition running dangerously low, and the troops obviously up against a superior force, a massacre of the entire command appeared possible. It is likely that the memory of the Custer disaster two years before, in which some of these same Northern Cheyennes had participated, came to more than one trooper's mind.

On the morning of the fourteenth, Rendlebrock and his officers determined on a withdrawal to Camp Supply, where the wounded could be cared for and reinforcements secured. With Rendlebrock at the lead, the dismounted command retreated back through the long, narrow defile by which they had arrived. Lieutenants Wood and McDonald with only a few troopers provided rear guard protection until ground conducive to the use of cavalry was reached. Then the two officers, along with Lieutenant Wilder, recruited enough men to make three mounted charges on the Indians. During one of these sorties, Private Burton, Company H blacksmith, was shot from his horse. The retreating troops made no attempt to rescue him, and he was presumed killed. Little more was ever said regarding the trooper. The Cheyennes withdrew only when the weary and severely parched command finally found a water hole and went into camp.[13]

The Fourth Cavalry detachment reached Camp Supply two days later on September 16. Makeshift drags had been constructed for carrying the wounded, which included Chalk and privates Burrows (or Borroughs) and Leonard of Company G.[14] Thirteen cavalry horses were lost. Rendlebrock optimistically estimated that about fifteen Indians had been killed and some thirty wounded. The Cheyennes were also believed to have lost twenty or more of their valuable horses.[15]

The Fort Reno troops had ridden 179 rough miles without letup or forage for their animals, fought a bruising fight against a tenacious force of Cheyenne warriors, and suffered casualties both in men and stock. Rendlebrock's near disaster was a wake-up call for the army, which realized anew that the Cheyennes were not only experienced fighters but also remarkably brave in battle.

But it was far from over. Camp Supply would be no rest haven for the weary Fort Reno troops. On the seventeenth, Lieutenant Wood and forty men of the command swung back into their saddles and headed north. They carried orders to make contact with Capt. William C. Hemphill and Company I, Fourth Cavalry, at the Cimarron River redoubt some thirty-eight miles above Supply. Hemphill's detachment had been sent out earlier from Camp Supply to search for the Cheyennes south of Fort Dodge. Finding that Hemphill was not at the Cimarron, Wood made a scout some seventeen miles to the east and north of the redoubt. Rendlebrock and Gunther arrived there the next day.

Rendlebrock now decided to make a forced march fifty miles to Fort Dodge, where they could take a Sante Fe train west to meet Hemphill. En route, however, two couriers arrived from Dodge with orders for the command to move east to where Hemphill was now camped on Crooked Creek.[16] Contact was eventually made, the Fort Reno command learning that Hemphill had found the Cheyennes on September 17 near a tributary of the Cimarron. He and his thirty or so troops had skirmished with some one hundred warriors inconclusively until dark with the loss of one man and two horses. Hemphill concluded that "the Indians were invincible and were fearless in the extreme."[17]

Pvt. Patrick Lynch, who was killed in the Battle of Turkey Springs, is buried in the Fort Reno cemetery. Arapaho scout Chalk was another victim of Turkey Springs.
Author photos.

Hemphill had since been joined at a water hole camp on Sand Creek, a tributary of Crooked Creek, by Company A, Sixteenth Infantry, from Fort Dodge under Capt. Charles E. Morse. The infantrymen were transported there in heavy government wagons accompanied by a civilian posse comprised of cowboys from the ranches of southern Kansas and Dodge City residents. The ranchmen rose to action when news arrived at the Comanche Pool headquarters on Medicine Lodge Creek that the Cheyennes had attacked and killed members of a family on the Salt Fork of the Cimarron and several cowboys on Bluff Creek. The cowmen galloped to Fort Dodge, where they were joined by some forty more civilians. From there they and their horses boarded a special Santa Fe train with Morse's infantrymen, wagons, and stock to a point west of Cimarron railway station some twenty-seven miles from Dodge.[18]

Rendlebrock's troops had no sooner unsaddled their horses than firing was heard within a mile or two of the camp. It was learned that the determined Kansans had pushed ahead, made contact with the Indians, and engaged them. Rendlebrock, senior officer of the combined military units, ordered his cavalrymen back into their saddles. Riding forth they found the posse being driven back by a large force of Cheyennes. The troops countercharged and forced the Indians into a ravine, holding them there until sundown, when Rendlebrock chose to withdraw.[19]

Rendlebrock's entire force, including the posse, renewed the engagement on the following morning, making a circular maneuver to attack from the south. The Cheyennes were now well entrenched behind breastworks and in rifle pits they had dug during the night. Gunfire was exchanged throughout the day until nearly sundown, when Rendlebrock broke off the fight. He ordered Morse to throw out eighteen-man picket detachments several hundred yards from the camp. Rendlebrock would be roundly denounced as a coward by the cowboys for breaking off the fight. They contended that the Indians could have best been whipped there and then. Rendlebrock argued later that it would have cost a considerable number of lives to storm the Cheyenne barricades. "The Indians fought like devils," he said, "and with as much system as if they had been drilled."[20]

Rendlebrock sent to Fort Dodge for supplies and ammunition, but when morning came it was learned that the Cheyennes had disappeared, their trail leading to the north. The troops took up pursuit at 7 A.M., trailing the Cheyennes, who were in sight ahead, westward. A skirmish took place when the warriors halted at a vacated stone work to delay Rendlebrock's advance. The infantry was sent forward as a skirmish line and a steady fire continued until mid afternoon.[21]

Rendlebrock, meanwhile, made camp some mile and a half away. Once again the Cheyennes slipped off during the night. The command remained in place during September 23, distributing the rations and ammunition that had arrived from Fort Dodge. On the next day, the march was resumed to a point on Crooked Creek two miles north of Meade City and from there on the twenty-fifth due north to the Arkansas River.

At Cimarron station they were joined by the command of Lt. Col. William H. Lewis, commander of Fort Dodge, with Companies B and F of the Fourth Cavalry and Company G, Nineteenth Infantry. The Fourth Cavalry was led by Captain Mauck, former commander of Fort Reno, who had made a hurried march from Fort Elliott to Camp Supply and on to Dodge.[22]

While Hemphill was at Dodge, Lewis had talked with Camp Supply interpreter and scout Amos Chapman. Chapman told him that the Cheyenne outbreak was caused by the Indians having such insufficient food that they were driven to eating horse flesh taken even from animals that had died of disease. In response, Lewis wrote a letter to Gen. John Pope for transmission to General Sheridan. In the letter, he defined the Northern Cheyennes as a people driven to the brink of despair.[23]

Lewis now assumed command of the Cheyenne-hunting expedition. Much to his chagrin, Morse was ordered to turn over his wagons for use by Rendlebrock and Hemphill and return to Dodge. The units were then consolidated while scouts searched for a crossing of the Arkansas River by the Cheyennes. Once the ford was located, the U.S. force pushed rapidly northward on the Indians' trail, following it for two days without event. At Punished Woman's Fork[24] of the Smoky Hill River, the Cheyenne warriors once again fell back to blunt the advance of the troops. Cheyenne riflemen set up an ambush by occupying the ridges along a deep ravine through which their trail ran. An eager warrior fired too soon, however, and the troops narrowly avoided the trap.

In the battle that followed, the troops suffered four casualties, one of them being Lewis, the officer who had spoken up for the Northern Cheyennes. Continuing to direct the fire of his men even after his horse was hit, Lewis was wounded in the thigh by a bullet that severed his femoral artery. He was placed in an army ambulance and sent off with a twenty-five-troop escort to Fort Wallace, Kansas. Already weakened by a two-week siege of dysentery, he died en route the day after receiving his wound.

Having failed once again to stop the determined Northern Cheyennes, the army made a desperate effort to do so at the line of the Union Pacific Railway that cut across southern Nebraska. A train was kept steamed up at Sidney Barracks ready to move troops to a point of interception. Gen. Wesley Merritt was ordered to move rapidly with Fifth Cavalry troops from Fort Leavenworth to Fort Laramie, Wyoming, and Col. Caleb H. Carlton to Fort Robinson, Nebraska, with Third Cavalry troops.[25]

When word came that the Indians had crossed the Union Pacific railway at Alkali station well east of Sidney Barracks, troops of the Fourth Infantry under Maj. Thomas T. Thornburgh were rushed to the crossing site by train. Thornburgh was met there by Mauck with a command that was totally exhausted. Mauck went on to Sidney Barracks while Thornburgh, his infantry troops riding in wagons, continued the chase into extremely difficult country filled with sand hills and devoid of grass or water. At the Niobrara River, Thornburgh joined with Carlton's Third Cavalry. Both units were suffering badly for want of food and water. After a futile chase, the joint command gave up the pursuit and retired to Camp Sheridan, Nebraska. The Northern Cheyennes, whose young men had committed numerous depredations in passing through Kansas, later told Ben Clark that they had fifteen of their people killed in the various engagements after leaving Fort Reno.[26]

At the same time that the Dull Knife/Little Wolf Cheyennes were making their escape from Indian Territory, another party of 186 Northern Cheyennes under Little Chief was being escorted southward to Darlington from Fort Abraham Lincoln, Dakota Territory, by Clark, who had been ordered from Fort Reno for that purpose. Fearing that the Little Chief group might learn of the retreat of the others and attempt to join them, the army detained Little Chief and his people at Sidney Barracks for a time. In December, after they had rested, Mauck and Fourth Cavalry troops H and G from Fort Reno and I and K from Fort Elliott were assigned to assist Clark in escorting the band on to Fort Reno and Darlington.[27]

After advancing beyond Camp Supply some thirty or forty miles, Mauck received orders from General Pope instructing him to disarm and dismount the Cheyennes. The demand that this be done before they entered the reservation had been made by Miles through the Office of Indian Affairs. To do so, however, was in direct contradiction to promises made the Cheyennes by General Sheridan. The Cheyennes, who had served with the U.S. Army against the Sioux and Nez Percés, had been told that in coming South they would be able to retain their weapons and horses.

The forty-eight Northern Cheyenne warriors led by Iron Shirt vowed to die first. They formed a semicircle around their women and children with their guns and knives in hand. Clearly they were determined to resist. Mauck wheeled his four troops of Fourth Cavalry into formation to enforce the edict but offered a reasonable time for discussion. An officer later described the scene: "The confronting lines were not thirty yards apart, and as we stood there looking into their eyes, flashing with resentment, our officers at least felt that their time had come."[28]

A dangerous confrontation appeared imminent until Clark talked with the Cheyennes and was able to mollify them by promising that the weapons would be returned once they were on the reservation. On December 9, the two companies of soldiers that had left the post on September 5 returned to Fort Reno after having traveled over a thousand miles in the saddle.[29]

Making the trip with them from Sidney Barracks, Nebraska, to Fort Reno was Lt. Herber M. Creel, Seventh Cavalry, who had been placed on detached service with the Northern Cheyennes for the purpose of learning the Cheyenne language and writing a complete grammar and dictionary of it. Also he was to make occasional reports on matters pertaining to the Cheyennes. His compilation of the Cheyenne language would be followed several years later by Mennonite missionary Rudolf Petter, who produced a Cheyenne-Arapaho dictionary.[30]

The chase after Dull Knife and his people had been extremely difficult on the Fort Reno troops, who had been forced to follow the

Indians north into freezing weather and snow and live on two hard tacks a day. When they returned to Fort Reno, the men were ragged, unshaven, and filthy.[31]

Their condition was well illustrated when a reporter for the *New York Herald* encountered Rendlebrock. The officer, who had been relieved of his command, was returning to Fort Reno in a Pullman car of a Union Pacific train from Sidney Barracks to Council Bluffs, Iowa. The correspondent described the officer as being "so sunburned as to be almost black, wearing a soiled uniform, with nothing to suggest that he was more than a private but a pair of worn shoulder straps, bearing the bars of a captain."[32]

When asked if he had given up the chase after the Cheyennes, Rendlebrock replied indignantly: "Do you think I was going to catch the Cheyennes alone? I'm going back to Fort Reno, sick and worn out. I haven't had my clothes off until I went to bed in this car last night since I started from Fort Reno September 10."[33]

The officer was bitter over his ordeal, blaming the Cheyenne interpreter (he probably meant Chapman, interpreter at Camp Supply) and Mizner, who he said could have prevented the outbreak if he had sent the artillery Rendlebrock had requested of him.

Though their long military careers in the Civil War and otherwise had been notable, the actions of Rendlebrock and Gunther at Turkey Springs and Sand Creek were challenged by other officers. Both men were tried by a Fort Reno court-martial for their performances during the fight. Rendlebrock was charged with misbehavior before the enemy, disobeying his commanding officer, and being drunk on duty. He was found guilty and ordered dismissed from the service. The sentence was remitted by President Rutherford B. Hayes; but because of his age and length of service, the officer was soon mandatorily retired from the service.[34]

Gunther, also a native German with a long U.S. military service dating back to 1855, had been a sergeant with Col. E. V. Sumner in 1857 and participated in a saber charge against the Cheyennes on Solomon's Fork, Kansas.[35] Gunther was accused by his junior officers of cowardly behavior for abandoning his troops after ordering a charge and, on another count, hiding in the grass when the Indians were thought to have fired into the camp. He was acquitted on both charges and eventually allowed to resume command of his troop at Fort Reno.[36]

Lieutenant Wood, who had preferred the charges against Gunther, would receive a brevet promotion to captain for his action at Sand Creek and Punished Woman's Fork. The army and the Fort Reno military in particular were subjected to a great deal of criticism over the Cheyenne retreat. A correspondent from Fort Reno defended the Fort Reno troops, pointing to the difficult circumstances under which they had acted. It was, the writer charged, Miles's fault for his "shilly shally conduct" with the Northern Cheyennes.[37]

Mizner cast blame on Rendlebrock, emphasizing to the committee that he had "*particularly instructed*" the officer to induce the Indians to return without using force and blamed other military brass for his not knowing the Northern Cheyennes were armed.[38]

There was enough blame to go around. Testifying before a congressional commission, Miles would point to the slashing of beef annuities for the tribes and rejection of his request for medical help. Still others could place a large responsibility on the nation at large for its government's consistent mishandling and maltreatment of native peoples.

On reaching their home ranges, the Northern Cheyennes had split into two main groups, one under Dull Knife and the other under Little Wolf. On October 24, 1868, Dull Knife's band was recaptured on the Niobrara River and incarcerated in a barrack at Fort Robinson, Nebraska. Dull Knife refused to return to Indian Territory, saying, "You may kill me here; but you cannot make me go back."[39] In an effort to force them to return, the commanding officer at Fort Robinson starved them to the point that the Cheyennes made a desperate attempt to escape and flee into the snow hills. Many were killed, and many others froze to death.[40]

The following March, Little Wolf and his almost naked and starving Cheyennes were taken captive on Box Elder Creek.[41] The government would send seven of the Northern Cheyenne survivors of the Fort Robinson outbreak to Kansas in an effort to prosecute them for crimes in Kansas during their flight north. Eventually it was decided not to press charges against them, however, and the Cheyennes were sent on south to Darlington.[42]

Still known as Camp Supply in 1878, this northwestern Indian Territory post shared Fort Reno's Indian monitoring duties. *Harper's Weekly,* February 27, 1869.

CHAPTER 7

Fort Reno and the Oklahoma Boom

Even as the army was still pursuing the Northern Cheyennes across Kansas during October 1878, 115 Southern Cheyenne and Arapaho men, women, and children were being welcomed with great enthusiasm by the citizenry of Wichita, Kansas. The visitors, who arrived from Darlington in twenty-six wagons under escort of Agent Miles, were to be the principal attraction at the Sedgwick County Fair. A huge crowd of people jammed the fairgrounds to see the display of farm equipment, animals, and produce and to applaud the winners in agricultural and home product contests. The Cheyenne and Arapaho mission school displayed a large exhibit of Indian manufactured items and relics of bygone warring days. Among them was the scalp shirt of Cheyenne chief Grey Beard, who had been killed by soldiers on his way to Fort Marion; Medicine Water's war shield; the war bonnet of Chief Whirlwind; plus a large number of tribal personal items.[1]

Additionally, Miles and his assistants, J. A. Covington and John H. Seger, presented a display of photographs depicting well-known Indian leaders and western Indian Territory sites. These included photographs of the Sand Hills battlefield; Kiowa chiefs Satanta, Kicking Bird, and Lone Wolf; Lookout Mountain near Fort Sill; and Arapaho chief Little Raven. There was also a picture of the Germain girls who had been held captive by the Cheyennes.

The mission school department displayed items made by Indian girls in the mission school: a log cabin quilt, a calico dress, five jars of pickles, notions, and fancy work. Items from the boys of the agency included specimens of penmanship, the Twenty-third Psalm copied from memory, and crops such as peanuts, beans, and corn that the students had raised.

Saturday was reserved for a grand exhibition of Indian war dances, racing, and shooting, all to be capped by a dog feast. The most spectacular event was the chase of two cows, one white and one black, that were driven onto the race track and pursued by mounted tribesmen. Charging their prey at a full gallop, the Cheyennes quickly dispatched the white cow with four arrows neatly centered in a small circle near the heart. The Arapahos had a more difficult time with their animal, however.

Despite this exhibit at Wichita of peaceful and productive agency life, the Northern Cheyenne retreat from Darlington aroused great concern in Kansas that the Indians of the territory could not be controlled with the existing military force. Capt. William G. Wedemeyer with the Sixteenth Infantry at Fort Wallace, who was ordered to investigate depredations committed by the Northern Cheyennes, conducted an extensive field inquiry into the matter. He reported a total of twenty-eight people killed, one missing, three wounded, and nine women and girls who had been raped.[2] According to a Kansas commission appointed to investigate the affair, the Cheyennes had killed thirty-two people during their retreat across Kansas. It also reported women who were sexually assaulted.[3]

On November 24, 1878, Lt. Col. Richard I. Dodge, who was returning to Kansas after serving on a court-martial at Fort Sill, stopped by Fort Reno, where he was welcomed by Colonel Mizner. Dodge continued on up the trail to Camp Supply and on to Fort Dodge. On January 5 following, he returned to Camp Supply, from where he and Amos Chapman explored down the North Canadian for a site at which to locate a new military post.[4]

As a result of the Cheyenne retreat, a great deal of political pressure in Kansas was brought to bear upon War Department officials to bolster the army's manpower in Indian Territory. In December 1878, Camp Supply was redesignated as "Fort Supply" and reinforced with three companies of Twenty-third Infantry under Col. Jefferson C. Davis.[5]

At the same time, a new military presence was established in western Indian Territory. General Sheridan originally proposed that the base be located at Sheridan's Roost on the North Canadian east of present Seiling, where he and journalist DeB. Randolph Keim had stopped to bag a large number of turkeys while returning to Kansas from Fort Sill in January 1869. Instead, Dodge chose a place known as Barrel Springs just downriver for a new post that would become known as Cantonment.[6]

Situated along the North Canadian sixty miles from Fort Reno and seventy from Fort Supply, it was initially founded and garrisoned by a detachment of Twenty-third Infantry under Dodge's command on March 6, 1879. The troops were quartered in tents at first, but soon cottonwood picket structures were erected. With the installation of a sawmill, frame barracks were erected. The small post also contained a two-story brick hospital and a stone bakery. Other frame houses and support buildings would also be built.[7]

Three miles north of Darlington at Caddo Springs, meanwhile, the Indian Bureau erected a three-story boarding school building with two transverse wings with deep connecting verandas. It was filled rapidly with Native American youngsters. In the fall of 1879, Miles joined other agents in leading a delegation of agency students to Muskogee, where they attended the Indian Agricultural Fair and met Secretary of Interior Carl Schurz.[8]

Fort Reno, too, made some physical improvements during 1881. New brick officers' quarters were constructed, along with a bakery. Water wells were dug and lined with stone. Dirt footpaths that connected the various buildings were graveled or macadamized.

In April, Mizner moved on to take command at Fort Sill, being replaced as commanding officer at Fort Reno by Maj. George M. Randall, Twenty-third Infantry. A native of Ohio, Randall had won three brevet promotions during the Civil War and two more for Indian fighting in Arizona in 1874.[9]

The Indians of western Indian Territory were now surrounded by a pentagon of military posts that included Fort Reno, Cantonment, Fort Supply, Fort Sill, and Fort Elliott, which lay just across the Texas Panhandle–Indian Territory border. The military effectiveness of these forts was increased immeasurably when in late 1881 telegraphic communication was completed from Fort Supply to Fort Dodge making a continuous line from Fort Reno with those posts and Fort Elliott. The line had also been extended from Fort Reno to Candee's store at Darlington. Not only did it serve military needs, but it was also of commercial value, permitting dispatches to be received "in something less than stage time."[10]

Though only a secondary post, Cantonment was for a time a danger flash point in Cheyenne relations. Not only was the trail crossing of the North Canadian there a key point on the cattle route between Texas and Kansas, but located in the Cantonment vicinity were the most recalcitrant elements of the Cheyenne tribe. Here was the locale of the Cheyenne Dog Soldiers as well as that of a band of young, war-ready Northern Cheyennes who were brought there in 1879.[11]

Henry C. Keeling, who came to Cantonment that same year as post trader, described his precarious relations with the Indians during his stay. When the Northern Cheyennes came into his store and helped themselves to goods, Keeling tried to bluff them by proclaiming that two troops of cavalry were on their way from Caldwell, Kansas. The warriors were not the slightest bit intimidated until their chief Black Wolf came in. Keeling had once taken the Cheyenne to a hospital at Fort Keogh, Montana, after the chief lost an eye in a fight with a wolf hunter. Keeling told how Black Wolf had befriended him at Cantonment. "He at once called the attention of all the young warriors," Keeling recalled," and stated to them that I was a friend of his, and had assisted him when he was in difficulty, and that if any of them should in any way cause me trouble, he would kill the offender. They stopped right there, as Black Wolf had a reputation for doing exactly what he said he would do."[12]

Officers from Fort Reno commanded the Cantonment post. Among those in charge during Keeling's stay were Maj. Richard F. O'Beirne, Twenty-third Infantry; Lt. Morris C. Wessells, Twenty-fourth Infantry; Capt. Charles Wheaton, Twenty-third Infantry; and Capt. Charles C. Hood, Twenty-fourth Infantry. The latter was in charge during the fall of 1882 when a pair of Texas drovers from a herd being held just across the North Canadian came to the post and became intoxicated. Filled with "brave-maker," they rode through the camp of the Indian scouts and fired into some of the tepees, killing a dog. They also shot up the trader's store.

Captain Hood, a veteran of twenty years on the volatile Rio Grande, mounted a troop of Ninth Cavalry and went after the cowboys. He surrounded their camp, arrested the pair, and threatened to send them to court at Fort Smith. The cowboys were released only when the herd foreman agreed to pay twenty dollars to the scouts for the dog and give their families five head of cattle to eat.[13]

On August 19 and 20, 1879, Fort Reno was visited by members of a select Senate committee, headed by Sen. S. J. Kirkwood, that was investigating the episode of the Northern Cheyennes. The solons took sworn testimony from Agent Miles, agency employees, Mizner, Ben Clark, Captain Gunther, Lieutenant Wilder, as well as Old Crow, Whirlwind, and Wild Hog's wife, who had since been returned to Darlington agency, and other Indians.[14]

The investigation did nothing, however, to improve conditions among the hungry tribespeople of the Darlington agency. With the country already beset by crop failures, the national financial entanglements of the Hayes administration fostered a severe reduction in the beef issue by the Commissioner of Indian Affairs. As a result, the Cheyennes and Arapahos at Darlington would be driven to near starvation. The situation, Miles warned, might well lead to another outbreak.[15]

The presence of Little Chief's band was at the heart of such a threat. Though he had vowed now to follow the example of Dull Knife and Little Wolf, the Northern Cheyenne leader was fully determined not to accept Indian Territory as a permanent home. Accordingly, he adamantly refused to send his children to school as the government wished.

At the same time, the military at Fort Reno was provided a new and difficult area of responsibility. Beginning in 1879, the troops at Fort Reno became the government's principal weapon in combating the white invasion of the Unassigned Lands, commonly known as the Oklahoma country. The task would prove to be an exasperating and frustrating experience for the U.S. Army, which found that military force was simply not sufficient to stop the intrusion of land-hungry whites known as Oklahoma boomers.

Following the initiation of post–Civil War treaties with the Creeks and Seminoles in 1866, a large portion of land in the center of Indian Territory had been left unclaimed by any Indian tribe. Public awareness of the fact was made by the publication of an article by Cherokee Elias C. Boudinot, a Washington lobbyist for the M.K.T. Railroad, in the February 15, 1879, issue of the *Chicago Times*.

National interest in the Indian Territory region was further aroused by the enthusiastic promotion of Dr. Morrison Munford, publisher of the *Kansas City Times*. Through news stories, editorials, and cartoons, Munford insisted that since the Unassigned Lands were owned by the United States, they should thereby be opened to public settlement. The federal government, aware of its long-established treaty promises that Indian Territory would forever be a haven of the Indian, stoutly disagreed with that view. Indian Bureau officials looked to the potential of settling Indian tribes in regions newly occupied by whites in the contested area.

As a result of the *Kansas City Times* promotion, the first boomer invasion of the territory was organized at Coffeyville, Kansas, in the spring of 1879 by Charles C. Carpenter, a flamboyant frontiersman of dubious character. Remaining safely in Kansas himself, he sent his caravan of homesteaders south past present Tulsa and up the Deep Fork of the Canadian. Lieutenant Sweeney was sent from Fort Reno with a detachment of Fourth Cavalry to investigate. About halfway between Reno and the Sac and Fox agency near present Chandler the troops found an abandoned settlement consisting of stakes driven into the ground, a few logs crossed for a cabin, and a site on the North Canadian selected for a mill. The site had been the proposed location of "Carpenter City, the new Capital of Oklahoma." Inspector John McNeil of the Indian Service appeared at Coffeyville and threatened arrest. Carpenter's people quickly acquiesced and retreated from the territory under escort of Maj. John A. Wilcox, Fourth Cavalry.[16]

Carpenter's invasion and another of the Quapaw reservation in far northeastern Indian Territory greatly concerned President Hayes, who ordered the military to use all the cavalry it could spare from Fort Reno, Fort Sill, Fort Supply, and Fort Elliott to stop the intrusions.[17] Troops at Fort Reno, however, would find another Oklahoma boomer leader that emerged in 1880 to be a far more difficult problem. This was David L. Payne, a former Kansas volunteer cavalry officer, politician, and recently a Democratic hanger-on in the Washington, D.C., political scene. There Payne had become acquainted with Boudinot and inspired with the potential of Oklahoma settlement. Returning to Wichita, Kansas, where he had once homesteaded and dabbled in local politics, ineffectively, Payne began recruiting down-and-out families who were desperate for a new start in life following the Black Friday of November 21, 1879.

In response to Payne's public threat to invade the Oklahoma lands, during February 1880 President Rutherford B. Hayes issued a procla-

David L. Payne, leader
of the Oklahoma
Boomer movement,
made numerous incur-
sions into the Indian
Territory. *Courtesy
Archives/Manuscript
Division, Oklahoma
Historical Society.*

mation warning that military force would be used to remove immediately all persons entering without permission onto the Unassigned
Lands.[18] Payne was undeterred and continued his recruiting.

The first of many Payne invasions took place on April 25. Slipping
across the Kansas border south of New Haven, he and twenty-one followers made their way south across what was then the Nez Percé
reservation on the Salt Fork of the Arkansas to the site of present
Oklahoma City. There on the south bank of the North Canadian River
they began laying off a town site they dubbed Ewing, after Payne's
Civil War commander Gen. Thomas Ewing Jr.

The jubilation of Payne and his men was soon interrupted,

however, by Lt. Julius H. Pardee, Twenty-third Infantry (mounted), who with twenty men had trailed the group from Caldwell. When Pardee displayed orders to remove intruders from Indian land, Payne countered that he and his men were on U.S., not Indian, land. Unsure of the legality of the matter, Pardee accepted Payne's argument and withdrew into camp nearby.

On the afternoon of May 15, however, a detachment of Fort Reno Fourth Cavalry troops under Lt. George H. G. Gale, guided by Fort Reno scout Tom Donnell, arrived at the Ewing site. Gale was unpersuaded by Payne's legalistic argument and ordered his men to round up and arrest the colonists. Payne was agreeable to arrest by U.S. troops, but not by the Indian scouts.[19]

Payne and his settlers were escorted to Fort Reno by the detachments of both Gale and Pardee. There the colonists were permitted to roam the post freely while the army determined what to do with them. Eventually orders came through to march them back to the Kansas line and release them. Pardee and his troops did so, escorting the boomers to Polecat Creek, where they were held for a time before being set free across the Kansas border.[20]

Lieutenant Gale continued to patrol the North Canadian as far east as the Sac and Fox agency. He reported that he found no settlers and heard of none.[21] But Payne had by no means given up on settling the Oklahoma lands. On June 6 he and twenty-one followers again crossed the Kansas line into Indian Territory and made their way to the North Canadian. Now Payne went first to the Council Grove area. From there he wrote a letter to the *Wichita Eagle* claiming that "surveying and laying of foundations going on at a lively rate."[22] Because he had sold lots to settlers at the Ewing town site, however, he moved on downriver to his original location.

Donnell soon arrived at the lead of a squad of Cheyenne/Arapaho scouts. When Payne again objected to surrendering to an Indian unit, Donnell sent for Lieutenant Pardee, who was camped upriver. Payne and his men good-naturedly served the troops breakfast, submitted to arrest, and let themselves be escorted back directly to Polecat Creek. There they were turned over to Capt. Thomas B. Robinson, Nineteenth Infantry.

Once again Payne was held while President Hayes and his cabi-

Cheyenne scouts were employed in the task of finding and turning back invaders of the Oklahoma lands. *Harper's Weekly,* April 6, 1889.

net debated a course of action. Finally it was decided to take Payne and his top lieutenants before Judge Isaac Parker's court at Fort Smith, Arkansas, where they could be fined one thousand dollars for their second violation of Indian Territory. The move was rendered useless by Payne's having no money with which to pay the fine.

The boomer leader returned to Wichita as a larger-than-ever figure and immediately began organizing another move into the territory. His effort in December 1880 was stymied by a strong show of military force at the Kansas border. However, some colonists did slip past the border troops without Payne and made it to the Oklahoma country. Donnell and his scouts found them and escorted them to Fort Reno, where they were held for a few days and then "sent on their way rejoicing back to Kansas."[23]

After Payne was faced down by the army, the boomer movement went into an eclipse for a time. The Fort Reno Fourth Cavalry troops, meanwhile, kept up their patrols. The *Cheyenne Transporter* listed Capt. Hanson H. Crews and Lt. Fred Wheeler with Company C; Lt. John W. Martin and Lt. Walter M. Dickinson with Company F; Lt. Abram Wood and Lt. Hugh J. McGrath with Company G; Lt. Stanton A. Mason with Company H, all of Fourth Cavalry; and Lieutenant Pardee with Company I.[24]

They were successful in arresting another group of eleven boomers, these led by Payne's right-hand man, Harry Stafford, south of the Cimarron. The boomers were taken to Fort Reno, where they were placed in the guardhouse for three days. They were then escorted to Fort Sill, held four more days, and then taken to the Red River and left to find their way home to Kansas as best they could.[25]

The Oklahoma boom, the paper complained, had called away the larger part of the garrison, leaving the post especially dull during the holiday season. A Kansas paper noted: "One company remains at Reno to watch the Indians while it takes six to watch the Boomers."[26]

Further complicating the situation, the Ute uprising in Colorado siphoned off considerable military manpower from Indian Territory during the spring of 1880. In order to reinforce Colonel Mackenzie in his campaign against the Utes, three companies of Twenty-third Infantry under Colonel Dodge were ordered to Fort Garland, Colorado, on temporary assignment. These troops would not return until the following September. Cantonment at the time was garrisoned by fewer than fifty men.[27]

A potentially dangerous situation had developed at Darlington. There had long been strong dissension between the army and the Bureau of Indian Affairs over the issuance of beef to the Indians. Officers such as Mackenzie contended that if the Indians were better fed they would be less likely to cause trouble. Reports had surfaced recently that the Cheyennes and Arapahos were suffering to the point of starvation from a shortage in their beef ration. It had become so bad that the military had stepped in to shore up the regular Indian Bureau issue, but with severely limited funds the army could purchase but little extra beef from the passing trail herds.

On one occasion, Miles had been intercepted on his way from the beef corral by a determined band of Cheyennes led by Mad Wolf, a Dog Soldier captain. The group, ominously brandishing pistols and Winchester rifles, demanded that they be issued the beef that they had not received because they were not present on ration day. By Indian Bureau policy they had forfeited their share by their absence.[28]

Miles issued the beef to the band, but when he reached the agency he instructed the Indian police to bring Mad Wolf and another Dog Soldier leader to his office. The police attempted to do so, but they found the two men now supported by a large number of angry tribesmen. Mad Wolf, who had thrown away his blanket and painted his body black, rode about on his pony declaring himself ready for war.

Miles called upon the newly arrived Major Randall for reinforcements. In response, Randall—described by a visiting drover as "a large blond Irishman"[29]—led two companies of troops forth to face the body of several hundred defiant Indians that had gathered in support of Mad Wolf. But Randall well knew that his command of some three hundred soldiers was totally inadequate to attack more than fifteen hundred well-armed Indians.

Randall ordered Capt. William H. Clapp, Sixth Infantry, to set up the post's Gatling guns on the bank of the North Canadian to cover a potential retreat. Randall then rode out ahead of his troops with Ben Clark to face the angry tribesmen. Keeling told of witnessing the confrontation through field glasses.

> I could see the Major with his cigar in his mouth standing up before those Indians seemingly as unconcerned as if he were in his own quarters, while surrounding him and Ben Clark were from fifteen hundred to two thousand Indians with their guns leveled on them. The least thing would have started the Indians to massacre these men, and possibly all the white men at the post, but the coolness and determination of the Major and Ben Clark averted a fight. It was a very exciting time.[30]

For a moment a calamitous fight appeared likely. However, Mad Wolf and his warriors were restrained by Cheyenne chiefs who counseled obedience. Randall then spoke to them, saying that Miles realized the young men thought they were making a just demand for beef rations but that they must not make any such threats in the future.

The Dog Soldiers continued to be an aggressive and powerful force among the Cheyennes, nonetheless. As time for the annual Sun Dance and Medicine Arrow Renewal approached in June, Dog Soldier traditionalists went about ripping tents of any tribespeople who refused to take down their lodge and move to the dance grounds.[31] They also heaped abuse upon those former students of Carlisle Institute who had returned to work in the agency shops or farms.

A correspondent to the *Army and Navy Journal* described the state of affairs at Fort Reno in January 1881:

> We have had some extremely cold weather. Lieut. Legget, 24th Infantry, C.O., succeeded in filling the ice house with a splendid quantity of ice, which will be very handy next summer, provided we are not hunting up lost Aborigines . . . Major Randall, 23rd Infantry, is out on the Kansas and I.T. line entertaining the Paynites. His command consists of Cos. G. H., I and C, 4th Cavalry, who are encamped at Caldwell, Hunnewell, Arkansas City, Kan., and Oklahoma, I.T. . . . Co. H, 4th Cavalry, are camped at Caldwell. They have had a rather unenviable trip, having participated in General Buell's expedition to New Mexico and Mexico . . . Co. G, 23rd Infantry, arrived here a few days ago from Cantonment, N. F., I.T., having been relieved by Co. F., 24th Infantry. I understand the latter company suffered from frozen feet, etc., on the march . . . Little or no amusement is going on at the post now. Last winter hops, etc., were common, but now the ladies are too scarce for such amusements, nearly all of our officers being young and unmarried.[32]

Domestic matters dominated another report in March. The Quartermaster Department was engaged in constructing new officers' quarters, barracks, and stables, while the companies themselves were busy planting gardens, hopeful that the growing season would be better than the past two disappointing ones. The fire guard around the post, aided by the prevailing wind, had successfully held off a grass fire. But there was concern among the troops regarding an army ban on the sale of spirits by the post trader. How were the men going to celebrate St. Patrick's Day, the correspondent worried, "without a wee drop of the craythur?"[33] And another domestic frustration had risen among the post laundresses when an administrative council limited them to the charge of only one dollar per month for washing the clothes of the enlisted men. Declaring such to be starvation wages, the women were threatening to form a Laundresses' Protective Union.

Payne made two intrusions of little consequence from Texas during 1881, one from Denison and another from Gainesville, without being detected by the Fort Reno patrols. Without the boomers to be concerned about, the Fort Reno/Darlington community turned its attention to other matters. Texas cattle continued to flow up the Chisholm Trail, and Red Fork Ranch reported regularly on the drovers and their herd sizes.

A frigid spell of weather that struck in late February revealed the danger of travel of that day on the open Plains. A mail driver on the Caldwell-Fort Sill route headed south out of Fort Reno in a buckboard wagon on a bitterly cold day. When he tried to cross the frozen Canadian River, his mules broke through the ice and became tangled in their harness. One mule drowned, and the driver was pulled out of the water by hanging onto the tail of the other mule. Soaking wet, he staggered on until he was found by an Indian woman and taken to a tepee. After cutting off his frozen clothes and boots, his hosts gave him a hot drink that made him sweat profusely. The Indians undoubtedly saved his life.[34]

In May, spring rains flooded streams of the territory, including the North Canadian, halting herds, stages, and Indian wagon trains headed for the agencies below. A large amount of freight piled up on the road between Darlington and the Kansas border. Mail was delayed by high water, and the carriers undertook great risk in crossing the flooded streams. A mail carrier on the Dodge City/Fort Elliott line drove his coach into the flooded Wolf Creek above Fort Supply and was drowned along with his team; and on another occasion mail was lost when the carrier attempted to cross the flooded North Canadian.[35]

Col. Edwin P. Pendleton (a lieutenant while serving at Fort Reno) later recounted how the mail arrived by stage from Caldwell once a day at about eleven in the morning, its arrival and distribution at the post trader store being an important event at the base. The Fort Reno military maintained a winter camp for evicting would-be settlers at present Oklahoma City, Pendleton said, he himself being stationed there during the winter of 1881–82.[36]

In June 1881, the famous Nez Percé chiefs Joseph and Yellow Bull with fifteen of their tribesmen were visitors to the Darlington Cheyennes. The Nez Percé and Cheyennes had an enjoyable time dancing and exchanging presents. The visitors were pleased to meet many old friends among Little Chief's Northern Cheyennes as well as Major Randall, whom they had known in the Northwest.[37]

Little Chief's resolve to return north had not lessened. Despite his promise to remain peaceful, the potential of another Dull Knife uprising hung over Darlington and Fort Reno. In June 1879, Mizner wrote to departmental headquarters at Fort Leavenworth to say that the strength of the Fort Reno garrison had "at all times been disproportionate to the number of Indians to be kept under subjection" and that "the post should never be without at least four companies of Cavalry."[38]

The problem of Little Chief and his band of Northern Cheyennes continued to hang over Darlington and Fort Reno. The Cheyenne leader was determined to return north to the Lakota Pine Ridge Reservation of South Dakota. He argued that he and his people had permitted themselves to be sent south to Darlington in 1878 only on the promise that if they did not like it there, they would be permitted to return north.

Like the Northern Cheyennes under Little Wolf and Dull Knife, Little Chief and his people had soon found they, indeed, did not like the North Canadian country or the situation there. There was no game to hunt for meat and skins as there was in the north. Their children were always hungry, and the government had taken their guns, making it necessary to kill issue beef with axes. Little Chief and his people totally rejected farming and the schooling of their children.[39]

An astute and determined leader, Little Chief complained forcefully to both Miles and Major Mizner at Fort Reno. Though he agreed that Little Wolf and Dull Knife had been wrong to leave Darlington without permission, Little Chief remained insistent on returning north. Miles was concerned over the negative effect of the Northerners on the Southern Cheyennes, while Mizner and his superiors feared that another outbreak might result. To diffuse the situation, Miles had arranged for Little Chief and a delegation of five other Northern Cheyenne chiefs to take their complaints to Washington during May 1879. Ben Clark was sent with them as an interpreter.[40]

Little Chief and his group had interviews with Interior Department officials and even with President Hayes, but nothing came of the visit. Matters at Darlington continued to deteriorate until finally the disgruntled band was permitted to return north to the Pine Ridge reservation. In October 1881, again escorted by Ben Clark and Company G, Fourth Cavalry, under Capt. William A. Thompson with seventeen six-mule wagons, Little Chief and his people were sent back north to the Pine Ridge agency.[41]

As Little Chief's band passed through Dodge City, a news reporter noted the entourage of 220 Cheyennes, escorted by a company of Fourth Cavalry. "There was a large train of wagons, ponies and dogs. A small bunch of cattle wound up the rear . . . The band and train was at least half an hour passing a given point, and was stretched out two miles in length."[42]

Clark returned to Fort Reno in December to report that Little Chief and his people had been well received by the Sioux and their agent, who had immediately issued rations and annuities to the newcomers. Even with Little Chief and his band gone, some 684 Northerners still remained at Darlington. Many of them wished to return north as well.[43]

Much to the chagrin of the Fort Reno military, in January 1882 Payne was back on the North Canadian with twelve men and three wagons. Troops from Fort Reno found the men encamped in a grove of trees on the river's north side and once again arrested them. They were taken to Fort Reno and held in the post guardhouse for two days before being released on Payne's promise to return to Kansas.[44]

Payne lived up to his promise, but he soon returned alone to spend several weeks undetected in a dugout cabin on Deep Fork near present Arcadia, Oklahoma. Wearying of the solitude and suffering from health problems, Payne made his way back to Wichita. By May he had organized still another caravan of settlers and led them to the Deep Fork. From there he wrote promotional letters back to Kansas with embellished accounts of houses and even hotels being erected. Once again the boomers were arrested and taken to Fort Reno, then escorted to the Kansas border.[45]

The Indians at Darlington agency still faced the serious problem of inadequate food rations. The commissioner of Indian Affairs, effecting policy of the newly elected Republican president, James A.

Garfield, announced that the department was cutting down one-third on beef rations for the reservations. The order created great alarm among the tribes, and a council was called with agency officials to discuss the matter. The chiefs told Miles they could not understand all the new roads of Washington. They said that they would do without blankets, clothing, and everything else so long as they could have enough beef to keep them and their children from starvation.[46]

Still the Indians at Darlington remained compliant. They took part in and seemed to thoroughly enjoy the Fourth of July 1882 celebration at the fort and agency. For one thing, all Indians loved a good horse race, and there were several held at Fort Reno on that day. The *Transporter* set the scene:

> In accordance with programme, the celebration of the Fourth took place at Ft. Reno, the weather being all that could be desired. The rain the night before had laid the dust, brightened up the grass and showed up the parade ground and the trim quarters and orderly barracks to good advantage; and the Post, with all its surroundings was a model of neatness and order. The country for miles around furnished a large crowd of sight-seekers and Darlington was well represented throughout the day.[47]

Foot racing between competing cavalry and infantry units were held during the morning. The noon meal was announced with a national salute of thirty-eight guns, one for each state of that time. After dinner came sack races, wheelbarrow races, tug-of-war contests, broad jumping and high jumping competition, and greased pole climbing.

These events were followed by a review of the agency Indian Police, who, mounted and carrying arms, passed smartly in review before Major Randall. By now the Indians had gathered in eager anticipation of the horse races. They came from all over the territory on horseback and in wagons, an estimated two thousand strong. "The running races, six in number," the *Transporter* observed of the Indian contestants, "consisted of a general stampede of at least a dozen starters, and it was wonderful to see the way in which the Indian ponies kept bunched together the entire race."[48] A saddle was awarded to each winner. The Indian races were followed by challenges for cavalry horses in quarter mile, six hundred yards, and half-mile events. Mounts of Company F, Ninth Cavalry, were winners in all.

That evening pyrotechnical displays—bouquets of rockets, showers of stars, colored lights, Roman candles, flying pigeons, wheels of fire, balloons, and other fireworks—were presented at both Fort Reno and Darlington, delighting a crowd that included many tribespeople. Before they dispersed, the people were treated to lemonade by agency personnel.

The U.S. Army hierarchy was becoming increasingly concerned about the additional expense of constantly removing Payne and his boomer followers. The boomer leader was living up to the tag of "Pertinacious Payne" put on him by the *Wichita Beacon*. General Pope referred to him as a "common criminal," while Secretary of War W. E. Chandler recommended a change in the federal statutes to add imprisonment as punishment for repeated incursions into Indian Territory.[49]

Expulsion from the territory and being hauled to court had failed to deter Payne; now the harassed Fort Reno military would try a new technique. It would harass Payne in return.

CHAPTER 8

A Fading Frontier

Throughout the decade of the seventies the Fourth Cavalry, supported by the Twenty-third Infantry, had been the mainstay of the
Fort Reno garrison. In October 1881, orders were issued for Troops G
and H, Fourth Cavalry, to transfer to Fort Craig, New Mexico, and
Troop C, Fourth Cavalry, to Fort Sill. Company G, Twenty-third
Infantry, was likewise reassigned to Fort Craig, Company I remaining. The infantry unit sent its equipment and baggage on by Indian
freighting wagons to Caldwell, from where it would travel by rail.
Before departing, the infantrymen were honored by being placed at
the front of the battalion as the entire garrison paraded under arms.
They were led down the hill toward Darlington by a drummer and a
fife player to the tune of "The Girl I Left Behind Me."[1]

Companies C and D, Twentieth Infantry, under Capt. Rodney M.
Taylor were brought from Fort Dodge to replace those of the Twenty-
third Regiment.[2] Soon after, two troops of Ninth Cavalry buffalo soldiers arrived from New Mexico to take over from the departing
Fourth Cavalry. Randall remained commanding officer at the post
until August 1882, when he was succeeded by Capt. Frank T. Bennett
and then Capt. Henry Carroll in December 1882. Both of these men—
Bennett of Ohio and Carroll of New York—were Civil War veterans
who had risen from the ranks to officer status. Carroll won a brevet
promotion to major for Indian fighting in Texas and in New Mexico,
where he was severely wounded.[3]

The return of Little Chief and his Northern Cheyennes to the
north ended the threat of another disastrous retreat through Kansas
and signaled a reduction of the Indian oversight responsibility for
Fort Reno. The principal role for the post now shifted to the acceler-
ating problem of white settlers intruding onto the Oklahoma Lands.
During the spring of 1882, the army high command issued orders for
the closing of Forts Wallace and Dodge in Kansas and Cantonment

in Indian Territory. The garrisons and equipment at these posts were transferred to Fort Reno, Camp Supply, and Fort Elliott in the Texas Panhandle. In June of that year, a party of Indian freighters began dismantling the Cantonment military effects and hauling them to Supply and Reno.[4]

In July 1883 Fort Reno was greatly enlarged by President Chester A. Arthur to an official designation as a military reservation consisting of 9,493 acres or 14 5/6 square miles. A topographical survey of the area, which lay within the Cheyenne and Arapaho reservation, was made by 2d Lt. Rowland G. Hill of the Twentieth Infantry. By these moves, the army firmly assigned Fort Reno control of the Cheyenne and Arapaho reservation and the Oklahoma Lands.

Of the Northern Cheyennes who still remained at Darlington, some four hundred accepted the government's offer for returning north. In late July 1883, Lt. Charles J. Stevens and a company of Ninth Cavalry escorted them to Fort Supply, from where they were taken on to Pine Ridge agency.[5] "The advance of civilization," commented the *Dodge City Times* regarding the closing of the posts, "is making its onward march. The Indian and the buffalo have gone, and now the soldier takes his departure. The peaceable character of the Indian no longer required the maintenance of a Fort so remote from the Indian country."[6]

Much the same could well be applied to western Indian Territory during the decade of the eighties. But in addition to the pacification of the tribes and the demise of the buffalo, there were other events that were spelling an end to the old frontier. For one, there were now distinct thoroughfares of white traffic beginning to lace the former buffalo range. The principal one was the Chisholm Trail that linked the non-Indian world of Texas to the non-Indian world of Kansas both in commerce and increasingly for general commuting.

Other cattle trails, notably the Western Trail, had come into existence as Kansas shipping points moved west with the expanding railroads and cattlemen looked to grazing potential in Colorado and elsewhere. Roads connecting the military posts with one another and the posts with Kansas supply points had also developed. A military wagon road ran from Fort Reno up the North Canadian past Left Hand Springs (the former Raven's Springs) and Cantonment to Fort

Former warriors of the Plains line up at Fort Reno to enroll as scouts for the army. *Archives/Manuscripts Division, Oklahoma Historical Society.*

Supply; another went west to the Wichita agency at Anadarko, then extended on either to Fort Sill or to Fort Elliott. Still another route along the North Canadian, which was also followed by the Star Mail Route on its Vinita to Fort Reno run, connected Darlington with the Sac and Fox agency and Shawneetown to the east.

A military road linked Fort Supply with Fort Dodge and extended on down Wolf Creek to Little Wolf Creek before turning south to Fort Elliott in the Texas Panhandle. Another army route ran more directly between Fort Dodge and Fort Elliott across No Man's Land, now the Oklahoma Panhandle. Even though Indian Territory was still the legal domain of the tribesman, these inroads of white transportation were clear signals of increasing dominance by people other than the native Indian.

In its effect on the innate personality of the vast open prairies of western Indian Territory, fencing of the land with barbed wire was a pronounced development. Nothing was more prohibitive to a countryside where once the great buffalo herds had ranged freely, Indian tribes had camped from river to river, and tribal hunters and warriors had roamed at will. Fencing also inhibited, but did not stop, the trail drives.

It had been the practice of the stockmen who grazed their herds on leased lands in Indian Territory to conduct annual spring roundups organized by pools that covered large general areas. This open range system, however, was slipshod in controlling stock. On one occasion a cattleman called in his neighbors to help cut out the strays from a herd of two thousand cows he had rounded up. The ranching community had a good laugh when the man's neighbors obliged him and reduced his herd by nineteen hundred head.[7]

The cattlemen began to realize the advantage of fencing in their grazing land for better control of their stock. During the spring of 1882, a surge of fence building took place in the Cherokee Outlet as ranchmen strung three and four strands of barbed wire around their respective ranges. Maj. Andrew Drumm, a Texas cattleman who had been the first to take up ranching on the Cherokee Outlet near present Cherokee, Oklahoma, in 1874,[8] fenced in his fifteen square miles south of the Kansas border. The Salt Fork and Eagle Chief Pool secured permission to run a fence on their south side in order to protect their range from trail herds.

During the spring of 1882, the Dominion Cattle Company let a contract for thirty-three miles of fencing in the Texas Panhandle. The Standard Oil Company, which operated a large outfit in the Cherokee Strip, caused a furor when it began fencing in range occupied by several small stockmen. That fall, an Arkansas City hardware dealer sold 45,000 rods of barbed wire to fence the Cherokee Strip lease of the Dean brothers north of present Stillwater.[9]

When the Cherokees complained to the government about the erection of fences and building of stock pens as well as the use of Cherokee Strip timber for fence poles, the secretary of war ordered troops to destroy all such improvements. In reaction, the alarmed cattlemen organized the Cherokee Strip Live Stock Association in 1883 and were able to lobby the federal government to make fencing subject to the wishes of the Cherokee National Council. Then, by bribery it was charged, they persuaded the Cherokees to permit the fencing to continue.[10]

Still another important influence upon western Indian Territory was the establishment of the U.S. District Court at Wichita with jurisdiction over much of northwestern Indian Territory—over all of the land lying north of the Canadian River and east of the 100th meridian not set apart and occupied by the Cherokee, Creek, and Seminole tribes. While the court did not hold any legal authority over the tribes, it did present another intrusion by the white man into their territory.[11] One of its earliest territory considerations was a charge against Philip McCusker for selling whiskey to the Indians. A grand jury, however, looked into the charge and failed to bring an indictment.[12]

Violence and murder still stalked the Chisholm Trail. In March 1882, trail boss Henry Stevens and Charles Parsons left Caldwell on their way to Texas to bring up a herd of cattle. With them were two men named Edward Derusha and Jim Morgan who had been hired at Caldwell. While sitting around a campfire on the trail after a Sunday morning breakfast, Morgan suddenly grabbed Parsons's revolvers, backed up against the wagon with the guns cocked, and ordered the others to leave. They did so, but Stevens turned and said something to Morgan. The other two men heard a shot, but they kept going and did not turn around to see what had happened.

Scout Tom Donnell was on his way from Caldwell to Fort Reno with a boomer-seeking detail when he met Parsons and Deruska. He went immediately to the camp and found Stevens dead where he had fallen. Morgan was gone, along with two fine horses, two saddles, four six-shooters, and a Winchester. Stevens's corpse and the trail outfit were taken to Fort Reno, where the trail boss was interred in the Fort Reno cemetery temporarily. A $500 reward was posted for Morgan, dead or alive. Not long after the murder, Morgan came into Red Fork Ranch and got a shave before heading west. He was intercepted near Cantonment by a company of Fort Reno soldiers and placed under arrest.[13]

A murder in September saw the reduction of a frontier stalwart who had been much involved in Indian Territory events. Half-blood Robert Poisal, who operated a farm just east of the agency, was returning from Sacred Heart Mission, where he and his niece Junnie Meagher had been to place some children in school. While there he mentioned that he was interested in buying a couple of horses. The remark was overheard by a young Creek Indian named Foster, who, thinking Poisal had money, followed and shot him from ambush along the trail. The killer was caught by the Seminole Light Horse

Police and taken to Fort Reno, where he was confined in the guard-house. While being taken from there to Muskogee for trial, Foster killed the deputy U.S. marshal and escaped.[14]

Oliver Nelson, who worked as a freighter and cowboy in western Indian Territory, explained how trouble sometimes came about. Cowboys in wintertime line camps, he explained, seldom had much to do. They often sat around their dugouts, read about famous "Wild West" outlaws, and thought up ways to steal Indian ponies safely. On one occasion four cowhands decided to waylay the army paymaster when he came down the trail to Cantonment with his iron money box and small military escort. As they lay in ambush, a bad storm came up. They were afraid to build a fire and almost froze to death. Later they learned that the paymaster had gone to Fort Reno first, taking the Chisholm Trail route instead of the more westerly Cantonment trail.[15]

During the spring of 1882, the Indian Bureau issued orders that the beef issue to the tribes would be reduced from 125,000 pounds per week to 83,000 pounds. At Darlington, the Cheyennes and Arapahos met with Miles and demanded to know why this was. Their crops had failed they said, and they had behaved well. Miles wired the War Department that the Indians were threatening another outbreak and requested more troops. General Pope paid a visit to Fort Reno during April to investigate the matter, and through his efforts a bill was introduced and passed in Congress to make up the deficiency. Still, two companies of Tenth Cavalry buffalo soldiers were sent to bolster the Fort Reno forces.[16]

In an effort to encourage Indian employees to establish residences at the agency, Miles had potential streets and lots between the agency and the Mennonite Mission marked off with a plow. It was hoped that the Indians would fence in their lots, dig wells, plant gardens, and begin an adaptation to the white man's style of residing in permanent homes.[17]

Railroad expansion was in full swing during the 1880s, and it was only a matter of time before they came in force to Indian Territory. A first rail line—the M.K.T.—had been constructed from present Vinita, Oklahoma, to Denison, Texas, during 1870–72. In 1871, a second line, the Atlantic and Pacific Railroad (A&P), was opened from Vinita west to the Arkansas River at present Tulsa and beyond to Red

Fork and Sapulpa. The line had been halted there, but there were plans to swing on westward across Indian Territory. Many early day maps of the region depicted its extended course along the Cimarron and Canadian Rivers.[18] During November 1882, the A&P's chief engineer arrived at Fort Reno and went out to where surveying crews were working. Word was received also that the St. Louis and San Francisco (Frisco) was nearing the Arkansas River.[19]

In late 1883, the Gulf, Colorado, and Santa Fe Railway (GC&SF) of Texas asked Congress for rights to construct railway, telegraph, and telephone lines across the territory. This soon-to-be subsidiary of the powerful Atchison, Topeka, and Santa Fe (AT&SF, or Santa Fe) would join with another subsidiary, the Southern Kansas (SK), in the enterprise during 1886 and 1887. The two divisions then embarked on a race—the GC&SF north from Galveston and the SK south from Arkansas City—to reach a juncture at Purcell, Chickasaw Nation. The contest was consummated by the driving of a silver spike at Purcell on April 26, 1887.[20]

The line, extending from Kansas to Texas directly through the Oklahoma Lands, would have great consequence upon the Fort Reno–Darlington region as an avenue to white settlement. At the same time, another Santa Fe line was building across the northwest corner of the territory from New Kiowa, Kansas, to the Texas Panhandle. Though less noticed, this route that ran southwestward through present Alva, Woodward, and along Wolf Creek slashed through the very heart of the Cheyenne-Arapaho hunting grounds. The Chicago, Rock Island, & Pacific (Rock Island), meanwhile, stood poised at Caldwell waiting to drive directly south along the Chisholm Trail.[21]

Indian education, despite its many problems, was slowly but surely growing among the tribes despite the strong resistance of many. It was traumatic for Cheyenne elders in particular to send their children to the white man's schools, where they would be taught to speak a new language and trained in a work regimen entirely foreign to their culture, where they would wear shoes and other clothes of the white man, and the hair of their young warriors would be cut short. All this was aimed at washing away the tribal being of the Indian children and stifling their ties to family and native culture—as Miles put it, "to kill much of the 'Indian' in the Indians of this agency in due time."[22]

Resistance continued among some tribal members even as others laid aside their old ideas and permitted their children to attend school. Whereas the Arapahos were more amenable to both the white man's work ethic and education, the Cheyennes remained severely split between those who were pliable to white ways and those who still held out fiercely against the breakdown of their traditional tribal ways. Many Cheyennes still remembered the attacks at Sand Creek and the Washita and harbored deep distrust and hatred for whites. However, one Cheyenne brought his only child, a little girl, to Miles, saying, "The whites killed my father and mother and only sister at Sand Creek and last summer took my only brother and sent him away from us. My heart has felt bad towards the whites many years but today I have thrown that feeling all away. Take my child as proof of my sincerity."[23]

Indian students who were sent off to eastern schools such as Carlisle and Hampton, Pennsylvania, however, often found it difficult to resist social pressures to reassimilate back into the old tribal customs once they returned home. John Seger found that once back in their home camps, where their newly learned skills were of little use, even some of the Arapaho boys cast off their white man's clothes in favor of native dress and returned to their old tribal habits.[24]

In February 1883 agent Miles returned from Lawrence, bringing with him Indian Inspector James M. Haworth, who had been Kiowa-Comanche agent at Fort Sill during the difficult time of the 1874–75 uprising. Now Haworth was making an official visit to inspect the Darlington operation, but he was also examining potential locations for a new Indian industrial school.[25]

Another visitor of great importance to Indian education arrived that fall.[26] After serving with the Tenth Cavalry at Camp Supply and Fort Sill during the 1874 uprising, Capt. Richard H. Pratt had been in charge of the Indians at Fort Marion. He afterward founded the Indian School at Carlisle, Pennsylvania, where many Indian Territory youngsters received formal schooling.

Pratt was extremely popular with the Indians, and a group of leading Cheyenne and Arapaho men gathered to hear him make a strong speech urging them to push for the education of their children. When he left he took six girls and five boys with him for enrollment at Carlisle. Among them were the sons of Arapaho chiefs Powder Face and Left Hand and two daughters of Yellow Bear.

Earlier in an interview with Mrs. J. H. Seger, Powder Face told of his past experiences as a warrior. He had, he said, killed and scalped many white men. He had been wounded four times, once almost fatally, and had fifty-five horses shot from under him. Since then he had been to Lawrence and Washington and now believed that the white man's way was the best, and he tried to go to Sunday school each Sunday. He had planted corn on his farm on the Canadian, thirteen miles from the agency, and now owned 107 head of cattle. He thought all the chiefs should wear white men's clothing in order to set an example.[27]

During the time of Pratt's visit to Darlington in the fall of 1883, the agency was also host to Dutch ethnologist Herman F. C. Ten Kate Jr. Ten Kate visited the Cheyennes' camp and smoked the calumet with the now-aged Dog Soldier chief Bull Bear, whom the ethnologist described as tall, bronzed, and silver-haired. Ten Kate felt strongly that Americans had no cause to feel proud of their "wars of extermination."[28] While he held great admiration for the tall, stoutly built Cheyennes and Arapahos, he felt that many of the tribespeople had been forced into little more than begging for government handouts at the agency.

The new Indian Industrial School, located six miles south of Arkansas City, was formally opened on January 19, 1884. Chilocco would have lasting memories for many Indian boys and girls of the territory in the years ahead. Its first student body consisted of twenty-two Cheyenne boys, twelve Cheyenne girls, eight Arapaho boys, and four Arapaho girls.[29] Chiefs Bull Bear, White Shield, and Big Horse had been among the first to bring their children forward to attend school in 1867. Bull Bear said that while he had raised his other children to be warriors, he was giving this son to the whites to educate. The boy attended Carlisle and took up the Anglicized name of Richard Davis.[30]

"Chief Whirlwind," the *Transporter* noted, "sports one of the top spring wagons in the country. The old chief, as well as the whole tribe, is fast abandoning the superstitious old customs and now believes the white man's road is the best."[31] Little Raven, the elder Arapaho chief who had long been adaptive to white ways, told an Arapaho school class, "If I were commencing life again, I would take the white man's road. I am now old but advise you to try to live like white people."[32]

Minimic, the Fort Marion prisoner who was now a spokesman for peace, died in May 1881. White Shield died at Kingfisher Ranch while returning from Caldwell with freight. The progressive Big Horse, who owned a sizable number of cattle and horses and was friendly with the whites, committed suicide. He had been suffering from a urinary infection and shot himself in the head with a revolver.[33]

Despite the conversion of these older chiefs, however, stubborn resistance remained among many elements of the Cheyennes. The most determined leader of these was Stone Calf, who spoke out strongly for improved rations and against horse thievery by whites, intrusion of the stockmen, the railroads, and other threats to Cheyenne sovereignty over their assigned reservation.[34] As leader of the Cantonment bands, Stone Calf, whose daughter was married to Amos Chapman, continued to defy the agent's authority when it came to the conversion of the Cheyennes to farming, to sending tribal children to the white man's schools, and other white influences over his people. In doing so, he had the strong support of the recalcitrant element of the tribe, the still powerful Dog Soldiers.

In February 1883, Maj. Thomas B. Dewees arrived at Fort Reno to take over as commander. A native of Pennsylvania, he, too, had risen from the ranks during the Civil War.[35]

A significant era at Darlington ended when Miles resigned as agent for the Cheyennes and Arapahos and moved to Lawrence, Kansas. Citing reasons of health and duty to his family, he had submitted his resignation to take effect the last day of 1883. It was not accepted, however, until the following February. His twelve years at Darlington had been both tumultuous and transitory in the government's attempt to acculturate the two roving tribes of the Plains.[36]

One of his innovations had been the issuance of rations to heads of families rather than to chiefs, a move that contributed to the dissolution of the tribe in a traditional sense. His programs of having the Indians transport their own goods from Kansas in their own wagons and having Indian children raise their own cattle had been successful. He had also promoted the placing of Indian students to work on white farms.[37]

Numerous changes were taking place in Indian Territory, all pointing to the eventual end of the frontier era at Fort Reno and Darlington. The presence of the *Cheyenne Transporter* newspaper not only interconnected the two communities but tied them more to the outside world. The paper was begun in 1880 by W. A. Eaton, who in May 1882 sold it to Kansas newspaperman George W. Maffet. Lafe Merrit was installed as editor. The *Transporter* opened an informative and colorful window into life at Fort Reno and Darlington until it ceased operation in June 1886.[38]

Another vital aspect of Darlington and Fort Reno were the missionaries. Their role was to meet with the Indians on a personal level and work with them not only to plant the seeds of Christianity among the tribal members, but also, in line with white thinking, to educate their children and improve their lives. The Cheyenne/Arapaho agency had been founded by a religious sect, the Society of Friends, or Quakers, who had undertaken those purposes as best they could while establishing and managing a foundling outpost on the frontier. The Quakers were entirely receptive to other religious sects working with the tribes and posed no opposition to the establishment of a Mennonite school at the agency in September 1881.[39]

Rev. S. S. Haury was assigned by the Board of Mennonite Missions to carry the Christian message to the Arapahos, educate Indian children and adults alike, and provide training in agricultural and domestic pursuits. The establishment and operation of a farm would not only provide that training but also help defray costs. "My reason for selecting the Arapahos are these," Haury wrote after visiting the agency and staying two months in a tent loaned him by Powder Face, "they seem to be more willing to receive a missionary than the Cheyennes."[40]

The first Mennonite school at Darlington consisted of two tents, one for classes and the other for dining. The male youths were housed in a barn loft, while the Haurys took up residence in a vacant wash house. With four helpers, Haury constructed a new church and mission a half mile north of the agency.[41]

The mission building was two and a half stories with a basement, containing dormitory and classrooms. Calamity struck in February 1882 when on a Sunday evening the building caught fire from a faulty chimney flue and burned to the ground. Haury, who discovered the fire, rushed to the second floor to evacuate the children who had already been put to bed there. The room was filled with poisonous gas, but Haury and others managed to drag all the children outside. Still

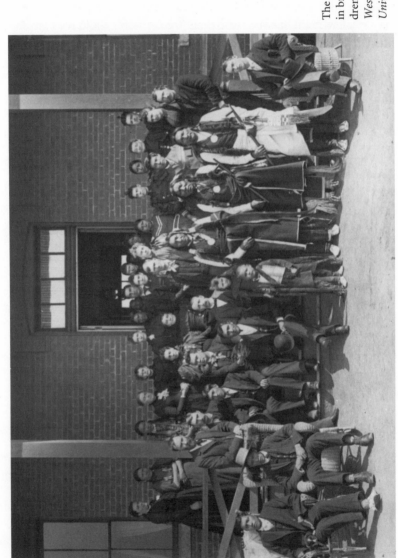

The Mennonites were leaders in bringing schooling to children at the Darlington Agency. *Western History Collections, University of Oklahoma.*

four of the children, including Haury's son Carl, died. The others who perished were Jennie Morrison, Emil Hauser, and a boy named Walter (last name unknown). In addition to the destruction of the building, the mission lost its winter's supplies and clothing, along with Haury's account books, papers, and clothing valued at $800.[42]

The hardworking Mennonites soon constructed a new four-story brick structure in replacement. Rev. Heinrich Voth, who would later become superintendent of the Cantonment and Darlington missions, recalled that his first work was felling trees and breaking rock for the school, which opened for classes on December 12.[43] The school featured a girls' playroom, an industrial teacher's room, a superintendent's study, a storeroom, and classrooms on the first floor. The second floor contained the sewing room and rooms for the mission employees. On the third floor were dormitory rooms. A bakery and laundry were in separate brick buildings.[44]

J. A. Funk headed the operation of the Darlington mission when Haury moved to Cantonment in February 1883; he was eventually replaced by Voth. The Cantonment buildings abandoned at the former military post were turned over to Haury, who adapted them as a Mennonite school. With the help of his male students, he established a fifteen-acre farm.[45] Haury also worked to place Indian children in white homes in Kansas and elsewhere. In June 1882 he escorted fourteen Indian boys to homes among Mennonite farmers near Halstead, Kansas.[46]

The Episcopal Church established a mission for the Cheyennes at Darlington under the Rev. John B. Wicks. Wicks arrived with his wife and children in September 1882 to take up residence in their newly constructed residence near the Arapaho mission.[47] Coming with Wicks was David Pendleton, a Cheyenne who had spent the past three years studying for the ministry at Paris Hill, New York. Pendleton stoutly refused to participate in the Sun Dance or other tribal ceremonies.[48] On June 16, Pendleton conducted the first ever Christian funeral for a Cheyenne. The deceased was the son of Chief Big Horse, and Pendleton conducted the funeral in the Cheyenne tongue according to the rituals of the Episcopal Church.[49]

A new age of communication came to the fort and agency in August 1884 when a telephone line was installed connecting the two sites. There was now at Fort Reno a hook and ladder company and a water wagon to fight fires. These accouterments were put to use when a fire destroyed the elegant brick quarters of Captains Bennett and Charles O. Bradley at the corner of the officers' square. When a cannon sounded the fire alarm, the hook and ladder wagon was rushed forth. Men were stationed atop adjoining buildings, and as fast as the water wagon could supply the pumps they kept a steady stream on each structure.[50]

Still another modernizing trend had begun at Fort Reno in June 1879 when a school for enlisted men was opened at the post. Supervised by Capt. William H. Clapp, an Ohioan who had risen from the ranks, but taught by an enlisted man, the school offered the often illiterate soldiers basic instruction in the three R's as well as geography and history. In 1884 the secretary of war concluded that, while such schools were good for post children, after-hour schooling was too much to ask of men in the military. The post school, however, led to schooling for Fort Reno children.[51]

Darlington now possessed a skating rink. And the installation in 1885 of a photographic gallery in a tent at Darlington by Duke and Decker began recording images of the residents there and making them even more a part of historical record.[52]

But most threatening of all to the once-native status of the region was the incessant flow of boomers across the Kansas border. Payne and his following of land-demanding settlers had by no means given up their dream of opening the Oklahoma Lands to settlement. They would return—again and again and again.

CHAPTER 9

Punishing Payne

A news dispatch from Kansas City in the fall of 1882, undoubtedly initiated by the *Kansas City Times,* had insisted that Payne and his colonists were getting along fine with the Indians of the territory, that the military would not molest the boomers, and that the cattlemen were their "bitterest enemies."[1] The claim was wrong. The one thing that the tribes, the cattlemen, and the military shared in common was their intense dislike of Payne and his followers. Many people in Kansas and the territory agreed with them, but Payne's enlistments of impoverished, landless agrarians steadily increased.

"Payne will learn afterwhile," the *Transporter* opined, expressing the prevailing frontier opinion, "that his Territory trips are unprofitable —but that will never be as long as he can dupe poor fools of farmers out of their hard earned money by his 'rights,' 'shares,' stock and privileges he sells them."[2]

In July 1882 Payne returned from a lobbying trip to Washington, D.C., to lead a party of some twenty boomers from South Haven, Kansas, southward to the Deep Fork River near present Arcadia. There they all pitched in and built a cabin for member W. H. Osburn, his wife, daughter, and a young female boomer named Dicy Dixon. Payne and the others then moved on to the North Canadian River opposite present Jones. They were industriously clearing land, digging wells, and building cabins when Lt. Charles W. Taylor arrived from Fort Reno at the lead of a ten-man detachment of Ninth Cavalry buffalo soldiers. Payne, who had been a captain with the Nineteenth Kansas Volunteer Cavalry during the Sheridan-Custer campaign in 1868–69 and felt a certain comradeship with other military officers, offered no resistance when Taylor placed him and his followers under arrest.

After dealing with Payne, Taylor rode to the Deep Fork to deal with Osburn. When Osburn stubbornly refused to get into his wagon

Payne and his lieutenants were escorted out of the Indian Territory by Fort Reno Buffalo Soldiers. *Courtesy Archives/Manuscripts Division, Oklahoma Historical Society.*

to be taken to Fort Reno, Taylor ordered his buffalo soldiers to over-power and bind the boomer and toss him into the back of the vehicle. The women were then placed in the wagon, and all were taken to Payne's settlement.

Learning of Osburn's resistance, Payne decided, more in a spirit of mischief than rebellion, that he would also give Taylor and his black troops some token resistance. Taylor waited patiently while Payne wrote a legal-sounding letter to the commanding officer at Fort Reno demanding that he contact his superiors regarding the use of force in making such an arrest.[3] Taylor agreed to deliver the letter, but he again politely requested that Payne and his group make ready to march to Fort Reno without making trouble. "I know nothing about your con-troversy with the government," the officer said. "My orders are to expel all unauthorized persons I find in the Territory."[4] "Then expel us, Lieutenant," Payne answered, "as best you can. We won't make it easy for you."

Taylor set forth to do just that. He ordered his men to harness Payne's teams to their wagons and load up the camp paraphernalia.

But when told to get into the wagons, Payne and his settlers sat down and refused to move. This delayed the operation, but they were eventually bound, carried up the hill to the wagons, and dumped into them. The affair went off with good humor, even when the gangling six-foot-four, two-hundred-plus-pound Payne was hoisted to the back of a muscular soldier and toted to a wagon.

Once the would-be settlers were all in the wagon, Payne smilingly promised that he and his followers would cause no more trouble. Taylor then ordered them untied and permitted them to either ride or walk on the three-day march to Fort Reno. A steady fall rain soaked the prisoners and troops alike. The boomers afterward charged that they were thrown into the guardhouse and otherwise abused by the military. However, some of them later admitted that they had been placed in quarters at Fort Reno and issued regular rations. A portion of the boomers were permitted to return to Kansas, but Payne and thirteen others were retained at the fort while the army decided just what to do with them.[5]

Pending a decision by government officials, new commanding officer Bennett confiscated the boomers' wagons, horses, guns, and other property. Though Payne had treated his arrest by Taylor almost as a lark, he spent his time during his incarceration at Fort Reno writing letters to newspapers attacking the army for arresting and holding his group for more than ten days without a trial.[6]

The secretary of interior eventually ruled that Payne and his followers would be taken to Fort Smith once more. Payne responded with a letter to Captain Bennett saying he and his people were willing and anxious to be taken to Fort Smith. But, he claimed, several of his people were too sick with chills and fever to make the trip. He argued further that there had been a bounty placed on his head in eastern Indian Territory, and he could well be assassinated if taken through the Indian nations. The army had an answer for Payne. The boomers would be taken to Fort Smith, not by way of the Indian nations but by a much longer route through Texas. Learning of this, Payne sent another letter to Bennett charging that such a move would be a great injustice and that Kansas was the safest and most practical route.[7]

But the army was not about to make it easy on Payne. On September 11, the Oklahoma boomer leader and his group, including Mrs. Osburn, baby Edna, and Dicy Dixon, left Fort Reno in army

ambulances on their way to Fort Sill under escort of Lieutenant Taylor
and a troop of Ninth Cavalry accompanied by two companies of
infantry. Payne undoubtedly found it interesting to revisit the post
that he had helped to found in early 1869 with the Nineteenth Kansas
Volunteers.

After a short rest there, Taylor put the prisoners on the road
again, this time marching to Henrietta, Texas, where railroad con-
nections could be made. Taylor made camp outside of town and
released all but six of his soldiers to return to Fort Reno. Little Edna
being ill, Payne secured permission from Taylor for Osburn to take
the child and two women to a hotel for the night. He also talked
Taylor into letting him and two others go into town to purchase some
needed items. He promised to return and make no trouble.

Instead of shopping, however, Payne went directly to the office of
a Henrietta lawyer, secured a writ of habeas corpus, and had it served
on Taylor. Taylor refused to accept the writ on the grounds that as a
military officer he could not surrender his prisoners to civil authority.[8] Payne and the other two men returned as he had promised, only
now they were gloriously drunk. Knowing that the local sheriff was
going to be after him, Taylor hurried his prisoners aboard an incom-
ing train. Finally the train finished unloading and loading its baggage
and passengers and picked up steam to depart. At that moment the
sheriff arrived with a posse and an order for Taylor's arrest. The carbines of the six soldiers held off the Texans as the train carried the
whooping cargo of Oklahoma boomers off eastward for Fort Smith.[9]

Once again Payne was taken before Judge Parker, who heard a
similar monologue from each of the boomers. Each member said, yes,
they knew the penalty for invading the Indian lands, but they were
on the Unassigned Lands, which was owned by the U.S. government.
They were merely exercising squatters' right. When he had heard the
same speech repeated several times, Parker looked over at Payne and
nodded. "Pretty good schooling, Payne," he observed wryly.

Parker scheduled a hearing on the matter for a later date, and the
boomers were released. The army's attempt to punish Payne had failed
miserably. He returned to Kansas a larger-than-ever figure and immediately began recruiting settlers for another invasion of the Oklahoma
lands. By January 1883, a much larger body of colonists gathered on

Walnut Creek south of Arkansas City. In Washington, D.C., the secretary of interior announced he would ask Congress to make it a criminal offense to invade Indian Territory. Congress, however, failed to respond even when President Arthur requested the new law.[10]

General Pope alerted Maj. Thomas B. Dewees, who had returned as commandant at Fort Reno, ordering him to wait until Payne and his followers had reached the territory. Dewees was to then arrest and eject them. Two companies of cavalry were rushed to Fort Reno to reinforce the troops already there, and patrols were increased. First contact was made by Lt. Charles J. Stevens and five Ninth Cavalry troopers on Coffee Creek.[11]

Stevens rode up to Payne. The two talked amicably for a few moments, then galloped off together ahead of the caravan. When the train reached Stevens's camp, Payne was in the officer's tent enjoying a glass of whiskey and a cigar. The boomers went into camp, and the word went around that Stevens had ordered them to halt there until more troops arrived under Captain Carroll. The colonists, many of them disgusted with Payne, who had made brave talk about resisting the military, met and voted to continue on to their destination on the North Canadian north of present Jones.

There the colonists established Camp Alice, named for a young girl in the group. Stevens issued orders that no one was to leave the camp. That evening Carroll arrived with over ninety more buffalo soldiers and called Payne to his tent. Payne later claimed that he exchanged some angry words with Carroll before submitting to arrest. But other boomers charged that Carroll and Payne "enjoyed a good smoke of peace and a good time was had at the tent."[12]

The next morning Lieutenant Stevens and several troopers were sent to bring the other colony leaders to Carroll's tent. Osburn refused to comply, and he was supported by a small crowd of Civil War veterans who crowded around his tent to prevent his arrest. Osburn's insurrection was derailed, however, by William L. Couch, who took to a tree stump to remind the boomers that they were peaceful citizens who came to build homes and not fight the army.

Most of the would-be settlers turned their wagons about and headed back up the trail to Kansas. Once again, Payne, Osburn, and a few others were marched off to Fort Reno. En route, another group of colonists was arrested on the North Canadian; they, too, were taken to Reno. The *Cheyenne Transporter* noted that these were "the hardest looking lot of Boomers we have seen."[13]

Carroll had intended to take Payne to Fort Smith still another time, but new orders arrived directing him to simply take him and his men to the Kansas border and release them. Payne was busy with speaking engagements in August 1883, but W. L. Couch led a 150-member colonizing party from Arkansas City to Payne's Crossing of the Cimarron near present Guthrie. The group was conducting Sunday morning religious services on the twelfth when a troop of Ninth Cavalry made a whooping charge on them. Lieutenant Taylor, wearing a white hat, moccasins, and leggings, was at their lead. He ordered his troops to round up the settlers and take their shotguns, rifles, and pistols.

Once he had his prisoners, however, Taylor was unsure as to what to do with them. Couch argued that Payne had filed for an injunction against their arrest by troops. The officer finally ordered the group to stay where it was, and he sent for Captain Carroll. Carroll arrived with Company F of the Ninth Cavalry and took charge. When he received word that Payne's injunction had been denied, he arrested the leaders and their families and escorted them to Fort Reno.

The colonists later charged that Carroll refused to let the men of the group ride in wagons and forced them to walk the entire distance to the fort. When two of the boomers resisted, they were tied behind the wagons and made to walk or be dragged. The boomers also claimed that the wife of one of the men was so distressed that she gave premature birth to a child that died. Those taken to Fort Reno were soon sent back to the Kansas line and released.[14]

The army was so pleased with Carroll's handling of the boomers that Gen. Edward Hatch from Fort Riley and Medal of Honor winner Col. Guy V. Henry, Seventh Cavalry, from Fort Sill came to personally express the gratitude of General Pope. The Fort Reno troops, aided by the post band, held a full-dress parade in honor of the visitors. On invitation, a contingent from the agency, mostly young women, came to view the military pageantry from the balconies of post houses and attend a grand reception held that evening in the home of Captain and Mrs. Bennett.[15]

By no means, however, were Payne and the boomers finished.

While Payne lobbied for settlement of the Oklahoma Lands in Washington during the spring of 1884, Couch organized another invasion of the territory. During April he led his colonists south from Kansas, dropping settlers off along Cottonwood Creek, Deer Creek, and the Deep Fork on his way to the North Canadian. There he established four camps, the principal one being at the site of present Oklahoma City. When word of this reached Fort Reno, Lieutenant Stevens and a thirty-man detachment of buffalo soldiers were sent to round them up.[16]

Some of the boomers offered resistance on this occasion, and Taylor's men were required to physically overpower both Couch's father and a New Yorker-turned-cowboy named Daniel J. Odell. The combative Odell had to be dragged from his horse and his hands tied behind his back. He was forced to walk with a rope tied around his waist and connected to the axle of a wagon as Stevens led his captured thirty-eight men and twenty-one wagons north across the head of Deep Fork to Payne's Crossing of the Cimarron, where he consolidated forces with Lt. Matthias W. Day. After waiting there a week in vain for other boomers to show up, the two officers marched Couch's band to Fort Reno. There they were turned over to U.S. marshals, who escorted them to Wichita, where they were arraigned before a U.S. commissioner on charges of conspiracy against the United States.[17]

Captain Carroll led a scout down the Deep Fork to Wells's store at the site of present Wellston, taking a number of prisoners. On May 16, Capt. Patrick Cusack arrested the wife and three children of settler J. S. Anderson, who was away at the time, and destroyed their cabin, corral, well, and fencing on Deer Creek. Also the log house, stable, and garden of J. W. Blackwood were demolished, and three men, who suspiciously claimed to be cowboys working for the Belle Plains Ranch, were placed under arrest.[18]

At Wichita, Couch and his men were released on their own recognizance, and their case was set for trial at Leavenworth on October 13. Undaunted, the determined boomer recruited still another large group of settlers and headed back for the Cimarron. The party was busy felling trees and snaking logs when Lieutenant Day appeared with a detachment of twenty black troops and six Indian police. When some of the soldiers approached with drawn pistols, Couch's men

raised their axes in defiance. A sergeant took Couch by the arm, saying, "Mr. Couch, I arrest you. You are my prisoner."[19]

Couch pulled back and the other boomers swarmed forth in his
defense, forming a "rail fence" of men three deep. Day faced them
with his troops, saying by his version of the incident, "This resistance
must cease right here. I will resort to arms." By boomer accounts, he
yelled, "If anyone moves an inch, blow their damned brains out!"

For whatever he said, the buffalo soldiers leveled their pistols at
the boomer crowd. When some of Couch's men broke for their wagons, Day ordered them to stop. All did but one man. "If you reach that
wagon," the officer warned, "you are a dead man." The man halted.
Day then established a guard point under four troopers and placed the
boomers in it one at a time while he searched their wagons and secured
their arms. Overnight some thirty-five of the boomers escaped, taking
with them some of the bolts and nuts from their wagons as a way of
resistance. Fifty of the settlers were still in camp under restraint.

It was back to Fort Reno again for Couch and the boomer head
men, this time to sleep on the bare floor of the guardhouse for five
days before being released and sent back to Kansas. At Wichita, Couch
filed charges against Taylor and Stevens for their actions against the
boomers.

There were other arrests of small parties of intruders by the Fort
Reno troops during the spring of 1884. However, an even larger confrontation between the military and the Oklahoma boomers was
shaping up at a place on the Chikaskia River known as Rock Falls,
south of Hunnewell. Located in the Cherokee Outlet and not the
Oklahoma Lands, Payne chose this idyllic, well-wooded spot as a site
for a major settlement effort.

Here his men erected a small shack to house the press of their
promotional organ, the *Oklahoma War Chief*. Its first edition to be
published there claimed the colony to number from 250 to 300 members. A small town soon emerged with structures for a restaurant, a
small hotel, and a drugstore, whose principal item of sale was alco-
holic beverages. These were surrounded by tents and dugouts, while
in the fields beyond, men were busy turning virgin soil to the sun-
light. Still another boomer settlement had been initiated twenty-six
miles to the east on Bois de Arc Creek near present Ponca City by
Payne loyalist Harry Stafford.[20]

On Sunday, July 13, General Hatch, accompanied by his staff, arrived at Fort Reno from Arkansas City to inspect and report on the settlement to the War Department. He shortly received orders to establish a base of operations from which he could monitor Payne's enterprise. He did so with six companies of Ninth Cavalry some ten miles below Rock Falls on the Chikaskia.

On August 1, President Arthur issued a proclamation warning that all intruders onto Indian lands would be forcibly removed, and orders soon reached Hatch: "Remove intruders from Indian country under the direction of the Indian Agent."[21] On August 6, the general, accompanied by Indian Inspector A. R. Green, rode to Rock Falls and informed a belligerent and argumentative Payne that he would have to move. The threat of military action was enough to cause some of the boomers to leave, but many others remained. On August 7, two troops of Ninth Cavalry under Capt. Francis Moore and Lt. Alfred B. Jackson arrived and began rounding up those settlers who did not manage to escape. When this was completed, the soldiers put the torch to Payne's settlement. The boomer leader was taken prisoner along with several of his lieutenants. At the same time this was taking place at Rock Falls, Captain Cusack was raiding Stafford's settlement, capturing several boomers.[22]

The majority of the boomers was escorted across the Kansas line. But for Payne and eight of his principal followers, the long-frustrated army had devised a special treatment. While it was now possible to reach Fort Smith by train from nearby Caldwell or Arkansas City, Payne and his men would be taken there across three hundred miles of sparsely settled eastern Indian Territory in a covered, springless army ambulance through the suffocating heat of August. They would be escorted by sixty Ninth Cavalry buffalo soldiers under the command of hard-drinking, tough-minded Lt. John H. Gardner and Lieutenant Jackson. One wagon carried the printing press of the *Oklahoma Chief*.[23]

The first day's march on August 11 led down the Chikaskia to the Salt Fork of the Arkansas. Here the troops were met by U.S. Deputy Marshal W. B. Williams, who held a civil warrant for the arrest of Payne and his men. Gardner adamantly refused to give up his prisoners, and an angry confrontation resulted wherein the cavalry officer brought his troops to formation and threatened to shoot the lawman and his one companion. Williams was denied the prisoners.

The cortege of wagons and cavalry continued on, following along the south side of the Arkansas River to reach the small trading post of Red Fork near present Tulsa on August 17. Here the more lenient Lieutenant Jackson took command. Payne and his men got their first drink of cold water and were permitted to purchase some fruit and vegetables at the Red Fork store.

After three more days in the cramped, jolting wagons, the prisoners arrived at Muskogee, where Jackson proudly drove through the middle of town to let people get a glance at the famous boomer leader. A visit was made that night to the high hill above the town were Union agency was located.[24]

From Muskogee, the entourage pushed on down the Arkansas River to Webbers Falls, where it crossed the river and continued on eastward to a point opposite Fort Smith, Arkansas. Jackson ferried the prisoner wagon across the river when it was learned that Judge Parker would no longer accept the boomers, deferring to the newly established Wichita federal court.

Thus rejected at Fort Smith, the captives were subjected to another grueling wagon ride through the rocky hills to Fort Gibson. En route, one of the boomers effected an escape. Following this, Jackson tightened up the watch over the prisoners, in part by leaving a fire burning just in front of their tents at night. Already confined in two small tents that were made almost unbearable by the scorching August sun, the fires only added to the boomers' misery. "My God," one of the boomers wrote, "we could Not Sleep aney at Night only to lay there and Die with heat we never suffered so in our lifes."[25]

Finally Payne rebelled and absolutely refused to reenter his tent. Jackson relented, permitting them to seek the shade of some trees. At Fort Gibson they were placed in the post guardhouse. On September 5 they were put on the march again, it having been arranged for them to be taken back to Fort Smith. The cavalcade traveled eastward to Tahlequah, where once again the boomers were displayed before "gawking" crowds with a parade through the streets of the town.

This leg of the trip through the Boston Mountains was even more torturous to the men in their wagon. Some three weeks after being arrested at Rock Falls, Payne and his men arrived back at Fort Smith. There U.S. Marshal Thomas Boles served a warrant on Payne for introducing whiskey into the Indian Territory. The boomers appeared before Judge Parker, who ordered them to return before the next term of the court and once again set them free.

It had, indeed, been a torturously painful ordeal, but the end result was that Payne was more of a hero to his followers than ever. And now, with the Kansas press denouncing the military's abuse of him, Payne had immensely more public support than before.

Rock Falls, though, would be his last intrusion into Indian Territory. On the morning of November 27, 1884—Thanksgiving Day—while on a speaking tour, Payne died of a massive heart attack during breakfast at the DeBarnard Hotel in Wellington, Kansas. His impoverished supporters were stunned as they buried him, wondering what would become of them now that their leader was gone.

Following Payne's death, William L. Couch stepped forward to assume leadership of the Oklahoma boomer movement. During December 1884, he was at the helm of a large colony of settlers that descended on Stillwater Creek at the site of present Stillwater, Oklahoma. Once again Fort Reno–commanded troops would be called into service, and it would be hard duty for the buffalo soldiers.

On orders to arrest the settlers, Lieutenant Day rode forth from Camp Russell on December 21 with forty men of Troop I, Ninth Cavalry, and two six-mule wagons. Reaching Halsell's Crossing of the Cimarron, Day found the river too flooded to cross. It was then that the troops were struck by a fierce norther with gale-driven snow and freezing temperatures. The tentless troops were forced to make camp in the scant shelter of a blackjack grove. The next morning they forded the ice-crusted river and, still battered by stinging north winds, pushed on to the Stillwater Creek settlement. They were met by some two hundred men who had fortified themselves in dugouts with their wagons lined in front. Only the night before, a wagon train had arrived from Kansas bringing shiny new Winchesters for those who had only shotguns.[26]

Day attempted to intimidate the boomers into surrendering by lining his troops up with their weapons displayed, but the determined settlers scattered and took up positions behind trees and wagons. With a woman and several children among the crowd, Day would not order his men to fire. Eventually he gave in to Couch's request that the army communicate with the president by telegraph regarding the situation. With no shelters, several of his men suffering from frostbite, and one man threatened with pneumonia, Day left behind a sergeant and six men and made his way back to Camp Russell over a countryside that was glazed slick with ice. The rain and sleet continued, and it was necessary for the troops to unload the wagons at every arroyo and help the smooth-shod stock across.

The intensely frigid weather still gripped the region when General Hatch, accompanied by a sizable force of cavalry and infantry and a large wagon train, marched from Caldwell to Stillwater Creek. The snow-packed roads soon turned into avenues of mud. Major Dewees, now commanding at Fort Reno, suffered the same difficulties of snowdrifts and frozen rivers in marching to Camp Russell, where he picked up Day and his troops and moved on to the boomer settlement to join Hatch.[27]

Couch remained as resistive as ever. His followers dug rifle pits in the frozen earth, apparently with the intention of opposing the

Medal of Honor winner Lt. Matthias W. Day assisted in the Fort Reno effort to restrain Oklahoma invaders. *Courtesy U.S. Military Academy Archives.*

army in battle. Hatch had already dispatched troops to cut off any supplies that might be sent to Couch and his people. But with only two days' rations remaining for his own men, Hatch decided to move boldly. First he sent a note to the woman in the camp begging her to leave. Then with orders to make their movements well observed, infantry companies were sent to seize a hill overlooking the boomer rifle pits. Dewees's four Fort Reno cavalry troops were dismounted and put into position, and three more under Captain Moore were dismounted on his left.

These threatening preparations made, Hatch and his adjutant then rode into the boomer camp and consulted with Couch. He hated to see bloodshed, Hatch said, but he would order his troops to fire at the first effort of the boomers to offer armed resistance. At first Couch refused to give in. He asked for more time, which Hatch refused to grant. Finally, the boomer leader submitted and the bone-chilled, famished boomers were loaded up and escorted back to Arkansas City. The *Arkansas City Traveler* announced the arrival of the bedraggled group—152 men, 1 woman, and 42 wagons—as it sloshed through the town's miry streets on January 29.[28]

Couch's capitulation was welcome news at Fort Reno, where a correspondent to the *Army and Navy Journal* commented:

> This recent "Boomer" excitement has created quite a stir here. We were left with only one company (with 11 men for duty) to guard the public stores and do the necessary police and fatigue duty of the post . . . For some years, has the demonstration of a few lawless individuals taken us from our comfortable quarters and families to face the bitter cold winds for days, only to feel after it is over that without punishment for such incursions we are liable to experience the same the coming year.[29]

Now another crisis, this between the Indians and the cattlemen, had developed in western Indian Territory. Both Fort Reno and Darlington would be caught directly in the middle of this new conflict.

CHAPTER 10

The Dog Soldiers and the Stockmen

In his *Autobiography*, one-time cowboy Charles Colcord relates an incident that illustrates the ongoing contest between ranchmen and Indians during the presettlement period of Indian Territory. After a spring multiranch roundup, a large herd was being driven down the North Canadian west of Fort Reno, where Arapaho chief Left Hand, now an old man, and his family resided in a house and several tepees. Left Hand and his men drove some eight hundred of the cows into his corral. When the cowmen arrived, Left Hand demanded a dollar a head for grazing on his land.[1]

Some of the seventy-five cowboys on hand began jerking down the corral gate bars. When Left Hand tried to stop them, the foreman of one outfit hit him in the head with an iron-handled quirt. Weapons were drawn on both sides, and a blazing gunfight between the cowboys and Indians was barely averted. Left Hand and his few men withdrew; but after the cowboys had driven the cattle into the main herd downriver, the chief appeared again accompanied by a sizable force.

"Indians! Indians!" Colcord wrote. "Every way one looked there was nothing but Indians, coming from every direction. seemingly coming out of the ground. I never saw so many in all my life."[2] Some 250 armed cowboys were on hand, but they were badly outnumbered and began circling their roundup wagons in preparation for a fight. One cowman dashed off to Fort Reno for help. Fortunately, however, some ranch entrepreneurs from Kansas City were present. Badly frightened, they quickly raised $350 and paid Left Hand off at 50¢ a head.

Miles was replaced as agent at Darlington in March 1884 by Daniel B. Dyer.[3] A curt man of little compromise, Dyer had previously served as agent for the Quapaws and Modocs in northeastern Indian Territory. He quickly encountered a major problem in his new job. Within two months of his taking over at Darlington, a clash between the Dog Soldiers and some Texas drovers proved far more deadly.

Arapaho chief Left Hand was a principal figure of early Indian Territory. *Courtesy National Museum of Natural History.*

On Sunday, May 4, 1884, Texan E. M. Horton, his brother, and two other men were herding some four hundred mares and colts from below Laredo, Texas, up the trail to Caldwell, Kansas.[4] Cheyenne chief White Horse helped by pointing him to the crossing of the North Canadian River. There, however, Horton found the quicksand was too much and came back down the river to ford at the Cantonment trail crossing. Some three miles from the river, he was confronted by Running Buffalo, a Cheyenne Dog Soldier.

By Horton's account, Running Buffalo demanded some ponies as a passage fee, which was permitted by agency rules; by other accounts the Cheyenne was attempting to turn the animals away from his garden patch by firing at them with his pistol. Horton claimed that the Cheyenne snapped his pistol in his face. Whichever was the case, it is certain that Horton pulled his revolver and shot Running Buffalo from his horse. Then as the man staggered to his feet, the Texan shot again and killed him.

Agent D. B. Dyer found himself caught squarely between the Indians and cattlemen grazing their herds on tribal land. *Leslie's Illustrated Newspaper,* May 18, 1889.

Some thirty or forty Cheyennes swarmed forth from their Cantonment village at the killing of their prominent leader. Now realizing his danger, Horton herded his ponies into the abandoned military corral at Cantonment and sought refuge from Rev. S. S. Haury in a building where a military telegraph line—constructed of iron poles because of prairie fires—connected Cantonment to Fort Reno and Fort Supply. Before the line was cut, Haury sent an urgent call for help to agent Dyer.[5]

He had tried to keep Running Buffalo's relatives from killing Horton, Haury said in his telegram, and finally succeeded in moving them to the temporary safety of a stone bakery. But the Cheyennes surrounded it and would not let any food or water through to the Texans. Also they took possession of Horton's wagon.[6]

Dyer asked Major Dewees to send troops immediately to rescue Horton and his crew. Lt. David J. Gibbon with twenty-five Ninth Cavalry troopers accompanied by William Darlington and five Indian police, left Reno at daylight on May 5 and hurried to Cantonment, some fifty-eight miles distant. En route they were met by a messenger, who urged them to hurry, as there were more Indians arriving and there was great danger that Horton would be killed. Gibbon also encountered a number of cattlemen who had gathered and were preparing to go to Horton's rescue. The officer told them it was unnecessary and advised them against such a foolish move.[7]

When Gibbon arrived at Cantonment, he found "much excitement and an ugly feeling" among the Indians. He talked with chief White Horse, who agreed to let him take custody of the horse drovers if he would guarantee they would not escape. Hungry, thirsty, and badly frightened, Horton's desperate party had even considered an attempt to dig an escape tunnel to the river. However, the only tool they had was an ax.

Gibbon's men surrounded the drovers and escorted them to another building through a gauntlet of furious tribesmen whose guns were cocked for a chance to shoot Horton. Prevented from getting at Horton, the Indians, now numbering more than one hundred, became even angrier. After a long parley, Haury and Amos Chapman, brother-in-law to Running Buffalo, persuaded the Indians to accept half of Horton's herd as compensation for Running Buffalo's death in line with the traditional tribal method of atonement.[8]

Realizing the impossibility of trying to drive his wild ponies off past the Cheyennes, Horton agreed. About half of the horses were released, and the Cheyennes went rushing eagerly in all directions after them. The buffalo soldiers then formed a double line of march and, with the Texans walking between them, drove the remaining animals away to the safety of Fort Reno. Because several of his horses had been used up in the dash to Cantonment, Gibbon's men were forced to walk and lead their mounts. Horton and his men were taken to Fort Smith and held for a time before being released. Acting on the secretary of interior's orders, Dyer eventually ordered the Cheyennes to return Horton's levied ponies.[9]

During the fall, a group of thirteen Cheyenne peace chiefs led by Whirlwind presented Dyer with a war shield and "medicine lizard" as a token of their goodwill.[10] This goodwill, however, did not last long for many Cheyennes. Determined to make the Indians of his agency more self-supporting, Dyer attempted to institute a farming program among the tribes, telling his charges that they would have to settle down on the reservation and go to work. He made some progress, but mostly it was with Arapahos. About thirty Cheyenne families took up farming, but most members of the tribe were either reluctant to do so or intimidated by the Dog Soldiers, who fiercely resented the work ethic of the white man as a challenge to tribal tradition.[11]

When the time approached for the Cheyennes to hold their annual Sun Dance and Medicine Arrow renewal, the Dog Soldiers acted to intimidate tribal members into attending the ritual. They burned fences, killed livestock, and withheld their children from the agency school. Further, they threatened tribesmen who farmed or worked in agency shops and ordered all breaking of land, building of fences, and other improvements by tribal members to cease.

When Dyer attempted to carry out orders from the Office of Indian Affairs to make a census of the tribes, the Dog Soldiers halted the proceedings by threatening to kill anyone who tried to enroll. They even posted two guards at the door of the agency office to intercept tribespeople.[12] The agency Indian police were powerless to act against the well-armed militants, and the Fort Reno troops were insufficient in number to act decisively. Dyer sent a warning to Dewees that the situation was dangerous and that if permitted to continue it could well cause the loss of "the lives of good innocent whites."[13]

Fearing a threatened Indian insurrection, during the spring of 1885 the army moved to reassign the existing forces at Fort Reno and replace them with an enlarged garrison. Company C, Twentieth Infantry, under Capt. Paul Harwood was ordered to Fort McGinnis, Montana, while Company D, under Capt. Charles O. Bradley was sent to Fort Assiniboine, Montana. On their departure in May, the units marched to the agency accompanied by the military band and conducted a farewell parade. A short time later Major Dewees led two companies of Ninth Cavalry off to Fort Robinson, Nebraska. Recently promoted Maj. Frank Bennett departed for a northern post.[14]

Replacements came in mid-June when Maj. Edwin Sumner, son of the famous pre–Civil War Indian fighter of the same name, arrived with three companies of Fifth Cavalry. He took command from Capt. Frederick M. Crandal, Twenty-fourth Infantry, who had filled the post temporarily. These units were followed a few days later by three companies of Eighteenth Infantry and one of Twenty-second Infantry. This brought the fort's strength to twelve companies, while four more companies of Fourth Cavalry were reported to be on their way.[15]

Indian affairs still continued to deteriorate badly. A Cheyenne named Flying Hawk attempted to withdraw his children from the Mennonite school at Cantonment. When Haury resisted, the Cheyenne began walking up and down in front of the minister's home with a pistol. He announced loudly that he would shoot Haury before sundown and outrage his wife.[16] Following this, Stone Calf, one of the most influential and resistive Cheyenne chiefs, led a party in ripping up fences and capturing cattle from a trail herd on the Caldwell route.[17]

George and Charlie Bent warned that if an effort was made to disarm the Cheyennes, the Indians would "sell their lives dearly."[18] Further, agency farmers reported that the Indians were well fixed for ammunition, having the best of quality by the gunnysack full. Cheyenne warriors were said to be herding their ponies together in the event of an emergency. An unsubstantiated story that appeared in Kansas newspapers told of two cowboys on the YL grazing range of the Cherokee Strip who had been found murdered with their bodies staked to the ground.[19]

Gen. Joseph H. Potter, commander at Fort Supply, was sent to investigate. He concluded that the discontent at the Mennonite mission at Cantonment stemmed from the granting of grazing rights there to frontiersman George E. Reynolds. An observer warned of dire trouble and noted that "The cantonment was always considered by Major Randall, Col. Dodge, Major Bennett and other experienced officers to be the right arm of Fort Reno and when it was abandoned a very grave mistake was made."[20]

The ugly mood of the Dog Soldiers continued, and the potential for serious trouble still loomed heavy over western Indian Territory.[21] The situation was intensified not only by the Horton affair but by the mysterious murder of Sitting Medicine, the son of chief Little Robe. His body was found by Indian scouts twelve miles from Fort Supply on July 28, 1885.[22] Rumors of a new Indian war swept across Kansas and Colorado. Newspaper accounts emanating from Fort Reno stated that six to seven hundred warriors were ready to resist confiscation of their arms. The medicine men, one newspaper story reported, were working like beavers to keep up the Cheyennes' war spirit.[23]

The situation was further agitated by rumors of an Indian uprising and panic among Kansas settlers. Gov. John A. Martin of Kansas claimed that several persons had been killed by Indians in Pratt

County, Kansas, and rumors flew that hundreds of families were fleeing north. It was later reported that outlaws may have helped stir up
the Indian scare in a scheme to plunder the vacated settlements. When
Cherokee Strip cowboy Oliver Nelson arrived at Protection, Kansas,
to find the citizens in near panic, he was asked his opinion of the Indian
danger. He replied that he had worked the territory from Supply to
Reno and he heard of Indians being shot but never a white man.[24]

Still reports and rumors of a pending Indian uprising persisted. A
telegram from Arkansas City claimed that several bands of Cheyennes
had been seen near town and that the local militia had been ordered
out with arms and ammunition. Another report said that a courier
from the Cheyenne agency had brought word that the whole Cheyenne
tribe was spreading to the north, east, and west in squads of twenty-
five to fifty and forcing cattlemen to provide them with rations.[25]

The *Army and Navy Journal* reported that troops had been hurried to the frontier from the departments of the Missouri, the Platte,
and Texas. Hatch had been sent to Ogallala, Nebraska, to guard the
old Cheyenne trail north. General Sheridan was confident, however,
the *Journal* said, that with a force of some four thousand men he could
surround the Cheyenne and Arapaho reservations and disarm the
Indians.[26]

Zach Mulhall, a future participant of the early Oklahoma scene,
announced that scouting parties had scoured the country around
Winfield, Kansas, for a hundred miles but no Indians were found.
The army declared that there were no Indians in Kansas, but directed
four companies of cavalry to the Kansas-Indian Territory border to
reassure the settlers there.[27]

Nonetheless Martin argued that Supply and Reno offered no protection for Kansas and demanded that forts be established on the
Kansas-Indian Territory line. The governor even went so far as to call
out the state militia at Larned and other western Kansas towns.[28] Gen.
C. C. Augur, now commanding the Department of the Missouri,
responded by ordering three companies of Fifth Cavalry to Fort Riley
ready to be sent south by rail to seal the Kansas border.[29] At Fort Reno,
Sumner's workforce expedited its activity on the steel-span bridge
connecting the fort and the agency across the North Canadian in the
event of an eruption of trouble.[30]

The situation on the Plains had reached the office of President Grover Cleveland. On July 10, he ordered Phil Sheridan, commanding general of the army, to go to the Cheyenne and Arapaho agency, hear the Indians' complaints, and right whatever wrongs he found there. In addition to his staff, Sheridan was accompanied by Gen. Nelson Miles; Col. Michael V. Sheridan, his aide-de-camp; Maj. Henry C. Corbine, Adjutant General's Department; and 1st Lt. Oscar F. Long, Fifth Cavalry. Also traveling with Sheridan were news correspondents from several metropolitan newspapers.[31] The military entourage, which came by army ambulance over the Chisholm Trail from the railhead at Caldwell, arrived at Fort Reno on July 15. They were met there by Colonel Potter and his interpreter Amos Chapman.[32]

On July 19, a council was held at Fort Reno with Stone Calf, Powder Face, Little Medicine, and other Cheyenne and Arapaho leaders who might lead a potential insurrection. Four companies of cavalry were drawn up some two hundred yards away just in case of trouble, but the assembled Indians were entirely peaceful. Still the three main leaders spoke bitterly of how the white men who leased their lands cheated and robbed them. Following the council, Sheridan ordered a census taken of the two tribes, it showing 1,360 Arapahos and 2,169 Cheyennes on the reservation.[33]

Sheridan was convinced that the matter of pasturing of Texas cattle on Indian lands was creating dissension among the tribes. Despite the recompense they derived from grass leases, Cheyennes, led by Chief Stone Calf, were demanding that the cattlemen remove their cattle from reservation lands. A government inspector who conducted an investigation of the situation on the reservation agreed that the leasing program resulted in far too many whites on Indian lands. He also stated firmly that additional military forces were needed at Fort Reno to head off a Cheyenne uprising.[34]

Texas cattlemen, who benefited greatly from the low cost of fattening their cattle for market on the reservation pastures, were adamantly opposed to giving up their leases. They vigorously lobbied the president and congressmen for support. The cattlemen also had the strong support of agent Dyer, who insisted that they had acted in good faith with the Indians. It was the Indians, he contended, who had taken the cattle lease money and then gone out and butchered the cattle for which grazing fees had been paid.[35]

President Cleveland, however, had already made up his mind to end the lease program in order to protect Indian sovereignty. The territory, he said, should be made into an Indian state.[36] In accordance with this policy, Sheridan conducted interviews with Indian leaders such as Stone Calf and Little Robe.[37]

It was charged by pro-cattle newspapers that he talked only with Indians and pro-Indian people and ignored informed sources such as George Bent, Edmund Guerrier, and Ben Clark, who were married to Indian women. Others claimed that these men were benefiting from arrangements with Fort Reno officers in regard to the lease program.

A story filed with the pro-cattleman *Wichita Eagle* related an incident that occurred between Dyer and Indian Inspector Frank C. Armstrong. Armstrong arrived at Darlington on July 5, held interviews with Indian leaders, and made his recommendations to Secretary of Interior Lucius Q. C. Lamar—and thus to the president—that white influence on the Cheyenne and Arapaho reservation be reduced. He described Darlington as a white town on an Indian reservation. Indian leaders such as Whirlwind, Big Jake, Howling Wolf, and Big Horse were demanding removal of the cattle herds.[38] The *Eagle* story said that Armstrong, who had been drinking heavily, cursed Dyer and accused him of not having control of his Indians. Dyer replied quietly that the Cheyennes had been out of control for years and that he could have made them mind if his request for troops had been sustained. "Cattlemen and reporters standing near," the story claimed, "told Armstrong they would sustain Dyer if he would slap Armstrong's face. A Kansas City Times reporter present afterward attempted to give the scene to his paper by wire but Sheridan refused to allow him to use the wire."[39]

In line with President Cleveland's wishes, Sheridan recommended the removal of Dyer on the grounds that the agent had alienated too many of his charges. A Kansas observer defended Dyer, saying that he was an honest man and a friend to the Indian but that he was a victim of jealousy between the Indian Bureau and the War Department. It was also suggested that a part of his problem was that he was a Republican and a civilian.[40]

Most importantly, Sheridan recommended cessation of the cattle lease program in accordance with the views of Stone Calf and other Cheyenne recalcitrants despite the desire of many friendly Cheyennes and Arapahos who wished to continue it. As had virtually been decided from the first, Sheridan recommended to the president that the lease program be halted and that the Cheyenne and Arapaho lands be cleared of cattle belonging to outside cattlemen. President Cleveland issued an executive order to that effect on July 23, 1885. He gave the cattlemen forty days to remove their cattle, horses, and other property from the Cheyenne and Arapaho reservation.[41]

Sheridan also recommended that the tribes be disarmed, but the chiefs were unanimously opposed to such a move. They had paid big prices for their arms with money received from their freighting operations and selling stock, and it always took the government a long time to make compensations.[42]

An enrollment of the Cheyennes and Arapahos was also put in place. Runners were sent out in all directions for all Indians belonging to the agency to come in and be counted and enrolled. All those who did not respond would forfeit their rations. Rev. S. S. Haury and Rev. H. R. Voth immediately began an accounting of the Arapahos, but the Cheyennes proved to be very obstinate in compliance. Sheridan agreed to provide regular employment to one hundred Indian scouts at thirty dollars a month. Guns and ammunition were issued to them.[43]

When he was asked later by a reporter how he had fixed things up in Indian Territory, Sheridan summed it up briefly: "Well, there is not much to tell. The cattle leases were at the bottom of the trouble. Several of the Indians have small plantations along the streams, which were included in the leases and their crops were destroyed by cattle."[44]

With these things done, a grand military review consisting of ten cavalry and six infantry companies was held at Fort Reno in honor of Sheridan and his staff. Shortly afterward, news reached Fort Reno of the death of former President Ulysses S. Grant. On July 23, 1885, eighteen cannon salutes were fired at sunrise, all business was suspended, and the firing of a cannon every fifteen minutes continued through the day. At sunset another round of eighteen shots was fired.[45]

Before leaving for New York to attend Grant's funeral, Sheridan named Capt. Jesse M. Lee of the Ninth Infantry as Dyer's replacement.[46] Lee had enlisted in the infantry as a private during the Civil War and had risen quickly to the rank of captain. He would continue in the service in the years ahead, being appointed as a brigadier general in 1902.[47]

Whatever the right or wrong of Sheridan's action, matters on the reservation and in Indian Territory settled down after his visit. Though thoroughly disgruntled, cattlemen rushed about to remove their cattle to other pastures in Texas, Colorado, Montana, and elsewhere to meet Cleveland's deadline. At the same time, Captain Lee arrived at Darlington on July 27, 1885, and took charge on August 15. He immediately set out to enforce the president's edict, sending soldiers to various ranch headquarters and key locations to oversee the cattle removal and maintain peace. When Cheyenne warriors stampeded a trail herd, the troops that had been sent to the Mennonite mission arrested thirteen Cheyennes. On November 6, Lee reported that the reservation was clear of cattle that had been there under the lease program.[48]

On November 12, the *Transporter* announced that Stone Calf had died near Cantonment, commenting: "Stone Calf had been a very bad man, but now he was a good one . . . Before his death he drew a plow from Agent Dyer and promised he would walk in the white man's path and be a good Indian."[49]

Ironically, the *Transporter's* own demise had already been set in motion. Removal of the cattlemen from the Cheyenne and Arapaho reservation meant the end of the newspaper's main source of revenue, the ranch advertisements. It would publish its last issue on August 12, 1886, closing an invaluable historical window to Fort Reno and Darlington.[50]

During the removal period, the agency was visited by a delegation of other government officials, a congressional committee headed by Congressman William S. Homan of Indiana, Commissioner of Indian Affairs D. C. Atkins, and four other congressmen. The committee was met a mile from Fort Reno and escorted to the post by an honor guard composed of Indian scouts. Half of the scouts were in military uniform and half were in native attire. An inspection review and parade was held, and cannon and musket salutes were fired in honor of the congressional committee.[51] "From here," the *Transporter* observed, "they went east through the Okalahoma [*sic*] country, doubtless noticing many parties of boomers while en route."[52]

Indeed, the land-hungry settlers were still as determined as ever. Payne was gone, but he had been the chief promoter of a changing attitude among the American public toward Indian Territory. For so long as the waters run, the government treaty makers had promised, it would be the Indians' homeland. But that was in the past. In his report to the secretary of war in the fall of 1885, General Miles expressed a view of the Indian lands that was growing more popular by the day. "The Indian Territory," Miles concluded, "is now a block in the pathway of civilization."[53]

CHAPTER 11

Prelude to Settlement

On the eve of the initial opening of Indian Territory lands to settlement, the Fort Reno/Darlington complex stood essentially as a nucleus around which the trappings of Anglo-American society had begun to develop. By a variety of means, the white man had invaded the excluded world of the Indian and made himself a part of it. Fort Reno, in particular, provided a protective cover for such integration as it, too, became less a rude, frontier fort and more a standard military post.

Fort Reno was at its apex during the 1880s. From the Darlington side of the North Canadian, it loomed handsomely atop a long, sloping rise. The Stars and Stripes fluttered over a grassy, tree-lined parade ground. On the east of the square were eight two-story officer residences fronted by comfortable piazzas and connected by stone walks. On the south were the long, frame soldier barracks, and on the west and north the post's administrative buildings. Separating the horse barns and corrals from the rest was a broad avenue that ran south toward Darlington past the large warehouse of the Evans brothers. Every morning at reveille, the roll of drum and blare of bugle sounded across the valley as the flag was raised, the process being repeated each evening as the flag was lowered at retreat. During the day, brass artillery pieces and cannonballs gleamed in the sun as sentinels with rifles to their shoulders marched their posts and other soldiers went through their daily drills or moved about tending to the herds of cavalry horses in the fields and stables.[1]

With the Indian situation now calmed, Fort Reno turned to internal matters. For one, soldiers put a sawmill in full operation at Council Grove and began sawing lumber for construction of buildings at the post and for the bridge that other troopers were constructing across the North Canadian.[2] With the river bridged, people would not have to depend upon the slow ferry in their daily lives, and

The bridge constructed across the North Canadian by Colonel Sumner is on the far right in this view of Darlington Agency. *Courtesy Western History Collections, University of Oklahoma Libraries.*

Indian tepees surround the grounds around Fort Reno. *Courtesy Western History Collections, University of Oklahoma.*

the movement of troops would be greatly facilitated. Further, it was hoped that there would be no more mail lost by carriers' having to ford the flooded river. Colonel Sumner, who was responsible for building the bridge, put up lamps at either end and assigned a corporal to keep the bridge in order. Persons were warned not to drive their wagons on the bridge faster than a walk, and a daytime guard was posted to enforce the rule.[3]

The history of Fort Reno, the Darlington agency, and the road to Kansas at this period of time is well served by the keen observation and descriptive acumen of Ida Marie Dyer, wife of the agent. Mrs. Dyer, the daughter of Sen. N. R. Casey of Illinois, followed her husband to Fort Reno in July 1885, traveling by stagecoach from Caldwell, Kansas. In a book that she later wrote about her experiences on the Indian Territory frontier, she provides graphic views of the fort and the agency as well as the stage route from Caldwell as it was then.

On her trip to Darlington, Mrs. Dyer found Pond Creek ranche to be elaborately furnished for such a "far-away retreat," the story-and-a-half frame building having carpet in one room and unbleached cotton drapes at the windows. She was immediately initiated into a truly Western scene there. Even as her stage pulled up at the station, another six-horse coach, which was loaded inside with passengers for Fort Reno and Fort Sill and atop front and back with mail and baggage, thundered off ahead in a cloud of dust. A big Cherokee Outlet cattle roundup was just finished, and some of the many cowboys hired for the affair were at the station. She wrote:

> They were typical in their corduroy pantaloons, high-heeled boots, with tops extending half-way up their thighs. The vicious-looking, jingling spurs attached, their white sombreros of umbrella-size shading their eyes, their extra cartridge belts and Winchesters lying across the horns of their saddles, made the *tout ensemble* of these Arabs of the plains formidable to look upon.[4]

Inside the station a motley but fearsome group of men were playing poker. To her eye and mind, they all appeared to be desperados and killers of various sorts. In the corner of the room, just beyond a beam lined with whiskey bottles, stood a stack of breech-loading rifles and other weapons. But even these rough denizens of the frontier were mindful of the day's code of respect to womankind.

Down the line, Skeleton ranche proved to be a lowly log cabin occupied by a sad-faced, worn-looking woman. Much as Hunnius had observed, the interior of the place was plastered with pictures from illustrated newspapers, show bills, and pinups of the day. Mrs. Dyer found her bedroom for the night to be noted especially for the smoke emitted from its coal-oil lamp and its abundance of ravenous mosquitoes.

The weeded mound of Hennessey's grave was still visible along the trail as the stage moved on to the stockade structure that was Bull Foot station. White-topped prairie schooners filled with the worldly goods of Oklahoma boomers and ox trains stretching out a mile or more were passed along the road. Many of the wagon trains belonged to Evans Brothers, post traders at Fort Reno. Of particular importance were their cargoes of "wet groceries"—liquor—for the post. "This was one branch of necessities," Mrs. Dyer noted, "most carefully watched, guarded, and pushed through on time at all hazards, for Army posts were exempt from the general stringent rules of the red man."[5]

River crossings, particularly at the Salt Fork of the Arkansas and the Cimarron, proved to be memorable experiences, as Mrs. Dyer described:

> A ride of fifteen miles brought us to the "Cimarron," a wide, swift-current river without bridge or boat. Fears were not to be indulged, and with eyes closed, and all sense of estimated distance obliterated by fright, the sure-footed and trusty horses plunged into this dangerous stream. Our carriage struck the high water-mark as we entered and it stayed with us to the end. The thing tumbled and tossed, first up, and then down, over boulders, and as the water rolled over the dash-board, and threatened to engulf us, it sputtered and splashed, and whirled around, the waves and spray dashing into our faces. The blood in our veins stood still, as we felt the wheels sink into the yielding sand, but after steady buffeting, we dragged through, and although the pulsation of the heart had quickened, we sped away toward the Cheyenne Agency and Fort Reno.[6]

As the stage approached Darlington, the glistening white tops of Indian tepees could be seen by the hundreds stretching along the river's treeless bank to the west. The romance of this view was dispelled, however, as the stage passed by the beef-issue post, where lay the scattered bleached bones of government-annuity beef herds that for nearly a decade had been killed and butchered here by the tribes. Buzzards, crows, and other birds of prey swarmed noisily among the carnage and filled the sky above, while packs of coyotes and wolves skulked about the periphery of the slaughter site waiting for night to fall for their turn at the feast.

Darlington, Mrs. Dyer found, sat comfortably in the North Canadian valley, its two streets forming a "T" against the river. The agent's home, with its whitewashed veranda, faced the street that ran along the river's north bank. The house was surrounded by the cottages of employees, their fenced yards and gardens giving the look of a small rural community. These residences were accompanied by a growing commercial center consisting of a hotel, physician's office, livery stable, three trading stores, and the building that housed the *Cheyenne Transporter*, a "bright newsy little home paper." The large building of the Arapaho school stood on the north end of the street perpendicular to the river. The brick Mennonite school was located apart at the east side of the agency grounds.[7]

Darlington's dominant structure, however, was the large brick commissary building, where annuity goods for the tribes were accumulated. Its cellar provided storage for bacon and oil; the first floor held such goods as flour, sugar, corn, and coffee; while the second floor housed wearing apparel, dry goods, school supplies for the agency children, and other commodities.

Mrs. Dyer soon found herself firmly involved in the social life of the agency and Fort Reno. One gala event was a masquerade ball held at the frontier fort on December 30, 1884.

On New Year's Day 1885, with the temperature hovering around the zero degree mark, some thirty-five officers and prominent men toured both the agency and the post in ambulances and carriages, calling at homes that had signified a willingness to receive guests. They were met with hearty greetings of "Happy New Year" and dishes of salads, turkey, jellies, fruits, and cakes.

It was during this period of frigid weather that the Darlington community was shocked to learn that the noted scout Philip

McCusker had been found frozen to death sitting by a tree on the banks of the Red River. After swimming his horse across the river in returning to Fort Sill from Texas, McCusker had unsaddled his horse, tied it to a bush, and attempted to build a fire but failed.[8]

In early May, the Dyers and the agency staff themselves hosted a grand ball and banquet for the Fort Reno officers, who, having been recalled with their troops from their boomer removal duties in the Unassigned Lands, were being reassigned to Montana and Nebraska. The agency hall was decorated, and Prof. Charles DeBra provided music for the entertainment of some thirty-five military and civilian couples.[9]

That same month the tribes had their own special celebration when $31,000 in grass lease money was paid out by lawyers representing cattlemen operating in Indian Territory. The money was issued in bills of small denomination to facilitate individual distribution.

"The distribution of the money," the *Cheyenne Transporter* observed, "is made on the Agency family ration tickets, upon which the Indian women draw their beef, flour, etc., and in the same manner they draw their grass lease money. After drawing their money, exciting times were had by the Indians changing and dividing their cash among themselves, after which they liberally patronize their traders in obtaining supplies and merchandise of every description."[10]

Chief Killer and Cloud Chief traveled to Arkansas City, where they purchased fine carriages for themselves; and Chief White Antelope procured a spring wagon along with harness.[11]

Even as the threat of the Cheyenne Dog Soldiers loomed over the reservation, the boys of the Cheyenne school were issuing a challenge for a football contest with the young men of Darlington, Fort Reno, and the Arapaho school.[12] They first found takers instead from Companies C and D, Twentieth Infantry, when those units were passing through Fort Reno on their way from Caddo Springs to new assignments in Montana in May 1885. Two games were played, and the Cheyenne boys, who had been drilled by Professor Potter, won both contests by a wide margin.[13]

Further social activity at Darlington was provided by the six-man agency string band, with piano accompaniment by Miss LaMonde, who gave a concert for employees of the Cheyenne school. On another occasion the band boys made the rounds of the agency, starting with

Fort Reno troops stand in formation during dress parade. *Courtesy Western History Collection, University of Oklahoma.*

the Dyer's house, and serenaded the village. They were fed and provided refreshments at various homes.

The Fourth of July was celebrated by an afternoon baseball game
between the Fort Reno and Darlington clubs with the agency winning
a close contest. A fireworks display was held that evening at the agency.
At Silver City on the South Canadian River crossing of the Santa Fe
Trail, rancher Montford Johnson sponsored a Fourth of July barbecue
and horse races open to all two- and three-year-olds and saddle horses
raised in Indian Territory. A few days later a dispute between Johnson's
cowboys and those of the Murray and Williams spread erupted into a
gun fight over a steer. Only two of Johnson's men had six-shooters,
while the Murray and Williams men had Winchesters. One of
Johnson's men was shot out of his saddle and killed before he could
draw his weapon, and another had his horse shot from under him.
Johnson himself escaped with bullet holes in his hat.[14]

Still another view of the Fort Reno-Darlington environs was provided by Father Hilary Cassal, a French priest of the Catholic Sacred
Heart Mission located just north of the Canadian River below present Shawnee, Oklahoma. During October 1885, Cassal was sent on a
tour of southwestern Indian Territory. Traveling in an old military
ambulance pulled by two mules and driven by a Potawatomi Indian
teamster named Pete Wano, Cassal traveled first to Fort Sill. En route
he visited in homes at the infant settlements of Johnsonville, White
Bead Hill, Erin Springs, Rush Springs, and Alex.

At Fort Sill, the Catholic priest celebrated Mass before a congrega-
tion composed largely of black troops from Louisiana and Mississippi,
many of whom spoke French, and some Irish soldiers. After Cassal had
delivered his sermon, Sergeant Franklin, who also served as a minister
for the buffalo soldiers, took up a collection of eighteen dollars.

From Fort Sill, Pete turned the hack to Fort Reno, where Colonel
Sumner permitted Cassal to visit the barracks and invite the soldiers,
white and black, to Mass on Sunday. It was left to the priest to find
his own lodging, which he did in the home of Capt. Alfred E.
Woodson, whose wife was Catholic. He accepted the invitation reluctantly, however, because Woodson was away on a hunting trip, and
Cassal feared the appearance of impropriety even though there were
servants in the house.

After baptizing the child of a Fort Reno dairyman, Cassal was rewarded with a five-dollar gold-piece from the godmother and five dollars each from both the father and mother. The priest was amazed: "I had never received so much money for a baptism in my life. It was just one hundred francs in French money. When I was assistant in Alsace, I used to get twenty-five cents!"[15]

Though it was considered the most dangerous part of his tour, Cassal was determined to visit Cantonment. Sumner warned him against it; but when the priest insisted it was his duty, he reluctantly gave Cassal a letter of introduction to the dashing Capt. Edward M. "Jack" Hayes, then commanding a detachment of Fifth Cavalry troops there. Pete was not at all pleased to go. In fact he was deathly afraid; the Potawatomis and Cheyennes had never gotten along very well.

The two men were sleeping on the trail under a buffalo robe when at three o'clock one morning they heard the sound of footsteps approaching. A Cheyenne chief appeared mysteriously out of the darkness, badly frightening the two travelers. Though the chief was suspicious of him, Cassal won his friendship with a breakfast and crucifixes. Later the priest met an aged Cheyenne woman who, through the use of sign language, conveyed information that her son was sick at the Cantonment Mennonite school and that her husband had gone there to get his sore eyes treated. Further on down the trail, Cassal met the husband, now wearing black glasses, who said his son had recovered.

The road along the way was totally void of other white men. A former ranch that consisted of a corral, a barn, and stacks of hay was eerily deserted even of livestock. There were hundreds of prairie chickens along the road, but the two travelers were weaponless and had no way of shooting them.

At Cantonment, Captain Hayes ordered a temporary chapel prepared for Cassal, who conducted Mass, heard confessions, and gave a short sermon before a group of some sixteen Indian boys. The priest also met missionary Haury. Haury described himself as a mere farmer who taught the Indian children only two things—work and prayer. Among other labors, the students at Cantonment operated a broom factory.[16] "More simple and more unsophisticated people I never met in my life," Cassal observed of the Mennonites, "and Captain Hayes said they did well with the children and that the parents all had a great respect for them."[17]

On another trip from Fort Reno, Cassal journeyed to Anadarko, where he had the pleasure of meeting and talking with the famous Comanche chief Quanah Parker, son of white captive Cynthia Ann Parker. The chief offered to help if the Catholics would come and build a school at Anadarko. A formal request for such from the Wichita agent soon followed.

At Darlington, Cassal met agent Dyer, himself a Catholic who had been schooled at Osage Mission, Kansas, by the Jesuits. Dyer escorted the priest through the classrooms and dormitories of the agency school building and took him to see the agency stables and stock pens. Cassal also met the Arapaho wife of rancher Benjamin F. Keith and was invited to visit the Keith ranch home that was located just down the North Canadian. Once there, he was led two miles away from the house to a huge tepee, where inside he found the ancient mother of Keith's wife lying on one of the eight pallets in the lodge. "When I came in," Cassal wrote, "she began to sign herself and showed me a big rosary hanging around her neck. 'This I got,' she said, 'from Father De Smet. He was a big white man with long hair. He baptized fifty of us in one day and to each one he gave a rosary.'"[18]

Another side trip made by the priest was to the small town of Silver City and the home of Montford Johnson. Johnson's father-in-law, Joe Campbell, also lived there. Campbell told the priest of hunting buffalo and wild horses in the territory with his father when he was a boy. Wild horses, he said, had been scarce some years; however, from 1860 to 1875 there had been large droves of them in Texas and Indian Territory. Campbell, whose father had come from Ireland and married a woman of Indian blood, shared the Indian's distrust of white people. "Before the white man came we were much happier in this Territory," he complained. "We never cheated our neighbor, never stole from him. But now, my Lord, it seems everybody steals and cheats!"[19]

From Silver City, Cassal and Pete rode south to Cherokee Town, a settlement established by some dissident Cherokees before the Civil War and for a time the home of Indian trader Dr. John Shirley. There the priest visited the Jennings's home from which would come Al

Jennings, Oklahoma's train robber and politician of the early 1900s. There were stops at other isolated frontier homes as the two men made their way back to Sacred Heart. One well-remembered night was spent in their hack surrounded ominously by a pack of yowling timber wolves.

Benjamin Keith, whose ranch Cassal had visited, was one of several intermarried whites and mixed bloods who had been permitted by agent Miles to establish themselves on the Oklahoma Lands in 1876. These included Hermann Hauser, former quartermaster's clerk at Fort Reno; Peter Shields; John Poisal; and George H. Johnson. The settlers also included some progressive Cheyenne and Arapaho families. Miles had mistakenly assumed that their homes would be inside the Cheyenne and Arapaho reservation when the eastern boundary was correctly surveyed.[20]

Another person to write effectively and provide invaluable insight into this period of Indian Territory history was a man who played a significant role in the affairs of the Cheyenne and Arapaho Indians. John Seger had been hired by agent Miles as a jack-of-all-trades to do masonry work, plaster, build chimneys, and the like. Smallish in size but determined and in good health, the twenty-nine-year-old Kansan would prove to be one of the most valuable persons connected with the Darlington agency. His energy and capacity to relate to the tribespeople of the agency would be a great asset to white-Indian relations. His crowning achievement would be the establishment of the Seger settlement at present Colony, Oklahoma.

Seger not only wrote informative articles—much edited, evidently, for Seger was far from well schooled—for the *Transporter* on his experience with the Indians but also eventually published *Early Days among the Cheyenne and Arapahoe Indians* through the help of professor and Western historian Walter Campbell (Stanley Vestal). Seger's book provides an excellent view of his life at Darlington and among the tribes.

When Seger had first arrived at Darlington on Christmas Day 1872, he was put to work tearing down the old cottonwood plank buildings and erecting new ones. It being too cold to do the masonry work he was hired to do, he was asked by the agency farmer to cut down trees and saw logs at Council Grove. Having once worked in the Wisconsin woods as a lumberjack, Seger was pleased to do so. His zeal and willingness to take on any task soon caused his promotion to assistant farmer. As such he helped teach the boys of the tribes to farm and was eventually named supervisor of the Cheyenne/Arapaho Training School, a position he held for five years.

In this charge, he was constantly challenged to keep the Indian children in school and the school free from the intrusive and disturbing visitations of parents and other tribal members. At times, this brought him face to face with imminent danger from angry Indians armed with knives and guns. Seger handled these situations with stout courage, and in doing so won the admiration and friendship of the Indians. His service at the agency, however, was forever shadowed by an ongoing, often physical feud with an old Cheyenne man named Hippy.

Seger's work at the agency was by no means the limit of his involvement in the affairs of the Indian Territory frontier. A scanning of news items in the *Cheyenne Transporter* reveals many of Seger's activities and enterprises. In 1880 he opened a buckboard and hack line carrying mail and passengers to Fort Elliott, Texas. At the same time he leased a large area of land (twenty-five by forty miles, some 300,000 acres) on the southern border of the Cheyenne/Arapaho reservation at the conflux of Cobb Creek and the Washita River. He referred to this as his ranch, where, he playfully boasted, he had ten thousand turkeys (wild turkeys, undoubtedly) and a whole creek full of fish.[21]

Seger sold a house he owned at Darlington to Thomas McDade, who established it as a hotel that he called the Cheyenne House. At one time Seger held an interest in a livery stable. It was he who suggested that the older boys and girls of the tribes be sent off to Carlisle for continued education. At the same time, the school cattle herd that he oversaw was successful, it growing to fifteen hundred head.[22]

Seger left the agency in 1882 to farm, run cattle, and raise horses on his Washita Cattle Company ranch. He resided in a dirt-roofed cabin he had built. During the next two years, he helped with cattle roundups in what is now the Oklahoma Panhandle and built fences for cattlemen in the Cherokee Outlet. Against the liking of Texas cattlemen, he employed Indian helpers in stringing some 275 miles of barbed wire.[23]

When the order came in 1885 for removal of all stock from leased areas, Seger's ranch, being on the Cheyenne and Arapaho reservation, was included along with those of the cattlemen. He now determined to move his family to Kansas, where his children could attend school. It was at that time that agent Jesse Lee approached him with a proposal. Lee wished to separate those Cheyenne and Arapaho families who wanted to farm and earn a living away from those who hung about the agency, gambled, and sponged off the others. It would mean starting a new settlement some distance from the agency. Lee thought that Seger would be just the man for the job and offered him the position of agency farmer at seventy-five dollars a month.[24]

Lee proposed that the Indians be moved to Seger's former Washita lease, which was enclosed with a four-strand wire fence. Accordingly, in the spring of 1886 Seger moved there from Darlington with twenty-five Arapahos and began putting in crops.[25] He would also establish an industrial school for Indian youths. The settlement would become known as the Seger Colony and ultimately feature a school and dormitory, a teachers' building, and a hospital, in addition to other attendant buildings, barns, pens, and the like. The enterprise was a success largely because of Seger's capacity to work effectively with and earn the high respect of his Indian charges. He would remain personally in charge of the Seger Colony for twelve years, and it would continue to operate after his retirement.[26]

Lee extended his program of dispersing the Indians out from the agency with other agricultural settlements. He also undertook a census of the two tribes and worked to stop the loose cohabitation and intermarriage of white men with Indian women without the agent's consent. Cantonment was still the hotbed of continued Cheyenne hostility. Chiefs such as Little Robe, Mad Wolf, and Bear Shield continued to confiscate stock from passing trail herds, sometimes at gun point, and take beef cows from herds in the Cherokee Outlet.[27]

The missionaries at Darlington labored bravely and determinedly to improve the lives of the Indian children they taught in the mission schools and, often, their impoverished parents as well. One such was Dian Lugenbuehl, whose story is picturesquely and touchingly told by Joseph Leroy Carter in his book *Dian Takes to the Indians*.

Deeply moved by a sermon at her Mennonite church in Tipton, Missouri, the then twenty-six-year-old Dian had determined to become a missionary among the Indians. In July 1885 she bravely headed off by train and stagecoach to Cantonment, where she taught in the Mennonite mission school for a time before being transferred to Darlington. Soon after she arrived at Darlington, the terrible blizzard of January 6, 1886, howled down from the north. Temperatures dropped to some twenty degrees below the freezing mark while the wind-driven snow swirled into great drifts across the open prairie. Cattle and horses were frozen to death by the thousands, their bodies piled high in ravines and against the barbed-wire fences.[28]

Oliver Nelson, who at the time was taking a respite from cowboying in the Cherokee Outlet to homestead a claim in Comanche County, Kansas, told how it was with the cattle:

> Sometimes a ball of ice would form on a cow's nose—a ball five inches across, with two small holes made by breathing. The poor things just walked the creeks and bawled. The mercury got down to 17 degrees below. In February their feet, and then their legs froze. When it would turn warm, the legs would break at the ankle or knee. Sometimes they would rest on the pegs a day or so before they would lay down. When, down, they could not get up. They died by thousands.[29]

Civilians and troops also suffered badly. Captain Hamilton, commanding a troop of Fifth Cavalry at Camp Russell near present Guthrie, reported that one of his men who had let his charger get away had been caught out in the storm. A four-man detail sent to look for him became lost and also lay out all night. The troopers managed to avoid freezing to death and eventually made it back to camp safely.[30]

During the summer of 1886, the mission, along with the agency and military post, was struck by still another disaster—a typhoid epidemic. After watching one of her Arapaho girls die of the disease, Dian herself went into a near-death coma before eventually recovering. Dian married Jacob Meschberger, who had long worked for the Mennonite missions, and took up residence in one of Cantonment's original cottonwood lumber houses, the picket bottoms of which were rotting away.[31]

Still other facets of life at Darlington and Fort Reno during 1886 were reflected in the columns of the *Cheyenne Transporter*. The March 15 edition described a friendly pugilistic contest between trader

William S. Decker, representing the Evans Brothers of Fort Reno, and the Darlington deputy postmaster Robert Fraser. The men fought four four-minute rounds, with Decker being declared the winner by the Fort Reno referee.

In the same issue, the paper devoted a full column to a dance party held at Fort Reno by Miss Sumner, the popular daughter of Colonel Sumner, Mrs. Foster (wife of Lt. Claiborne L. Foster), and Mrs. Almy (wife of Lt. William E. Almy). The east wing of the adjutant building was beautifully decorated with flags and Japanese lanterns and the floor waxed for dancing. The night proved to be stormy, but the blazing fireplaces were cheerful to the thirty persons who attended the affair. The party was billed as a "calico hop," and those in attendance wore calico costumes. Of particular notice was Lt. Samuel E. Adair, a favorite with the ladies, who arrived in "a neatly fitting 'dolly varden,' low cut vest and diamond studs." The costumes of the ladies were likewise described as being original and elegant.

Another column featured a narrative by John Seger, who recounted the journey of his first group of Arapaho "pilgrims" from Darlington to what would become his colony settlement on the Washita River. The North Canadian was crossed on Sumner's bridge, but it required a whole day just to ford the main Canadian. One of the Arapaho women, fearful of crossing the river in a wagon, waded across with her child on her back. Another woman, the wife of Bear Robe, was very ill in her wagon but did not want to be left behind. She died en route. "Our party took a last look at her; then Bear Robe wrapped her in his blankets and buried her while the oxen were being yoked for our onward journey."[32]

Later that summer, Seger again wrote to report that despite a drought, his Arapaho colonists had produced new potatoes and watermelons. He was pleased that the girls had proved themselves quite apt in learning domestic details, and the boys were paying close attention to their milk cows. He was concerned, however, that one of the members arranged for a medicine dance for a sick family member. Seger suggested a way of breaking up the medicine dance practice:

> Let all the whites on the reservation take hold of the matter
> by giving the Indians a Fourth of July celebration about their
> time for their medicine rites; let them march in the procession;

let the chief of the dog-soldiers be marshal of the day with a colored sash; let the chief medicine man carry the national flag at
the head of the procession; let the beaters of the tom-tom beat
the infantry drum, and at the grand stand let their Agent explain
to them that the occasion is for their pleasure in honor of the
birth of nation, etc.[33]

Eventually the tribes themselves would pridefully adopt the
essence of Seger's idea in celebrating the Fourth of July. During 1886,
however, the 110th anniversary of the nation's birth was celebrated at
Fort Reno by a huge white crowd. Red, white, and blue trimmings
decorated the post as military and civilians joined in watching a
greased pig chase, tug-of-war, and racing contests during the morning. Commemorative exercises were conducted at noon; and afterward the excited crowd flocked to witness the troop horse racing on
an oblong course that Captain Woodson had prepared just south of
the garrison. Company K of the Twenty-fourth Infantry (black)
improvised with music for the occasion, and the evening was concluded with fireworks furnished by the Evans Brothers post traders.[34]

CHAPTER 12

Monitoring the White Deluge

The basic responsibility of the Fort Reno garrison was still its military support of the Cheyenne/Arapaho agency. But the Oklahoma boomer problem had not gone away with the demise of Payne. It having been determined on authorization of the president that it was legal to use military troops as "posse comitatus" in arresting Indian Territory intruders, the United States looked to the Fifth Cavalry as its principal tool in holding back the boomer tide from Indian Territory.[1]

In line with this, Troops C, E, I, and L of the Fifth Cavalry at Fort Robinson, Nebraska, were ordered to Fort Reno during the summer of 1885. The command arrived there on July 2, 1885, after marching 468 miles. Within two weeks, the troopers were in the saddle again, this time making a sixty-two-mile ride to the Cimarron River and back. In August they marched to Cantonment, scouring the country from there to Kiowa, Kansas, from where they patrolled the Kansas–Indian Territory border until October, when they continued on north to Fort Riley.[2]

Troop L of the Fifth under Capt. William C. Forbush performed garrison duties at Riley until November 1886. At that time the unit was sent to Camp Martin on Bois d' Arc Creek in northern Indian Territory. There during the next eleven months, scouting parties of the unit patrolled against illegal invasion of the territory, arresting not only boomers but cattle rustlers, horse thieves, timber thieves, and hunters who entered without official permits. John D. Brandt, bugler for Forbush, described one incident that occurred.

A party of twenty-six Kansans led by a Winfield businessman invaded the territory on a Christmas hunting trip. When they refused to pay a ranch woman for cooking their breakfast, her son raced to the cavalry camp and reported the matter. Brandt was ordered to take a detail of four men and arrest the intruders. It was snowing when the detail caught the hunters returning home with four wagons loaded to the brim with game. Brandt ordered the intruders to dismount and drop their guns and ammunition belts to the ground.

The men complied. Brandt then had their horses unsaddled and tied behind the wagon. Still Brandt began to worry that he had no handcuffs and feared that his small detail would be unable to stop the men if they chose to run. He posed the problem to a Corporal Dunn. Dunn had an answer. The corporal ordered the prisoners into a line, then proceeded to cut all of the buttons off their coats, shirts, and pants. As a result, the hunters were forced to hold their coats closed with one hand and their pants up with the other. They caused no trouble as they were marched to the cavalry station, where Forbush commended Brandt and Dunn for their ingenuity.[3]

The Oklahoma boomer movement had now moved largely to a political effort, with William Couch spending much of his time in Washington, D.C., lobbying for the cause. There was, however, one last boomer invasion in October 1885 when Couch somehow evaded the border guards and led a large party to the North Canadian. This time a hundred or more troops marched from Fort Reno under Major Sumner. One band of intruders was arrested at Council Grove and sent to the post guardhouse. That afternoon the troops found another

a Chase after Boomers

Artist Rufus Zogbaum sketched Fort Reno troops as they monitored the Oklahoma Lands prior to the Run of 1889. *Harper's Weekly*, April 18, 1889.

group of some forty-five men, women, and children at the site of present Oklahoma City. These and other stragglers who came in to the camp were captured and disarmed. Couch was away at the time, but his brother Abe was among those taken prisoner. The conclave was escorted to Caldwell and released.[4]

A new type of boomer intrusion into Indian Territory took place during 1886 and 1887. The Southern Kansas Railway of Kansas and the Texas, Gulf, and Santa Fe line of Texas began grading and laying rail in a race to meet at Purcell, Chickasaw Nation. The new line ran directly through the Oklahoma Lands, creating stations that would later become the cities of Guthrie, Edmond, Oklahoma City, Moore, and Norman. Simultaneous to the building of this line was another Santa Fe extension from New Kiowa, Kansas, across the northwestern corner of Indian Territory cutting south of Camp Supply. This line would establish station points that ultimately would become the towns of Alva, Waynoka, Woodward, Fargo, Gage, and Shattuck.[5]

Still other lines had been approved by Congress. Surveyors for both the Fort Worth and Denver Railway and the Chicago, Kansas, and Nebraska Railway companies had been seen laying out routes across the Cheyenne/Arapaho reservation. In December 1887, a much-disturbed delegation of chiefs from the two tribes visited Fort Reno to discuss the matter with Col. James F. Wade, Fifth Cavalry, who had become commander of the post in August 1887. The Indians had not been aware that the tribes had agreed to the building of railroads and telegraph lines across their lands by their Treaty of Medicine Lodge in 1868.[6]

For a time there would be a lull in the boomer activity, and life at Fort Reno returned to more routine matters such as rifle practice, marching, and litter-bearer drills. New recruits from New York and fresh mounts from Fort Leavenworth arrived by train at Oklahoma Station for delivery to Fort Reno. Loads of timber were hauled in by ox team from Council Grove, where a guard detail was regularly posted; other soldiers escorted paymasters and agents carrying annuity funds to various locations. A trooper was court-martialed for signing the commanding officer's name on three orders for ammunition (twelve dollars in all) with the post trader; another for sleeping while posted as a sentinel at his troop's stables.[7]

Saddler George Walter, on duty at Camp Martin, was reported to be of unsound mind due to an opium habit acquired before his enlistment and was ordered sent to Fort Riley for medical attention. The very angry wife of another trooper responded to an inquiry from the post surgeon as to how long her husband had been in a lunatic asylum before entering the service. The St. Louis woman answered that her husband had been incarcerated for nine months with "the snakes from whisky and beer." When he got out he had stolen her $150 savings and absconded, leaving her with five children. Her oldest boy had sworn that one day he would get satisfaction of the man. "He is one of Jeff Davisess gang," the distraught woman charged, "and you take him in the Republic army! He ought to be hung on a sour apple tree."[8]

An October 1887 inspection listed some of Fort Reno's deficiencies: an offensive cesspool in back of the quarters; the worst bathing facilities of any post in the department; officers' quarters that had fallen into dilapidated condition and badly needed paint; post buildings full of dust in consequence of the strong prevailing winds. Field guns and carriages were not properly housed, and the post cemetery was in need of repair.[9] Eventually the Department of the Missouri authorized two thousand dollars for the erection of two double sets of noncommissioned staff quarters at the fort.[10]

During 1887 and 1888, Couch and other leaders of the Oklahoma movement concentrated on gaining public support and influencing Washington politicians. There had always been political overtones to settlement of the Oklahoma Lands. In Kansas, Democrat David Payne had been stoutly opposed by Republican editors such as Marsh Murdock of the *Wichita Eagle* and well-known Kansas journalist Milton W. Reynolds, who wrote under the pen name of Kicking Bird. Reynolds had taken the pen name from the Kiowa chief of that name whom he had met during the Medicine Lodge treaty council. But now these men and others began to see Indian Territory not as a population drain on Kansas but as a potentially lucrative market area and a vast field of opportunity for white enterprise. This shift of political thinking began to break down the barriers to settlement of Indian Territory among the non-Indian public and politicians alike. It had never been difficult to convince white Americans that the government should reward them with Indian lands. And soon it would once more do so.

Fort Reno, the military establishment most immediate to the Oklahoma Lands, would play a key role in the continuing search for and arrest of intruders and in monitoring the momentous event from various locations around its borders. The military was aware that Couch and his large family, as well as many other boomers, had attached themselves to the Santa Fe work crews that during 1886 and 1887 were grading and laying rail south from Arkansas City.[11] Couch, who carried a railroader's pass, was arrested and confined at Fort Reno. After what was termed a "harassing delay," he was taken to circuit court in Wichita and released. He declared his treatment by the military had been an outrage.[12]

In November 1886, even before the rails of Santa Fe's Arkansas City extension had reached the site, William Decker erected a story-and-a-half trading store at the site of present Oklahoma City. By the time the Southern Kansas line reached the site in March, the location had begun to develop as a small settlement around the railroad's section house, loading platform, pump house, and water tank. Also arriving were a number of white squatters who camped about in tents, dugouts, and sod houses.

In February 1887 Santa Fe officials notified Colonel Wade that the Arkansas City extension would soon be arriving on the North Canadian and the newly created Oklahoma Station would be open for passengers and freight. In line with this, the quartermaster for the Department of the Missouri recommended that Fort Reno erect a small house and corral at that station to serve as office and lodging for a quartermaster agent engaged in shipping stores to the fort.[13]

During April 1887 Lieutenant Adair arrived from Fort Reno with a detail of Cheyenne scouts and destroyed the squatter camp leaving only "half-burnt poles of sod houses and the stumps from which the trees were cut."[14] East of the station and tracks, the army erected an eight-room house for the new forwarding agent, C. F. Sommers. Decker built a small stockade structure that would serve as the first post office at the location; and in December 1887, boomer Samuel H. Radebaugh became the first postmaster in a two-story frame structure. These settlers were evidently allowed, for Lt. Augustus C. Macomb, Fifth Cavalry, commanding a company of Cheyenne and Arapaho scouts, reported from Oklahoma Station in March 1888 that the country along the North Canadian was clear of intruders. He was concerned, though, about four men who were seining fish and shipping them by rail to market in Arkansas City.[15]

Once the Santa Fe line had entered the Oklahoma Lands, Wade saw the need for guards at every station to prevent boomers from riding the trains in and disembarking. He proposed to send Capt. James N. Morgan of the Twenty-fourth Infantry and a detachment of Indian scouts to perform that duty.[16] In order to more closely monitor boomer infiltration, various temporary posts such as Camp Chilocco, Camp Guthrie, Camp Schofield, Camp Price (south of Arkansas City), Camp Purcell, Camp Kingfisher, and Camp Russell (near Guthrie) were established.

On September 18, six Fifth Cavalry troops left Fort Reno and marched to a place called Taylor's Springs—named for Capt. Alfred B. Taylor, Fifth Cavalry—six miles west of Guthrie and established Camp Rockwell, where they remained for a month before returning to Reno.[17] Capt. William P. Hall was sent first to Willow Springs just south of the Kansas border from Arkansas City; later he was moved to the ox-bow bend of the Arkansas River near present Marland to intercept boomers coming from that direction. Troop G under Captain Hayes patrolled the Oklahoma Lands, while Troop B under Capt. Robert H. Montgomery scoured the Cherokee Strip for hunters, woodchoppers, and other intruders.[18]

Hall was replaced at Willow Springs by Captain Woodson and Troop K, Fifth Cavalry, in January 1889. On January 15 Woodson led his command of fifty-two men of Troop K from Fort Reno to Guthrie Station and then followed the route of the Santa Fe railroad to a point on Chilocco Creek near Willow Springs Station. From there he could watch all the roads leading out of Arkansas City and interdict all travelers who appeared to be boomers.

A detachment of troops was also posted at the Rock Springs crossing of the Chikaskia to oversee the trails leading south from Hunnewell and Caldwell. By this, Woodson felt he was covering all the trails frequented by Oklahoma boomers.[19] He found, however, that it was difficult to intercept some of the boomers who had quickly learned just where the troops were and often evaded them. Still he snared many, some of them with homes built onto their wagons.[20]

Oklahoma Station was soon populated by an assortment of land-hopeful whites, including the Couch family and old boomer faithfuls. A warning was issued from Fort Reno for them to leave, but few did. During late December 1888, Lieutenant Macomb arrived there with a detachment of Fifth Cavalry and Cheyenne scouts.[21] A visiting *Wichita Eagle* scribe wrote that Macomb placed himself on friendly drinking terms with the boomers and sympathized with them.

Setting up headquarters in a tent, Macomb cheerfully read the orders for them to vacate the Oklahoma Lands. At the same time, there were "intelligible winks that were translated into Oklahoma vernacular and meant that they could just make a move on or before the third day thereafter, come back or do what they liked, as that would relieve the officer of his 'painful duty,' and he would, you see, stand in with them on the deal."[22]

Some of the boomers caught a train north to Kansas or south to nearby Purcell, Chickasaw Nation, but many took temporary refuge in the underbrush along the river. One boomer who was chopping wood refused to comply when he was invited by a Cheyenne scout to depart. As a result, he received a rifle butt to the head, eliciting a complaint that the scouts took entirely too much pleasure in ordering white men about. When Macomb returned in February 1889 he found many boomers still there, including one man who was selling lots from a large plat of the "Oklahoma Co-Operative Townsite and Homestead Company."[23] Once again the boomers took to the woods, only to return again when Macomb and his troops had departed.

The Oklahoma Station crowd found considerably less geniality from Lt. John M. Carson Jr., who arrived there with some seventy-five soldiers of Troop B, Fifth Cavalry, and Indian scouts on March 16. Carson had strict orders to remove all unauthorized persons, and he was determined to do so. Finding some forty men loitering around the Santa Fe Station, he arrested them and put his men to tearing down their tents and dugouts. Everyone but government and railroad employees were ordered to be gone by nine the following evening.

Dismounted patrols searched the woods and brush along the North Canadian, and some Indian scouts reconnoitered along Mustang Creek. An old Civil War veteran named W. A. Arnold, who was well ensconced on Crutcho Creek, tried to resist arrest until quelled by a pistol butt to the head. An Afro-American man discovered at a wood-cutting camp and an elderly Afro-American woman, whose husband was away, were arrested along with a number of whites. Many of the settlers again escaped into the woods and some left on trains. Carson took the ones he had rounded up and marched south across the South Canadian into the Chickasaw Nation.[24]

Various bills to establish Indian Territory as the Indian state of Oklahoma had been introduced in Congress for a number of years. None, including the one then being debated in the House of Representatives, was successful. The political battle to open Oklahoma Territory to white settlement was essentially won in 1888 with the defeat of Grover Cleveland's Democratic administration, which had stoutly rejected the opening of Indian Territory lands, and the election of Republican Benjamin Harrison.

Settlement of the Oklahoma Lands succeeded only as a last-minute rider, known as the Springer Amendment, on the Indian Appropriations Bill in early 1889. The measure left it up to President Harrison to issue a proclamation declaring the region open to settlement. This he did on March 27, 1889, establishing the following April 22 as the day that U.S. citizens could line up on the borders of the Oklahoma Lands and make a run to locate and claim 160-acre homesteads.

After Harrison issued his proclamation, the problem of monitoring intrusion became far more complicated. Thus far the principal influx had been from the north in Kansas. Now the wagons of hopeful settlers were filling the trails from Texas as well, and it became necessary to guard the southern line of the Oklahoma Lands additionally. On April 16, Gen. Wesley Merritt was ordered from Fort Leavenworth to Indian Territory to take command of troops as any emergency might require.[25]

The army now undertook a large movement of troops to the territory, some by rail and some by forced marches. These involved two companies of Thirteenth Infantry from Fort Elliott; three companies of infantry (Sixth, Thirteenth, and Eighteenth) from Fort Leavenworth under Capt. Arthur MacArthur, father of Gen. Douglas MacArthur; three companies of infantry (two of Tenth and one of Eighteenth) under Lt. Col. Simon Snyder from Fort Lyon; two companies of Seventh Cavalry under Maj. Theodore A. Baldwin from Fort Sill; and two companies of Thirteenth Infantry from Fort Supply.[26]

On April 20, General Merritt sent a wire from Oklahoma Station to divisional headquarters saying that, because the telegraph line there was badly overworked, he was establishing a line of couriers from the Santa Fe station at Woodward to Fort Reno, which would serve as a command post and communications center for the military operations.[27] Couriers on foam-lathered horses arrived hourly as others dashed off with orders and dispatches. Here also came newspaper "specials," as reporters were then known, to send their accounts off to eastern newspapers via the telegraph line at the fort.

During the month or so that Merritt was at Fort Reno, likely before the run, a photograph was made of ten Fifth Cavalry and three artillery officers from Fort Reno and eighteen Seventh Cavalry officers from Fort Sill mounted in a line behind Merritt. Among the group are a number of men who would eventually rise to the rank of general. Some of the Fort Reno officers, who were evidently away on land rush duties, are not in the photo.[28]

The event of a land run into Oklahoma, or "Harrison's Hoss Race" as it became known to many people, was a novel and untried method of opening a vast area of land to settlement. The military, like everyone else, was uncertain as to the precise nature of the rules that it was to enforce. For a time, the army continued to operate under the preproclamation guidelines and attempted to hold the boomer tide in check at the Kansas line. As a result, huge buildups of would-be rushers accumulated at Caldwell and Arkansas City. Both of these two border towns were fed by railroads (though as yet Caldwell had no line into the territory as did Arkansas City) and offered the most direct entry across the Cherokee Outlet to the Oklahoma Lands.

As the date of the opening neared, a clamor of protest went up from the camps over being held at the border. Finally, the Interior Department decreed that at eight o'clock on the morning of April 19, the rushers would be permitted to cross the Kansas border and advance across the Cherokee Strip to the borders of the Oklahoma Lands. On that date, two great wagon caravans, one from Caldwell and one from Arkansas City, began their sixty-mile overland journey. Both groups would be escorted and controlled by troops from Fort Reno.

At Arkansas City, it was Captain Hayes who gave the signal for a thousand or more wagons and even more horsemen to start. With Troop G, Fifth Cavalry, at the lead, the long line of covered wagons

These Fifth and Seventh Cavalry officers, some from Fort Sill and centered by Gen. Wesley Merritt, include several Medal of Honor winners and other famous names of the Indian Wars. *Courtesy U.S. Military Academy Archives.*

headed down the Ponca Trail. Recent rains had turned the trail muddy and flooded the streams. At the Salt Fork of the Arkansas, Hayes attempted to build a pontoon bridge across the raging stream. It proved to be too hazardous, however, and it was decided to snake a rope across the river so that the wagons could be taken apart and ferried across on a makeshift boat. This effort was ended when a group of men from Winfield cut the rope to dash on ahead. Hayes sent a squad of cavalry after them and forced them to hold up and wait for the others.

Not far away the four-span trestle bridge of the Santa Fe Railroad loomed temptingly. A settler attempted to force his frightened team across, but one of his horses fell through the ties and broke its leg. When railroad officials refused further passage, Hayes wired the superintendent of the line, saying he would not be responsible for harm to his bridge, which the rushers were threatening to sabotage. Instructed to act on his own discretion, Hayes sent men to the Ponca Station some six miles away and had them rip planking from its platform to fill in between the ties of the bridge.

The settlers then unharnessed their teams, the wagons being pulled across the bridge by squads of men and the horses either led behind or made to swim. It was estimated that some seven thousand men, women, and children and more than two thousand horses, mules, and cattle crossed over the bridge within a twenty-four-hour period. When at one point some men attempted to push their way to the front of the line and cross out of turn, Hayes made them go to the very back of the line. He remained at the bridge until the last wagon was across.[29]

At the less difficult Black Bear, the troops joined the settlers in cutting down the banks and making a corduroy bridge across the stream. It was there that young Lt. Fred W. Foster and ten of his men at the lead of the caravan were challenged by a band of sixty rushers who did not want to make camp as Foster had ordered. They displayed their weapons and declared that Foster had no right to make them go into camp. Foster responded by forming his men in line with carbines ready. One of the settlers stepped forward to argue the matter. "The next thing we know," he growled, "you'll be objecting to my taking my shirt off without permission." "I have no objection to your taking it off," Foster replied pleasantly, "if you wear a clean under-shirt." The crowd broke into laughter, and the rebellion was ended.[30]

Once across the Black Bear, the caravan split into two segments. One group, led by Hayes, veered off toward Stillwater Creek, and the other, under Foster, cut southwestward on a route that followed the Santa Fe line. Both groups reached the northern border of the Oklahoma Lands at sundown on April 20.

At Caldwell, Troop K under Woodson had arrived ahead of the planned departure to take up positions from which the officer could monitor all of the roads, bridges, fords, and other avenues of exit from the Caldwell area into the territory. It was impossible to cover them all, however. The tracks of a group of wagons that had eluded Woodson's patrols were discovered, and a squad of Fort Reno troops was sent in hot pursuit. The intruders were found on Turkey Creek and escorted back to Caldwell. There their names were recorded and their photos taken.[31]

On the morning of April 19, Woodson sent a bugler around the camps announcing that the border would be crossed at ten o'clock. The settlers arrived there to find the troops drawn up into line, waiting. Sharply at ten, Woodson gave the command, "Forward—March!," the bugle sounded, and, with the cavalry at the lead, the cavalcade of wag-ons, buggies, and horsemen headed south into Indian Territory.

Slowly but steadily the long wagon train moved along the Chisholm Trail, camping the first night at Pond Creek. The flooded Salt Fork was reached the next morning, halting the procession and causing the wagons and teams to pile up on the river's north bank. Following the military style of river crossing, Woodson had his men ride out into the swollen stream and set stakes to follow. In a spirit of happy cooperation, the settlers then pitched into a mass effort of unloading the wagons, floating the goods across, and, by wading or riding, giving assistance to the wagons and teams in fording the swift, red-muddied current to the south bank. "That was the happiest bunch of people I have ever seen in my life," one participant com-mented later.[32]

The Caldwell group reached Buffalo Springs on April 20 and were held there by Woodson to await the opening. The settlers passed the twenty-first, Easter Sunday, with religious services, singing, and sport-ing contests, including a baseball game.

Hayes and Foster were thus posted at the eastern end of the north border as the day of the great run, April 22, approached. Captain Hall and his troops were situated on the western flank opposite Kingfisher; Captain MacArthur, with four companies of infantry, was located at Guthrie Station; Lieutenant Adair arrived at Purcell on the eve of the opening, posting troops at the main ford a mile north of town and at the Santa Fe bridge five miles to the north. Fort Reno garrison troops patrolled the North Canadian valley, while four companies of infantry under Lieutenant Colonel Snyder were sent to Oklahoma City; two troops of cavalry under Major Baldwin were on the main Canadian north of Purcell; four companies of infantry under Capt. William Auman at Kingfisher; one troop of cavalry east of Oklahoma Station; two troops on the line south of Arkansas City; and one troop north of Kingfisher. Merritt set up his headquarters in a railroad car on a siding at Oklahoma Station.[33]

Even with this amount of troops monitoring the Land Run of 1889, there were still vast stretches of border surrounding the Oklahoma Lands that were totally unmonitored. This was especially true along the South Canadian River, which formed the southern border and the eastern side, abutting Indian reservations. Numerous people would enter the Oklahoma Lands ahead of the high noon, April 22, time restraint, leading to another popular term of the day—the Oklahoma "sooner."

The military would share authority with civil officials in attempting to control the situation before and after the run. It would ultimately be revealed, however, that all too often those civil officials themselves—particularly the deputy U.S. marshals who were on the ground at the various locations—would abuse their trust and stake claims ahead of the historic frenzy that was about to descend upon the Oklahoma Lands.

CHAPTER 13

They Came Running

The year 1890 is often cited as the year the American frontier ended. It is a valid date in relation to western Indian Territory, for during the period of 1888 to 1891 two significant events reshaped its destiny. They were the opening of the Oklahoma Lands to settlement in 1889 and the allotment of lands within the Cheyenne and Arapaho reservation in 1891. These two events, in which Fort Reno played a major role, threw open the gate to non-Indian population and ended with finality the migratory, buffalo-hunting life of the Plains Indian.

On the eve of these historic events, Darlington and Fort Reno were visited by two well-known roving artist-correspondents. They were Frederic Remington and Rufus F. Zogbaum. Their narratives and drawings, which appeared in *Harper's Illustrated Weekly* and *Century Magazine,* offer a final transitory view of a western Indian Territory that would soon no longer exist.

When Remington arrived at Fort Reno in 1888, Colonel Wade provided him with a mule-drawn buckboard in which to visit the Cheyenne camp. The officer further sent for Ben Clark to serve as a guide. Remington viewed Clark as the "perfect type of the frontier scout," a man who had been acquainted with the Cheyennes for more than thirty years and spoke their tongue fluently.[1] In many ways, Clark epitomized the Fort Reno/Darlington frontier. An interviewer once asked General Sheridan who was the best scout he ever had. Sheridan replied:

> Ben Clark is the best scout I ever had. I don't know where he came from, but he dropped down upon me like a Godsend just when I needed him most. It was when I was starting on the Washita campaign and could not find anyone who knew the country. Ben proved to be the very man I wanted. Clark is a man of great intelligence, has a good education, and I have always tried to give him something to do.[2]

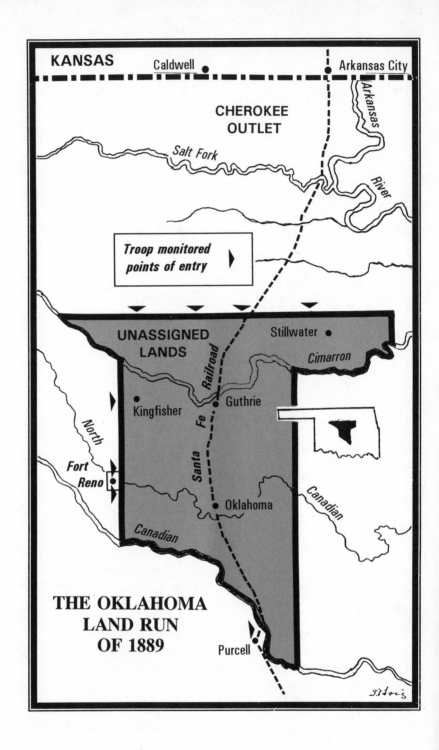

KANSAS Caldwell Arkansas City

CHEROKEE OUTLET

Salt Fork

Arkansas River

Troop monitored points of entry

UNASSIGNED LANDS

Stillwater

Cimarron

Railroad

Kingfisher Guthrie

North

Santa Fe

Fort Reno

Canadian

Oklahoma

Canadian

THE OKLAHOMA
LAND RUN
OF 1889

Purcell

And so did others, the military records being filled with orders for Clark to ride off on long trips in attending Indian and military needs. In December 1875, he was ordered to escort the Indians on their buffalo hunt at the request of the Arapahos; in August 1876, to carry dispatches to Fort Dodge. In October 1876, he was reassigned from Camp Supply to Fort Reno as interpreter.

In January 1877, Clark was sent to Cheyenne, Wyoming Territory, as a judge advocate witness. In March 1877, he was ordered to establish the shortest route from Fort Reno to old Fort Cobb. In September 1877, he accompanied troops to Fort Elliott. In November 1877, he was ordered to Chicago on temporary duty. In April 1878, he was sent to Fort Leavenworth on temporary duty. In July 1878, Clark escorted the Northern Cheyennes from Fort Lincoln, Nebraska, to Fort Reno. In November 1878, he was again sent to Fort Elliott.

In May 1879, Clark accompanied a delegation of Northern Cheyennes to Washington; in July 1879, he was ordered to Kansas City, Missouri, for interviews by a congressional fact-finding committee. In August 1881, Clark accompanied Agent Miles to Washington as interpreter. In September 1881, he escorted Little Chief from Darlington to Pine Ridge. In November 1881, he was sent with five Indian scouts to eject cattlemen from the Cheyenne/Arapaho reservation. In February 1887, he was ordered to proceed by stage and rail to Washington to report to the commanding general of the army.[3]

Ben Clark was reportedly born in St. Louis on February 2, 1842. He enlisted in Albert Sidney Johnston's expedition against the Mormons of Utah, serving with the U.S. Volunteers from December 3, 1857, until August 13, 1858. By some accounts, he was a courier at Fort Bridger before joining the Sixth Kansas Cavalry during the Civil War, serving from October 18, 1861, to December 31, 1863. Upon being discharged at Fort Smith, he reenlisted as a veteran volunteer again at St. Louis.[4]

After the war, Clark took up life among the Cheyennes in the Colorado Rockies, learning both their ways and their language and taking a wife among them. In 1868, he joined John Simpson Smith and Amos Chapman as a guide and scout for the expedition of Gen. Alfred Sully into northwestern Indian Territory. That same fall, he helped lead General Custer and the Seventh Cavalry to the Washita, and in 1874 served with Generals Miles and Crook against Crazy Horse

Scout Ben Clark received glowing praise from Gen. Sheridan and other officers for his many services on the frontier. *Courtesy Western History Collections, University of Oklahoma.*

and the Sioux.[5] General Miles, who knew Ben Clark for more than twenty years, said of him: "His record is remarkable for courage during various campaigns and his influence for peace among the Indians is well known."[6]

As Remington's escort at Fort Reno and Darlington in 1888, Clark led the artist on a tour of the Cheyenne village, around which were scattered pony herds, wagons, and brush sheds. The shrouded forms moving about the camp, Remington learned, were Indians who had replaced their winter blanket with a white sheet for summer. His artist's eye made note that Indian riders now used the light cowman's saddle in lieu of their old wooden "tree" saddle. He met the ancient and toothless Bull Bear, once the leader of the powerful Dog Soldiers, and talked at length with Chief Whirlwind, who expressed the Indians' great fear of losing their land. Remington was highly impressed with the chief's knowledge on the situation of the Indian.

The artist admired the Indian scouts, some of whom were "strikingly handsome" in their army uniforms; but he was less than entertained upon observing the brutal dispatch of some beef cows at the issue corral by a band of young tribesmen armed with revolvers and rifles.

He described the agency as a group of stores and little white dwelling-houses that gave much the effect of a New England village except for the saddled ponies, wagons, and Indians that reflected its frontier character. Remington's drawings of the agency, its inhabitants, and daily activities contribute much to the historical record of the location just prior to public settlement of Indian Territory.[7]

Zogbaum added to Remington's account with still more scenes of Fort Reno, Darlington, and the Oklahoma country. He also provided a narrative description of the agency as it existed in 1889:

> Here the agent resides, and here—in a great brick building fronting a wide unpaved plaza or square, on the various sides of which stand the stores of the Indian traders, a hotel, and the livery and stage stables, whence the stage line carries the mail and passengers to the railroad [Oklahoma station], thirty miles away—is situated the main office or agency for the two tribes. On some streets branching off from a park of rather ragged and forlorn appearance, in which a few trees raised their crooked branches into the air, are placed the residences of the employees, the schools, the saw-mill, the blacksmith shop, wagon, and tin shops.[8]

In addition to the agent, Zogbaum noted, agency office employees consisted of a chief clerk and two assistants. Two engineers operated two sawmills that produced lumber for building farmhouses for tribespeople. The agency employed two blacksmiths, a wagon maker, five farming instructors, and a large number of Indians who worked as apprentices, drivers, herders, and the like. The thirty Indian policemen,

all full-bloods, owned their own horses. The captain and two lieutenants each received ten dollars monthly; the privates eight. Five sub-
agencies operated on the reservation along with two government and
two mission schools. Like Remington, Zogbaum found the Indian
method of slaughtering the beef on the brutal side but interesting to
sketch.[9]

Fort Reno and the Darlington agency were center posts around
which western Indian Territory was transformed from raw frontier
and the assigned home of the Plains Indian during the 1870s to an
agricultural/commercial domain of the white man by the end of the
1880s. For the Indians, who had been promised the land in perpetu-
ity, this meant not only a loss of their reservations but a drastic altera-
tion in their tribal way of life.

The linchpin of this metamorphosis would prove to be the
Oklahoma Lands. Once this core piece of land was removed from the
whole, both Indians and whites knew full well, the rest was certain to
follow sooner or later. The mechanism for such had been put into
place with the Springer Amendment to the Indian Appropriation Bill.
By it the president was authorized to appoint a commission to nego-
tiate new agreements with tribes of the territory. At the heart of such
agreements would be the allocation of individual homesteads to tribal
members within their reservation area and the sale of the remaining
land to the general public. With tribal members thus spread apart
from one another and surrounded by non-Indians, the old tribal village and social system that had long ruled here was doomed.

The Oklahoma land run of April 1889 was a national affair in
which the Fort Reno troops played a key role in controlling the horde
of settlers that descended upon Indian Territory. The army's most
dramatic act, perhaps, was to serve as starters for the great headlong
dash for homesteads and town lots. Some officers did so by the firing
of a pistol or a rifle, some with their troop buglers, and, at Fort Reno,
by the booming of cannon.

At the Santa Fe rail line just north of present Orlando, Lt.
Henry D. Waite placed his mounted troops in a cordon extending
east and west away from a Fifth Cavalry red, white, and blue guidon.
Wagons and anxious horsemen crowded the line in front of the blue-
clad Fort Reno troops. Taking a position in an open space, Waite sat
on his horse with his watch in his gloved hand, counting the minutes

as they ticked slowly away to twelve o'clock high noon. When finally the hands of the watch overlapped, Waite signaled his buglers posted on either flank of the line. The bugle notes of "Dinner Call" sounded across the prairie, the troops swung gatelike to the railroad, and the mass of settlers surged forth.[10]

Lt. Claiborne L. Foster, who had set off a similar crowd from his position to the west, reached the railroad just before the first of eight settler-laden trains from Arkansas City arrived at the north line. He and his men climbed aboard to ride to Guthrie station.[11]

On the north line to the east, Captain Hayes arrived to find the crowd on Stillwater Creek greatly disturbed that some sooners had gone on ahead across the line. Hayes pacified them by agreeing to take the names of those present and forwarding them to Washington, D.C. His troopers went about collecting signatures in the nose bags used to feed their mounts.

In addition to the settlers that had come down by wagon from Arkansas City, this group included some three hundred cowboys from the Cherokee Outlet ranches. Mounted on their favorite ponies, the ranch hands were confident and anxious for the great race. Sergeant MacDonald of Hayes's troop described the start: "The order was given, the bugle blew the blast—charge—forward. And that line broke with a hurrah and rush, an impetuous onward movement—the cowboys firing their pistols and yelling, making a scene never before witnessed in this or any other country, settling up a country by the aid of a bugle call."[12]

On the western flank of the boundary at Buffalo Springs, twenty miles north of Kingfisher, Woodson sounded a bugle call for the two thousand wagons and eight thousand settlers to begin their two-mile movement to the line. He and his soldiers waited there dismounted until the fateful moment approached. When he ordered his men to mount up, a false start was made by some of the anxious crowd. A squad of troopers went galloping after them, and the miscreants were shoved back into the line just in time for the start. A hush came over the affair as Woodson raised his hand, then brought it down sharply to signal his bugler. The race was on, and the sound of the rushing horses and wagons was "like the roaring of thunder."[13]

A similar moment of history was enacted on the line a mile west of Kingfisher by Captain Hall and Troop C. His bugle call was

backdropped by the distant boom of cannons at Fort Reno. A reporter
described the scene he witnessed from the Kingfisher land office:

> Presently out of the dust cloud, the forms of racing horses are
> seen. On comes the mad crowd of rushing horsemen. The cloud
> of dust sweeps along. Several riders have fallen and horses gen-
> erally have stampeded. Nearer and nearer thunders the caval-
> cade, until at last straight down Chicago Avenue, a mad crowd
> of excited men, with teeth set and plying whip and spur, rushes
> into the newborn City of Lisbon [Kingfisher].[14]

Many settlers, some of them desperate farmers driven from no-
man's-land and the Texas Panhandle by drought, formed along the
lower western boundary only a short distance from Fort Reno. All able
men of the post were ordered to be mounted and ready to help monitor the run. So many men of the fort's garrison were on duty elsewhere
and the ranks so thin, however, that only a scattering of soldiers could
be posted across the North Canadian valley. At ten minutes of twelve,
the soldiers began yelling for everyone to get on the line. Cannons had
been primed and readied, and when the moment of high noon came,
their booming set the swarm of land seekers rushing forth.[15]

It was from there that speculators rushed to establish two town
sites immediately adjacent to Fort Reno. One of these was the present
city of El Reno. The other, called Reno City, was short-lived when
neither the Rock Island nor the Choctaw Railroad extended its line
through the site.[16] A citizen of the time later recalled the town's
demise:

> Finding itself left off the new railroad line (the Rock Island)
> by almost two miles, the boom town suddenly took to wheels
> and moved across the river (North Canadian) to the new town,
> which was to be El Reno. Even the new three-story Caddo hotel
> migrated to the railroad town, detained for several weeks when
> half-way across the river, when the outraged and sometimes
> bemused guests came and went over a footbridge in order to
> catch a cab to the new city.[17]

The El Reno site, with its potential as a railway crossroad and as a
choice farming center, was one of the prime locations of town site
speculators. Two such town site groups vied for it, but it was the claim
of John A. Foreman, a prominent Cherokee, that was recognized by

Thousands of eager citizens rushed to grab 160 acres of virtually free land in the Indian Territory. *Courtesy Archives/Manuscripts Division, Oklahoma Historical Society.*

the General Land Office. On February 6, 1892, this decision would be overturned by Secretary of Interior John Noble, who denied Foreman's right of entry. As a result, claim jumpers swarmed onto the El Reno town lots, and the new town sprang into being overnight.[18]

The town, as the fort, was named for Gen. Jesse L. Reno, the "El" in El Reno coming from the general's middle initial. Moreover, many of the city's streets bear the names of Fort Reno Fifth Cavalry officers of that day and persons connected with Darlington. Officers for whom streets are named include Colonel Wade, Capt. Charles H. Watts, Lieutenant Carson, Lieutenant Foster, Captain Hayes, Asst. Surg. John V. R. Hoff, Lt. Robert London, Lieutenant Macomb, and Maj. Gerald Russell. A street is also named for Gen. Nelson Miles. Other namesakes were H. L. Bickford, a Darlington freighter; Ben Clark; Neal Evans; Ben Keith; and W. G. "Caddo Bill" Williams, the Minco rancher.[19]

In preparation for the opening at Purcell, the blue-and-gold uniformed Lieutenant Adair, at the lead of Troop L, posted himself on his mount in the middle at the main ford of the Canadian River facing the line of wagons and horses waiting there. A half hour before noon, a lone settler attempted to cross the river and was quickly escorted back by a trooper. With ten minutes to go, the engineer of a special boomer train made up at Purcell's station sounded his whistle, and the train began moving slowly northward along the river's west bank to the bridge that led across and into the Oklahoma Lands. As the minute hand of his watch neared twelve, Adair raised his hand and then on the hour waved briskly to his bugler, John Brandt.[20]

The clear trebles of the bugle resounded against the towering bluff of Red Hill and echoed back across the Canadian valley, mingling with the great shout that went up from the crowd along the river and the train that carried hundreds of exuberant hopefuls toward the place where nine years earlier David Payne had first established his colony of Ewing on the banks of the North Canadian.[21]

That site, which had already become unofficially known as Oklahoma City to many, was occupied by General Merritt and his staff, four companies of Tenth Infantry under Lt. Colonel Snyder, and Troop L of the Fifth Cavalry under Captain Forbush. U.S. Marshal William C. Jones and some thirty-two deputy marshals were also on hand.[22] Thus far, the only duty of the soldiers had been to arrest authorized persons who got off either a northbound or southbound passenger or freight train. One man who tried to evade arrest by jumping off a train before it stopped at the station broke several ribs.

It was later shown that Jones and many of his deputies spent their time at Oklahoma station before the run in staking out claims for themselves. Quartermaster Sommers also tried to grab a choice quarter section near the depot. He requested that Forbush provide a starting signal for himself and two women from the quartermaster's reservation.[23]

Forbush did so by firing his pistol. Sommers's claim, however, would ultimately be ruled illegal, as were those of Jones and his lawmen. Couch and his family also made the run from the railroad right-of-way on the contention it was not part of the Oklahoma Lands. The U.S. Supreme Court would eventually rule against this ruse, and all who acted likewise would lose their claims. The military left these and other land run issues for the civilian authority to handle.

The problem of maintaining law and order among the multitude at Oklahoma station, however, was left to the military by default when Marshal Jones and his deputies were nowhere to be found, and general pandemonium prevailed. Almost everyone was armed, and when disputes over claims erupted, gunplay resulted. Liquor was dispensed openly, and there were many drunken men. Gamblers operated freely, and many people were swindled or robbed. Water was scarce and fought over, and there were only two places that served food. In the absence of other authority, Colonel Wade appointed Capt. Daniel F. Stiles, Tenth Infantry, as provost marshal. Stiles later detailed the situation:

> Upon April 22, I was directed by the commanding officer to go to town and to preserve order. I was also directed to render such assistance to the United States marshals as might be called for. I established a guard at the railroad depot shortly after 9 A.M., and at about 2 P.M. found United States Marshal Jones, with whom I conferred in regard to the situation. Colonel Jones gave me the names of some half dozen deputies and it was understood they were to keep the peace and the military was to assist them. I reported these facts to the commanding officer, Col. J. F. Wade, Fifth Cavalry, but as the day progressed the crowd increased and the marshals disappeared. Colonel Jones, I was informed, went to Guthrie and his deputies could not be found.[24]

Stiles would continue to act as provost marshal at Oklahoma City through the year, but he soon became enmeshed in the virulent conflict among settlers and political groups. When an attempt was made to hold an illegal election, troops dispersed the crowd. "Some two or three persons," Stiles reported, "were slightly injured by bayonet thrusts and by being struck by the butts of muskets, but none seriously."[25]

Fort Reno would also maintain a presence on the military reservation just east of the Santa Fe depot in Oklahoma City until December 1891, when Lt. Thomas J. Clay notified the secretary of interior that the troops stationed there were being moved back to the fort.[26]

On May 21, several hundred people attempted to locate a town site on a homestead claim, and a dozen soldiers managed to eject them. A similar incident occurred on May 22. This time a company of infantry and a troop of cavalry were dispatched by Wade. When a shooting affray on June 14 resulted in the death of the city marshal of South Oklahoma City and the wounding of two others, troops were sent to disperse the crowd.[27]

Capt. Harry G. Cavenaugh, Thirteenth Infantry, served as provost marshal at Guthrie and exercised law enforcement there.[28] That place also experienced rampant soonerism and insider manipulation. Not only officers of the U.S. marshal's command but other high-ranking officials as well took advantage of their positions by attempting to grab choice land. Troops under Captain MacArthur had arrived there prior to the run, set up a tent camp, and monitored those arriving by train or otherwise. They were supported by the arrival of Troops H and K of the Seventh Cavalry under Major Baldwin.[29]

One group of men who arrived by train on Sunday evening included a number of prominent figures, several of whom staked claims for themselves. Among them was Col. D. B. Dyer, the former Cheyenne/Arapaho agent, who said he now represented the Wells-Fargo Express Company. Dyer would be elected Guthrie's first mayor, largely through the support of the deputy U.S. marshals, one of whom reportedly told Captain MacArthur regarding their grabbing of claims: "Everybody here is interested except you military men."[30]

The former Indian agent was the principal subject of a report by Inspector J. W. Pickler, who charged him with being a sooner lawbreaker and a profiteer.[31] Dyer also looked to other opportunities. The dust of the run had barely settled when he became involved in an effort to persuade the Cheyennes and Arapahos to make claim against the government for the Cherokee Outlet lands once assigned to them by the Treaty of Medicine Lodge. Colonel Wade evicted Dyer from the reservation in May, at the Indians' request, he claimed.[32]

Dyer had the support of another former agent, John D. Miles, who had been elected mayor at Kingfisher, and Samuel J. Crawford, former governor of Kansas, in influencing the tribes. During May 23 and 24, 1889, these men joined a group of Cheyenne and Arapaho leading men at Oklahoma City to work out a contract with the government whereby the two tribes would receive $1.25 an acre for the lands of the Cherokee Outlet—or "Cherokee Strip" as it was known popularly. Though they attempted to hide the fact from the Indians, Dyer, Miles, and Crawford reaped a healthy 10 percent of the government payment as a reward for their legal services.[33]

The United States, meanwhile, was pressuring the reluctant Cherokee Nation into selling the Outlet. An important move in that direction was made by President Harrison when on February 17, 1890, he issued a proclamation forbidding cattle grazing in the Outlet and ordered all cattle removed by October 1, 1890. Fort Reno's Fifth Cavalry was ordered to join with troops from Fort Supply in searching for and removing all cattle herds and settlers in the Outlet.[34]

Even as Fort Reno troops were providing law enforcement in the Cherokee Outlet and the newly occupied Oklahoma Lands, the government was moving to carve new areas for non-Indian occupation out of the reservations of Indian Territory. On July 7, 1890, the Jerome Commission arrived at Darlington. Its purpose was to work out an agreement relative to the huge 3.5-million-acre Cheyenne/Arapaho reservation whereby tribal members would be placed on 160-acre allotments of land within their assigned reservation. The remainder of the tribes' lands would be declared surplus and sold to the federal government for homesteading by the general public and added to a newly created Territory of Oklahoma.

The three-man commission, headed by former governor of Michigan David H. Jerome, had already secured such an agreement with the Sac and Fox, Potawatomi, Shawnee, and Iowa tribes. The reservations of these tribes, which were located just east of the Oklahoma Lands, would provide the stage for a second Oklahoma land rush on September 22, 1891.[35]

At Darlington, the commission found the tribes badly split. Cheyenne traditionalist Old Crow told them: "The Great Spirit gave the Indians all this country and never tell them that they should sell it ... I don't want money; money doesn't do an Indian any good."[36] His view was supported by Young Whirlwind, Little Big Jake, and many other Cheyennes. Arapaho chief Left Hand and Cheyenne Cloud Chief and other progressive tribal members bargained for better terms but, in the end, led in signing the agreement that offered some fifty cents an acre for their surplus lands. Former Cheyenne/Arapaho agents Miles and Dyer were among those who helped the commission garner Indian signatures for the contract by paying off influential men of the tribe.[37]

When Old Crow and others appeared at Darlington to contest the cession agreement on the grounds that a majority of their people had not signed, they were ignored. The measure was passed by Congress on March 3, 1891. On June 19 Cheyenne and Arapaho tribespeople began arriving at Darlington to receive their portions of the government payment for the surplus lands of the reservation. When they departed their wagons were loaded with silver dollars—the only form of recompense they would accept.[38]

Reports soon began to surface of the Indians being charged outrageous prices for broken-down carriages and wagons and being cheated badly in other deals. The *Kingfisher Free Press* observed that: "It is quite probable that the Indians have ... paid thirty thousand dollars for about fifteen thousand dollars worth of horses and mules."[39]

The surveying and assignment of the 160-acre plots now began. Principally they were located up the North Canadian River from Darlington to the north boundary of the reservation, along the north bank of the Canadian River to present Taloga, and along the Washita River basin. The tribespeople began going to their new homes during the summer. The faction under Old Crow, however, rejected both the money and allotments and moved to the western end of the reservation.[40]

When the allotments were finally completed, the Cheyennes and Arapahos were left with only 529,692 acres of their 3.5-million-acre reservation—a little over one-seventh of the original land.[41] The government had already made plans to hold its third big land rush, this time for the remainder of the Cheyenne/Arapaho lands.

CHAPTER 14

The Cheyenne/Arapaho Opening

Despite their extensive duties with the settlement of the Oklahoma Lands, troops at Fort Reno continued to be involved in rounding up and removing cattle from the Cherokee Outlet through most of 1891. During August, two troops of Fifth Cavalry were sent to join Fort Supply units at Enid. Within a week, the soldiers had gathered some fifteen thousand head of cattle and shipped them out over the Rock Island Railroad or sent them north to Kiowa, Kansas.[1] This, however, was only a portion of the remaining outlet cattle, and both Fort Reno and Fort Supply troops would still be occupied with the chore as the opening of the Cheyenne/Arapaho reservation approached in the spring of 1892.

The land rush into the Cheyenne/Arapaho lands was nothing less than an upheaval of life and conditions for western Indian Territory. Though it brought with it the authority of civil officials, the military force of Fort Reno's Fifth Cavalry and the influence of Darlington would continue to play major roles in adjudicating the inevitable conflicts between the tribesman and the white newcomer during and well after the opening.

There was much that was the same about the run of April 19, 1892, as with that of April 22, 1889, and there was much that was different. Once again hordes of land-hungry Americans flocked to the borders of the new lands, again there were those who entered early, some of whom were caught and evicted by troops, and again the troops gave the signal for a frantic onrush of hopeful land seekers.

This opening, however, featured some entirely different conditions than before. One significant fact was that the borders of the Cheyenne/Arapaho reservation were even more extensive than those of the Oklahoma Lands. Monitoring entry totally into such a great body of land was not remotely possible. Further, this time there were native people residing on the premises—a people who had just been

Fort Reno and Darlington line the horizon behind this Indian encampment along the North Canadian River. *Courtesy Archives/Manuscripts Division, Oklahoma Historical Society.*

dispossessed of the land that others were rushing forth to grasp. The potential for bloody conflict was apparent to both military and Indian Bureau officials, particularly since Cheyenne leaders still contended that the allotment agreement had not been approved by a majority of the tribe.

Awareness of this potential prompted Charles F. Ashley, who had become the Cheyenne/Arapaho agent succeeding Gilbert B. Williams (September 1886 to May 1889), to prepare the tribes for the coming onslaught. April 18 being issue day, some thirty-five hundred Cheyennes and Arapahos were at Darlington on the day before the run to receive their rations. Ashley advised them to go to their allotments and remain there to prevent settlers from misclaiming them. Further, he encouraged the tribespeople to direct the newcomers to unassigned land and be of as much assistance as possible.

At Darlington, all of the Indians were supplied with government plats showing the location of their lands. Whites were surprised at the ability of the tribespeople to understand the plats and find their precise locations. The Indians were cautioned to carefully guard their ponies and cattle against the possibility of their being stolen by settlers.[2]

The tribespeople departed immediately after slaughtering the beef annuity and taking their family's share. The allocation for the two tribes had been cut for the year, and, fearing trouble, the Indian Bureau had asked for and obtained an additional food supplement. This action undoubtedly contributed to the lack of interference from tribesmen during the land run of April 19, 1892.

The Indians were further occupied by their ghost dance revival that was under way at various locations. The largest dance, featuring more than two hundred dancers and a large assembly of tribespeople, was conducted at the allotment of Arapaho chief Left Hand some fifteen miles from Darlington.[3] The idea was generated at these dances that an Indian messiah would ultimately arrive, sweep away the white man, and restore the Indian to his former greatness. "He will come," the prophets said, "when grass grows tall and the sun draws hot. He will come and drive the white man from the Indian country."[4] This belief helped mollify the Indians' anger at the white invasion and maintain an "imperturbable indifference to the rush and bustle and hurry and excitement" of the opening.[5] Such an attitude was expressed by a tribeswoman who stood on a knoll and watched the galloping teams, bounding wagons, and frantic-faced settlers begin the mad dash for claims. "Heap big fools," she observed in disgust and turned away.

Colonel Wade received orders to be ready to place in the field two troops from Fort Sill, two from Fort Supply, and all of those at Fort Reno. Three days before the event, soldiers burned off much of the tall, dry grass at points within the reservation to help settlers find the survey corner stones that told them range, township, section, and quarter section—information the settlers had to have to register their claim. And once again the Fort Reno Fifth Cavalry, with the assistance of federal marshals, was responsible for preventing illegal entry. People found to be inside the reservation borders prior to starting time were arrested and escorted back to the line.[6]

One instance of this involved Nannita "Kentucky" Daisy, who in 1889 had gained national attention by riding the cowcatcher of a train out of Edmond Station, jumping off, and laying claim to a homestead. Again, in the Run of 1891, the petite advocate for women's rights had made the front pages of *Police Gazette* when she was thrown from her horse during the stampede into present Chandler and mistakenly was reported killed. Prior to the Cheyenne/Arapaho opening, Kentucky Daisy arrived at El Reno at the lead of a colony of eleven other female rushers, all armed with rifles and revolvers.[7]

The women sooners attempted to hide out in County "F" (essentially present Roger Mills County) at the bottom of a deep ravine from which they planned to make their run. Daisy, riding alone and leading a packhorse with provisions, was en route from El Reno to the camp when she was discovered by two cavalrymen who were on night patrol. She was arrested and escorted back to the line. Returning to El Reno, Kentucky Daisy gave a vivid account of her capture to the press and vowed that she would try again to join her friends.[8]

Newspaper coverage was confined largely to the main gathering points on the east end of the reservation, where the largest crowds accumulated, though these were by no means the only points of entry. As the fateful day approached, people flocked to the existing towns of Dover, Kingfisher, El Reno, Reno City, and Minco, all except Reno City being serviced by the Rock Island Railroad.

The railroad scheduled trains both north and south so that they would cross the border precisely at noon where the rail line swerved into the run area west of Kingfisher.[9] Three special trains brought many of the nearly two thousand people there to await the hour of noon on the line just opposite a place that speculators had already chosen for the location of a new town. The town was to be called Okarche, the name being compiled by taking the first two letters from the words Oklahoma and Arapaho and the first three of Cheyenne. When the signal was given, a race ensued between the trains and horse conveyances over the two miles to the Okarche site, which was quickly laid out into town lots.[10]

Another very popular location was Caddo Springs, which lay just inside the reservation's east line a half mile north of Darlington. Newspapers were reporting that the site offered the only pure water in the region—enough for a "million people." A *New York Times* reporter wrote before the run that "Standing on the summit of the Caddo Springs site, a dense line of anxious people could be seen for a distance of twelve miles, north and south."[11]

Many rushers crowded the north line above present Okeene and along the North Canadian above Cantonment. Settler W. C. Broady later recalled the scene there on a day that was misty and cool with a brisk wind out of the north:

> At that point was the camp of troopers, at least thirty-five in number, which comprised two large wagon outfits with mule teams. As the forenoon wore on, the cavalrymen began deploying west to the gypsum hills and east across the Cimarron and down that river until the fartherest trooper sighted one riding north from the Kingfisher camp. The soldiers were posted at intervals a mile apart. All the troopers, save one at the campsite on the Strip line, rode out in front of the throngs with a watch in one hand and a carbine gripped in the other. Instantly at high twelve the guns were fired and the excited homeseekers were off whooping and yelling.[12]

One group of five hundred people moved up the Canadian River to the northwest corner of the Wichita reservation, where they wanted badly from lack of provisions.[13] A group of black settlers who had gathered at Cimarron City near Langston had paid all their money out for railroad fare and were suffering from lack of food. Collections were being taken up for them in Kansas and Oklahoma churches.[14] Most of these people made the run on foot from the Dover area.

Even before the run began, disaster struck the family of James McFarland of Iowa, who was camped on the line near Dover. He had loaded his wife, four children, and all of his possessions into his wagon in order to move south for a dash into County "C" (Blaine County). His horse suddenly became frightened and bolted. He was run over by the heavy wagon and suffered an arm and both legs broken. Worse still, the wagon turned over while caroming downhill. It fell on McFarland's family, crushing and killing his wife and three of his children. His seven-year-old son suffered head injuries and a broken arm.[15]

A second rail line, the Oklahoma City, Ada, and Atoka (known as the Choctaw Road) had been extended into the reservation area some ten miles past El Reno.[16] A *Wichita Eagle* scribe wrote:

> The rush into the territory from El Reno took place from five locations along the line which separated Oklahoma from the Cheyenne and Arapaho country. The biggest crowd was stationed about four miles south of town and consisted of about 3,500 homeseekers . . . The next largest of homeseekers assembled at the line directly west of the townsite of Reno City; the next at the line north of El Reno, near the track of the Choctaw road, and the fifth crowd stationed themselves in coal cars on the Choctaw track ready to be pulled in by a Choctaw train to a townsite between El Reno and Fort Reno. Soldiers were in charge of each crowd, having been detailed to give the signal to enter. So that all the boomers in the valley could start simultaneously, Lt. Almey of the army brought out a field piece from Fort Reno and stationed it on the line west of El Reno, ready to fire when the sun reached his meridian height.[17]

Consternation rose along the eastern line when it was reported that a number of Texans were preparing to make their entry from Greer County. As a result, many men broke camp and, in the absence of troops at their location, crossed the line to head for the southern and western borders.[18]

Minco was the viewing point for a sizable portion of the run into the southern areas of the reservation. It was reported from there on the eighteenth that a steady stream of wagons, horses, and men had passed that way headed for County "H" (essentially Caddo County) just west of the Wichita reservation.

Three colonies were camped and waiting on the north-south line. An Arkansas colony contained 440 people, a colony from Texas numbered 400, and one from Kansas 600. These groups were camped about a mile apart just across from a proposed county seat for County "H," called Rossmore, forty miles west of Minco. Troops were already stationed there, and U.S. marshals had also been sent to monitor this section of the opening. Some people feared much trouble from this mixing of Texas Democrats and Kansas Republicans.[19] The *New York Times* wrote:

> In addition to these colonists eager for town locations, a ride along the line this morning revealed fully 3,000 families encamped. Women and children occupy the miniature towns, and are apparently as happy as they were in their abandoned homes.
>
> The young men and professional boomers have not yet left the towns and cities. They start to-night, with their horses in light marching order, and will add 2,000 to the large number encamped within sight of the territory.[20]

It was arranged that the initial signal for the opening would be made by Colonel Wade at Fort Reno. This would be done by the firing of a cannon and would be extended north and south by troops of the Fifth Cavalry placed strategically along the eastern border of the former reservation.[21] Ulysses B. Roberts, trumpeter for Troop C under Captain Hall, stated that he fired the shot for the run on the Canadian River south of El Reno. During preparation for the event, he said, he carried mail and orders between a temporary split-log headquarters at Capital Hill in Oklahoma City to Colonel Wade and troop commanders of the Fifth Cavalry some six miles in from the eastern line of the run area.[22] The Arkansas City *Weekly Republican Traveler* described the opening along the east line:

> The Cheyenne and Arapahoe reservation was opened to settlement at noon today. At that hour a cannon which had been taken to the border from Ft. Reno boomed forth the signal that noon was at hand. The signal was taken up by the cavalrymen who were stationed within hearing distance all around the border, their carbines repeated it and the race for homes had begun. The old fifth cavalry which had in years past conquered many

tribes of Indians by force of arms, officiated today at the peaceful subjugation of the lands of the Cheyenne and Arapahoes . . .
Simultaneously with the booming of the cannon and the cracking of the carbines there was heard the shouting of excited men,
thundering of horses hoofs and creaking wagons, and the groan-
ing of prairie schooners."[23]

Five minutes after the signal had been given at Darlington, the
New York Times reporter at Caddo Springs was "surrounded by 2,000
people, digging, driving stakes, measuring lots and streets, and erecting tents."[24] As with many locations, there was talk of Caddo Springs
becoming the capital of Oklahoma, but the rushers soon discovered
that the core of the area belonged to the Concho school.

Former Cherokee Outlet cowboy Laban S. Records and his
brother made the 1892 run from the northeast corner of the reservation three miles west of Kingfisher, where a large group of land seekers gathered along the Cimarron River. Records provided an account
of his participation:

> I let the horse go at a good gait until I was satisfied I was on
> the first full quarter from the river . . . I did not slacken speed
> but jumped to the ground, rolled on my back as I held to the
> long hitch-rein. The horse circled around me three times before
> I could get him stopped. He pulled me to my feet again. I stuck
> my four-foot cedar stick into the soft earth. It bore a penciled
> inscription, "This claim is taken by L. S. Records."[25]

By Ashley's estimate, some 25,000 people entered the Cheyenne/
Arapaho lands on April 19. The boundaries of new counties with letter designations from "C" through "H" had been previously surveyed
and platted within the reservation and sites for county seats designated. Within only a few days, villages sprang into existence at most
of these and other locations.[26]

For all of its chaos and potential of violence, the Run of 1892 took
place with little conflict between Indians and whites. The seeds for
trouble, however, were deeply implanted in both groups. The media-
tion of Agent Ashley and the muscle of Fort Reno troops would be
called upon more than once in the months ahead to settle differences
between the two races. Being greatly in the majority and often having

A Fort Reno officer queries a sooner intercepted by his troops. *Harper's Weekly*, July 6, 1889.

the force of civil law on its side, the white population was often the main perpetrator of friction.

One such case occurred when county officials at Cheyenne telegraphed Territorial Gov. A. J. Seay at Guthrie that Cheyenne chiefs White Shield and Red Moon, accompanied by eighty to one hundred warriors, had been there intimidating the settlers. The chiefs supposedly insisted that they had not sold the land and warned the whites to leave within three days. County "F" officials claimed that many of the badly frightened settlers were leaving and requested that a company of soldiers be sent to protect them.[27]

Ashley conferred with Colonel Wade at Fort Reno, stating that he knew that there were only forty-six males over the age of fifteen in the bands of White Shield and Red Moon. Inquiries by both John Seger and Amos Chapman indicated that there had been no trouble with the Indians in County "F." Ashley called the Cheyennes to a conference at Cantonment, and they further denied having made any threat against the settlers.

Whites on the other hand, the agent reported, "have stolen the Indian's fence posts, wire, burned and shot through his tepee, abused and misrepresented him and, in one instance when the husband was not at home attempted to assault his wife."[28]

Agency farmer H. Kliewer reported from Cloud Chief that he had found eighty-three trees cut down on the lands of a Cheyenne named White Turtle and one of his relatives. During his investigation, Kliewer also found a sign on an Indian allotment that read: "To all whom it may concern. We hereby give you notice that thirteen of us are going to move on this creek at once in spite of hell and high water."[29]

The Cheyennes and Arapahos had long been plagued by white horse thieves, and the practice only increased following the opening. On June 30, 1892, four white men stole two horses from an Arapaho herd ten miles from Cantonment. When two Arapahos followed, one was shot in the foot by the thieves.[30]

The matter was reported to officials at Cantonment, and agency police pursued them to the Cherokee Outlet, where their jurisdiction ceased. The chase was then taken up by a posse under the U.S. marshall at Guthrie. Three of the thieves were eventually captured, but in the process one of the stolen horses was killed.

The Run of 1892 drastically and dramatically changed the mid-section of western Indian Territory, wedding it to the new Oklahoma Territory and cutting deep into the native culture and dominance of the land with towns, farms, fences, and the beginnings of Oklahoma's road system. To the south the Kiowa/Comanche reservation and that of the Wichitas would remain aloof from non-Indian settlement until 1901. Greer County, a nonreservation area under dispute with Texas, was already peppered with small white communities.

On the north, the Cherokee Outlet was still essentially unpopulated except for the military garrison at Fort Supply and the Indian school at Chilocco. Its eastern fourth had been assigned as reservations for the Osage, Kaw, Ponca, Otoe, and Missouri tribes. Three major rail lines now crossed the region, their stations offering prime locations for future town sites.[31] The no-man's-land of the Panhandle had already been established as a part of Oklahoma Territory by the Organic Act of May 2, 1890, and designated in its entirety as Beaver County.

Even as the dust was settling from the Run of 1892, plans were well under way for still another great land rush into the Cherokee Outlet. At Fort Reno, Colonel Wade received orders in February to exert military force to stop unauthorized settlements in the outlet.[32] When time came for the opening, however, the territory would be without the services of the Fifth Cavalry. On June 24, 1893, the *El Reno Eagle* reported the regiment's departure for Texas in special trains over the Choctaw and Santa Fe railroads. "El Reno hated to see the Fifth go," the paper noted. "For eight years it had been stationed here, and the people of the city were acquainted with most of the soldiers; but El Reno extends a hearty welcome to the Third (Regiment U.S. Cavalry) and trusts that the relations between soldiers and civilians will be pleasant and agreeable."[33]

CHAPTER 15

This Land Is Our Land

"The Indian Territory has long been a barrier to Kansas growth and progress," a Kansas newspaper would observe upon the opening of the Cherokee Outlet to settlement, "and every citizen of the state should note with pleasure the removal of the obstruction."[1]

With congressional approval having been given to the opening of the Cherokee Outlet pending a proclamation from the president, the army was ordered to remove all unauthorized persons from the region. Fort Reno and Fort Supply Third Cavalry units were reinforced by four additional troops from Fort Riley under the command of Col. Dangerfield Parker, commander of Fort Supply. The task, encompassing as it did some nine thousand square miles and more than four hundred miles of border, was momentous.[2]

On August 19, President Grover Cleveland issued his proclamation declaring the outlet open to settlement at noon on September 16, 1893. The outlet was divided into seven counties by the Department of the Interior, they being designated K through Q. Land offices were established at Perry station on the Santa Fe's Arkansas City extension, at Enid station on the Rock Island, and at Alva and Woodward stations on the Santa Fe's Kiowa, Kansas, extension. Men were put to work digging water wells at each of these locations, while parties of surveyors ran lines and established corner stones within the outlet.[3]

One principal variation in the Cherokee Outlet opening was the requirement that all home seekers must first apply for and receive certificates of eligibility. These were to be issued at locations bordering the outlet, which was known to people of the day as the "Strip," though the Cherokee Strip was actually a section of land across lower Kansas that was once owned by the Cherokees. Registration would be done at tent booths set up at nine points in the one-hundred-foot strip of land that had been held in reserve just inside the outlet boundaries. Sites chosen for the registration booths were at Stillwater; north of Orlando; north of Hennessey; south of Goodwin station near Higgins, Texas; Kiowa, Kansas; Cameron, Kansas; south of Anthony, Kansas; Hunnewell, Kansas; and Arkansas City, Kansas. Here land seekers would make application for a homestead or a town lot or file a soldier's statement of declaration. The booths were thrown open on the morning of September 11, and immediately long lines began to form at each.[4]

The summer of 1893 had been one of severe drought in the West, with temperatures above one hundred degrees. The heat and dryness had continued on into the fall, adding to the despair created by an economic depression. There were no wells or water supply at the application booths. With one-hundred-degree temperatures in the shade and hot winds filled with suffocating dust, the tiresome wait in the shelterless lines was a miserable, sometimes deadly experience. Numerous people were overcome, and six people reportedly died at Arkansas City, two at Caldwell, one at Hennessey, and two at Orlando. No rain had fallen for more than four months, and the extremely dry vegetation was easily set afire. Whether set by homesteader campfires, sparks from locomotives, or on purpose by sooners to retard the run for others, prairie fires raged at several points.[5]

Colonel Parker organized the outlet into four military districts. Section 1, which lay east of the Rock Island rail line, was commanded by Capt. John B. Johnson with Troop B, Third Cavalry, from Fort Reno. Section 2 was bordered on the east by the Rock Island Railroad line and on the west by a line running due south from Kiowa, Kansas. It's southern half was under the command of Fort Reno's Lt. Charles A. Hedekin, Troop A, Third Cavalry, with headquarters at Enid station. Section 3, which ran westward from the west line of Section 2 to a north-south line at Fort Supply, was divided on a slant east to west by the Santa Fe line from Kiowa. The southern half of this section was assigned to Capt. George K. Hunter and Troop K, Third Cavalry, from Fort Reno with headquarters at Waynoka station.[6]

On September 13 Hunter's troops herded fifty-three intruders into Orlando. The men claimed that they had certificates of registration and thought that entitled them to enter and take up homesteads. Instead they were relieved of their certificates and made ineligible to claim land in the outlet. When they pleaded to have their certificates

restored, the arresting officer referred them to the president's proclamation, which allowed no leniency to sooners.[7]

The main task of the troops was controlling the borders against
the press of thousands of home seekers and early entry. Hedekin spread
his men some thirty miles along the southern border of the outlet
south of Hennessey at intervals of three-quarters of a mile. Efforts to
clear sooners out of the area of Enid station was made difficult by the
need to monitor the fifteen thousand home seekers massing on the
outlet's southern line. In support, Fort Reno's Company C, Thirteenth
Infantry, under Capt. William M. Waterbury was assigned to provide
guard at the Enid station land office.

On September 2, Hunter marched from Fort Reno to Hennessey
on his way to Section 3, east and south of Woodward. One technique
of finding sooners was to post lookouts with binoculars on high points
of the terrain. When a rider or wagon was sighted, troopers were sent
flying after them.[8] Three sooners were found on September 3 and
ejected, as was another on the tenth. Hunter made camp at Waynoka
station, from where his troops conducted patrols. Several Texans were
discovered and ejected.[9]

Similar functions were carried out at other sections of the outlet.
The northern half of Section 2 was patrolled by Capt. George A. Dodd
with Troop F, Third Cavalry; the northern half of District 3 by Capt.
Francis H. Hardie with Company G, Third Cavalry; and Third Cavalry
Troop D under Lt. Kirby Walker guarded the registration booth at
Goodwin station, opposite Higgins, Texas, and just west on the Santa
Fe line from Shattuck station. Walker's detachment also patrolled the
western and southern borders of Section 4. The land offices were
guarded by units of the Thirteenth Infantry under 1st Lt. Marion B.
Saffold at Alva; Captain Cavenaugh at Woodward; Captain Waterbury
at Enid; and Capt. Benjamin H. Rogers at Perry.[10]

In addition to those people lining the borders on horses and in
wagons, many others planned to make the run by way of the railroads.
Controls for this were issued by Secretary of Interior Hoke Smith,
who decreed that no railroad trains would be permitted to enter the
outlet during the six hours preceding the time of the opening. Trains
were required to be ready at the borders at least thirty minutes ahead
of time, and no passengers would be permitted to board them earlier

The opening of the Cherokee Outlet saw another mad scramble for Indian Territory homesteads. *Leslie's Illustrated Newspaper*, September 28, 1893.

than that time. Only those with certificates would be allowed on the train, and no one would be taken onboard inside the outlet. The trains, their speed limited to fifteen miles an hour, would be required to stop at each station and at intermediate points not more than five miles apart. Smith further issued orders prohibiting the carrying of deadly weapons on the day of the run.[11]

As it had been with other openings, it was necessary to guard against the sabotage of railroad bridges that crossed the streams of the outlet. Reports surfaced that a group of men who planned to make the run by horse had organized at Arkansas City and Guthrie for the purpose of going into the outlet the night before the opening and burning the railroad bridges. Train engineers were ordered to run cautiously for it had been reported that straps and spikes had been removed from some bridges. Crews were out all night before the run inspecting and repairing the bridges.[12]

Other dire rumors swept through the crowded gathering points. At Arkansas City, stories were told that racehorses were being poisoned by some of those who were to ride trains. At Guthrie, a rumor made the rounds that the outlaw Dalton gang planned to rob all the banks in town while everyone's attention was on the run. In Orlando, new arrivals were alarmed by the story that Iowa and Pawnee Indians had been hired to make the run and kill off the first white men to stake their claims.[13]

Boomers carrying blankets, provisions, and even small tents, jammed trains out of Kansas City, Wichita, Guthrie, and other railroad stations for border destinations. Special trains of boxcars, cattle cars, and flatcars were made up at Wichita and other points. Huge crowds, including many mere sightseers who had come to view a historic event of their day, accumulated at virtually all of the towns along the outlet borders. Arkansas City's crowd was estimated roughly at 30,000; Caldwell, 15,000; Hunnewell, 3,000; Kiowa, 10,000; Stillwater, 7,000; Orlando, 25,000; Hennessey, 7,000; Perry, 20,000; and at other points another 12,000.[14] The *New York Times* reported from Arkansas City:

> All night the rumble of teams could be heard as they moved out to the Strip. At the railway stations men stood in line at the ticket office awaiting the slow movements of ticket sellers, who could not sell over 2,000 tickets an hour. The trains filled rapidly. At first there was an attempt to examine the registration certificates, but this was soon given up as the rushing thousands pushed those ahead of them, the trainmen giving all their time to collecting tickets.[15]

Several trains stood ready at the Guthrie depot, but every hopeful desperately wanted to be on the first. When boarding time came, the shouting crowd rushed forth to swarm over the engine and tender, under the platforms, and on the roofs of the coaches. The soldiers moved forward with bayonets and cleared the train. Still people pushed, crowded, and elbowed to get near the cars. Men were knocked down, women had their clothes torn, and several people were trampled and injured. "Every train was jammed not only in respect to seats, aisles, and platforms, but also on the roofs and tenders and in the baggage cars. In every conceivable nook, on every imaginable perching mount, was a human being."[16]

Much to their chagrin, all who boarded at Guthrie were forced to disembark at Orlando and take their lot among the multitude of people who had arrived there earlier. During the night the registration booth at Orlando had been robbed of certificates and the official stamp. Thousands of forged certificates were on the market.[17]

The weather changed drastically on the night before the run, a cold north wind driving temperatures down considerably. People in the boomer camps who had suffered so badly from the heat now shivered from the cold. Without sufficient blankets, many of them spent the night around their campfires in an attempt to keep warm. The wind continued to gust during the morning of the run, raising dust clouds and threatening rain as people began moving toward the line.[18]

As the fateful hour approached on September 16, scenes were much the same from one point to another along the borders of the outlet. There the course of American empire had once again caused a portion of Indian Territory to be surrounded by an invading host of some one hundred thousand people on horses, in wagons and buggies, on trains, on foot, and a few even on bicycles.

From his position on the east of the line south of Arkansas City, Lt. Frank M. Caldwell gave the initial signal to start the run by firing his pistol at high noon. His signal was echoed by reports from the carbines of his men who were stationed every six hundred yards along the line. The rush was launched in good order except for a point west of the Chilocco reservation, where a false start was launched four minutes early by a pistol report from among the crowd. A man named James H. Hill of Kingborn, New Jersey, jumped the line and was three miles inside the outlet when, after he ignored an order to halt, he was shot and killed by a soldier. This did not stop the nervous crowd from bolting.[19]

A similar premature rush was made on the line at Hunnewell when a moment before noon a rider broke through at a hard gallop, causing a large portion of the crowd to bolt. Lt. Tyree R. Rivers realized he could do nothing to stop them and fired his pistol to start the rest.[20]

The start went smoothly at Caldwell, where Capt. Oscar Elting gave the signal. Pond Creek and Enid stations were the destinations of choice among the crowd. A reporter for the *Wichita Eagle* described the scene:

> Today 15,000 people, who had gathered at the border south of
> here, were rushing helter-skelter into the strip, in every direction
> as far as the eye could reach. Five minutes later the foremost and
> fleetest horsemen were specks in clouds of dust in the distance,
> while behind were hundreds of white-covered wagons and drays
> and buggies trooping into the land that had long been promised,
> leaving behind them great clouds of dust to mark the line.[21]

The anxious "strippers" who rode the trains were extremely unhappy with the slow speed of the locomotives. It was reported that in the race to Enid station from Caldwell, the train was outrun not only by saddle horses but also by many buggies and lighter vehicles. Yet, slow as they were, the trains could not stop for people who jumped recklessly off while the train was in motion. Though soldiers were on the train to prevent it, all along the line, even as the train was moving, people would drop off the coaches. One of these was a "respectable looking woman" whose excitement led her to make such a leap from the top of a car. She hit the ground somersaulting and was left stranded with a broken leg while the train rolled on down the tracks.[22]

Another prime starting point along the Kansas border was at Kiowa, which featured both horse and train entry. Captain Hardie had spread his troops in a cordon east and west along the line south of Kiowa, though he confined the run to one four-mile section. Here, too, a premature discharge of a pistol started the crowd early. Believing that killing three or four people would fail to stop the estimated eight hundred, Hardie fired his own pistol so that the rush was launched evenly. The opening also went smoothly west of Hardie's position above Pond Creek, where Captain Dodd gave the signal according to time on watches that had been set by telegraphic communication.[23]

Both the Missouri Pacific and the Santa Fe had lines to Kiowa, but it was the Santa Fe that extended across the northwest corner of the outlet to Higgins in the Texas Panhandle. As noon approached, three Santa Fe trains stood boarded a mile west of Kiowa. When the signal was given they, too, headed off toward boxcar stations that would soon become towns.[24]

On the south border of the outlet, the major points of entry were north of Stillwater, Orlando, and Hennessey. The estimated crowd of 22,000 at Stillwater was held in check by Capt. J. B. Johnson, who had spread his men along the border between Stillwater and Orlando. Two men who started out early were caught and arrested. The line held at that time, but a few minutes before noon a shot was fired and the rush was on.[25]

The crowd at Orlando was estimated at 25,000, it being bolstered by many people who, despairing of the crush at Arkansas City, had come there on the train. The boomers on horseback, in wagons, and on foot got off evenly at the crack of carbines of cavalrymen, while

Capt. Francis H. Hardie, Third
Cavalry, shown in this sketch by
Frederick Remington, helped moni-
tor the Cherokee Outlet opening.
Harper's Weekly. March 26, 1892.

hundreds more followed on the Santa Fe special trains. Territorial
Gov. William C. Renfrow was among the dignitaries who had come
to witness the event.[26]

Wharton and Perry stations were the favored town site locations
for this group, and freight trains were soon hauling large quantities
of provisions, lumber, household goods, and other items to those
places where tent residences and shops quickly sprang into existence.

Another estimated 15,000 strippers massed along the Rock Island tracks north of Hennessey. Lieutenant Hedekin and Troop A, Third Calvary, restrained the line there. A shot was fired at 11:55 A.M., and many people rushed ahead. "The earth trembled for five miles," a reporter wrote, "and the three or four soldiers who tried to stop the moving avalanche of animals and vehicles had no more effect than if they had tried to harness Niagara."[27] Hedekin refused to give the signal early, and some four thousand law-abiding citizens remained in place until he did so.

Captain Hunter started a thousand persons from the outlet border west of Cantonment. Farther west, between Higgins, Texas, and Goodwin station in the far southwest corner of the outlet, the signal was given by Lieutenant Walker of the Third Cavalry. The run there consisted only of some thirty men on horseback and in wagons and about three hundred people on a Santa Fe train.[28]

Fire fueled by the dry prairie grass and high winds posed a serious threat, and deaths resulted from it. A settler named Osburn had no sooner driven in his stakes west of newly founded Ponca City than a prairie fire swept in upon him and his wife. As he hurried to move his team from danger, Osburn yelled to his wife to take refuge in a gully. Mrs. Osburn did so, but sparks ignited the tall grass around her and burned her to death. Osburn took her body to Ponca City, where it was buried on the prairie. A Baptist minister was called forth from the town's lot seekers to perform the ceremony.[29]

Another woman had a similar death near Perry when a contesting claimant fired the grass as she prepared a makeshift shelter for the night. Instead of fleeing, the woman tried to beat back the flames. But the strong wind pushed the flames over her. Two men hurried to her, but she had already been burned to death. Even as they were bending over her, a new claimant galloped up and, upon learning what had happened, proceeded to drive his stake into the ground and begin throwing up a mound of dirt to make his claim. [30]

The concentration of newspaper correspondents at Arkansas City and Guthrie and the resultant weight of publicity from those points, plus the familiarity that stemmed from being in between two town-lined borders, made the eastern end of the strip far more popular to land seekers than the lesser-known western end. It did not help the cause of the western section that it was often described as being little more than a series of sand hills.

The towns that bordered the eastern end, particularly Arkansas City and Guthrie, were flooded with gamblers, pickpockets, and thieves who preyed upon the bankrolls of homestead hopefuls. Soonerism was rampant, and stories were told of men who buried themselves in holes, exposing themselves only enough to breathe.

Charges persisted that troops were selling registration slips on the sly. "It was a rich man's opening," a *Wichita Eagle* scribe commented later, "and twelve hours before high noon of the 16th the sooner had the best of everything. Many had bought certificates right under the noses of government officials, and if those officials did not know it they are chumps. Many hired the best horses, and got them in at the right starting points, many induced the government soldiers to permit the fast horses to start before 12 o'clock, and many made it possible for those who were not sooners to beat the plain, sovereign squatter in the race . . . The sooner got the outlet."[31]

Soldiers were charged in the press with drunkenness and accepting bribes, though government officials congratulated Colonel Parker on managing such a momentous affair with so few men. For the Fort Reno military, the Run of 1893 meant an end to the chore of patrolling the Cherokee Outlet for contraband cattle or illegal intruders. The garrison settled down to a more normal peacetime pace.

Medal of Honor winner Frank D. Baldwin served as Indian agent at Anadarko from October 1894 to May 1898. He and his wife, Alice, were often visitors at Fort Reno. In a book, she later hinted at some of the personal interplay among the officer corps:

> The post was in command of Colonel Pierson [Pearson], colonel of the 10th Infantry. Reno was a sociable and gay station. Private theatricals were much in demand, and the actors and actresses astonished their friends by their ability. I regret to say that, notwithstanding their ambitious efforts, jealousy became so rampant that the Romeos and Juliets, together with other immortals, disbanded and the places that knew them, knew them no more. The colonel and his charming wife were popular in the garrison, with the exception of a few malcontents and disgruntled ones which is always the case in every military post.[32]

The Cherokee Outlet region now joined the former Cheyenne and Arapaho reservation area as a part of the new Oklahoma Territory and was operated primarily under civil law. Still Fort Reno troops would stand ready to quiet conflicts between tribesmen and whites when civil law did not function.

CHAPTER 16

One Last War

Fort Reno and Fort Sill alone existed as U.S. military posts within the twin territories that divided present Oklahoma during the 1890s. Upon these garrisons fell the responsibility of controlling any disturbances that arose within the various Indian tribes. But the day of Indian uprisings had passed. In 1892 the *El Reno Democrat* took notice of the passing of the frontier. "The great camping ground of the Cheyennes and Arapahos," the paper observed, "is slowly dwindling away and the military at Fort Reno will never again witness these tribes encamped within her gates."[1]

Troops at Fort Reno were called to a new duty in the fall of 1892 when a political quarrel among the Choctaw Nation erupted into virtual civil war. When several supporters of Wilson N. Jones, who was running for reelection as Choctaw governor, were murdered, his followers took up arms. An armed force of some two hundred men was headed by Jones's opponent, Green McCurtain. In order to avert a bloody conflict, the War Department sent a company of Fort Reno troops under Capt. E. M. Hayes, Fifth Cavalry, by rail to Tuskahoma, where they remained for almost a month and quelled the disturbance.[2]

Still another serious altercation developed among the Choctaws the following spring at Antlers, again requiring the use of troops from Fort Reno. When a hundred or so men attempted to rescue a prisoner being held by the Choctaw government, they were resisted by Choctaw militia. Several men were seriously wounded in April 1893, when a detachment of Thirteenth Infantry under Capt. John B. Guthrie was loaded aboard cars of the Santa Fe line and rushed to Antlers. The Fort Reno soldiers remained there until order had been restored.[3]

Nonetheless, the War Department continued to maintain Fort Reno as a cavalry/infantry post. For a time yet, Fort Reno and Darlington would continue to be much involved in Indian affairs in the ever-enlarging Oklahoma Territory. An 1893 brochure by the El

Reno Commercial Club claimed that the government disbursed more than $500,000 annually to Fort Reno's soldiers and Indian police and for military supplies. The expenditures at Darlington were estimated at $500,000 in addition to that spent on three Indian schools and a large agency farm. Indian annuities for the past season amounted to $260,000, most of which was spent at El Reno.[4]

The Kiowa/Comanche and Wichita/Caddo reservations were still unsettled by non-Indians, though settlers and hunters invaded the area regularly. In October 1894, General Miles (whom the Northern Cheyennes called Nok-ko-ish-cha, meaning Bear Coat)[5] arrived at Fort Reno for a hunting expedition to the Wichita Mountain region with Captain Woodson.[6] The Fort Reno garrison at this time consisted of Troops A and B of the Third Cavalry and Companies A, B, H, and F of the Tenth Infantry, whose commander, Col. Edward P. Pearson, was also post commandant.[7]

At Darlington, difficulties had beset the administration of Charles Ashley from the very beginning. He had stirred up considerable resentment by halting the old method of issuing beef whereby tribesmen were allowed to chase and kill the steers as they had buffalo. When he withheld rations from families who would not send their children to the agency school, a Cheyenne named Pawnee Man invaded the commissary building with a cocked rifle. Ashley had him arrested by the Indian police.

The agent worked hard but experienced much difficulty in getting the tribes to take their allotments. His tolerance of the Ghost Dance revivals as a step toward Indian acceptance of Christianity brought the disapproval of the Mennonites, who charged that he was too lax with the tribes. When the government cut beef rations 50 percent in 1892, it prompted many tribal leaders to withhold their children from school. Concluding that more forceful leadership was needed, in July 1893 the Indian Bureau replaced Ashley as agent with Fifth Cavalry officer Woodson.[8]

During the following November, a flare-up of interracial trouble occurred at Cheyenne, Oklahoma Territory, requiring the interdiction of both the Darlington agency and Fort Reno. A young Cheyenne named Wolf Hair had come to town in his wagon to purchase provisions. There Tom O'Hara, a Texas cowboy known as Red Tom, tried to intimidate him with a drawn six-gun. When Wolf Hair left town, O'Hara followed and murdered him. Furious Cheyennes among the bands of Red Moon and Spotted Horse threatened to avenge Wolf Hair's death.

In response to an urgent request for protection from white citizens at Cheyenne, Woodson urged the Cheyenne leaders to restrain their young men from acting unlawfully and promised to bring O'Hara to trial. Whites in Cheyenne demanded O'Hara's arrest, and while he was being held in jail there a large band of Cheyennes rode to the jail and demanded that the Texan be turned over to them. The sheriff refused, whereupon the tribesmen fired their guns in the air and returned to their camps. O'Hara was eventually tried in a Canadian County court and found not guilty by an all-white jury.[9]

The potential for more trouble in the region existed in the continued practice of cattlemen pasturing their herds on Indian-owned allotments—herds from which the hungry tribespeople would occasionally help themselves to a beef or two. Stockmen also charged that the Indians were stealing their horses. At the same time, it was not-so-jokingly said among whites that ranchmen would often buy one Indian pony and steal four.[10]

The situation led to still another affray during the spring of 1894 when a western Oklahoma Territory rancher named J. Cotter, accompanied by cowboy William S. Breeding, invaded Chief Hill's Cheyenne camp in an attempt to take an unbranded pony that Cotter claimed. Chief Hill insisted the pony was his and grabbed the horse's halter, whereupon Breeding shot the Cheyenne twice in the chest with a rifle.[11]

Some accounts say that though he was direly wounded, Chief Hill staggered to his lodge, grabbed his Winchester, and killed Breeding. Other reports state that other Indians came to Chief Hill's aid and began firing on the two men, who attempted to escape. By this version, Breeding was knocked from his horse and killed after fleeing some seventy-five yards, and Cotter's left arm was hit and broken. The irate Indians bashed Breeding's head in with a rifle butt and set fire to his body.[12]

Cotter managed to escape and spread the news of the fight. Within three or four hours after the shooting, Deputy Marshal William Banks arrived at Chief Hill's camp and took charge of Breeding's corpse, sending it home wrapped in a blanket. After hearing Cotter's account of the affair, Banks returned to the Cheyenne camp and recorded a statement from the wounded Chief Hill. While he was there, word came that a large body of armed white men were a mile away. Banks mounted his horse and rode out to meet them.

Though no warrant had been issued, the posse declared its intention of storming the Cheyenne camp. Banks put them off until the next morning, at which time he joined the posse in riding to the camp. Banks persuaded the main portion of the group to hold up while he took three or four men in to the camp to talk. After consultation, two Cheyenne men, Roman Nose and Thunder, were identified as participants and taken into custody. Banks placed them in a dugout for safekeeping until Sheriff Malone of County G arrived.

Members of the posse sent Banks a note giving him fifteen minutes to turn the prisoners over to them, but the lawman firmly refused and ordered the posse to disperse. It was at this point that Captain Hunter and two troops of Third Cavalry arrived from Fort Reno.[13] The whites subsided only when Hunter, a twenty-year veteran officer, declared that if they wanted trouble they could not start it soon enough for him. Roman Nose and Thunder were taken to Fort Reno, where, despite lack of any evidence against them, they were charged with manslaughter and ordered to stand trial. Agent Woodson put up $500 of his own money for their bond and secured them an attorney for their trial in November. At that time the two men were declared innocent of any charges and released to return home.[14]

Reporting on the matter, Fort Reno commanding officer Col. George A. Purington concluded that the settlers were clearly at fault. The officer also lauded highly the services of Ben Clark in his contacts with the Indians. "His knowledge of the country is of much and frequent value to the officers in command here."[15]

During the affair, stories appeared in Oklahoma Territory newspapers reporting a bloody gun battle between the whites and Indians. A trader, who arrived at El Reno from Seger's Colony, claimed that Cheyennes under Red Moon had come to Seger's store to purchase three thousand rounds of ammunition and that afterward a fight had taken place with a white posse in which 15 Indians were killed and as many whites.[16] Another account claimed that 150 armed men had surrounded the Cheyennes' camp and demanded their surrender; another that 28 Indians and 14 soldiers and settlers had been killed; and another that the Indians had burned Abernathy's store at Cantonment. The fight supposedly took place on Panther Creek, eight miles west of Arapaho, Indian Territory, but in fact it never occurred.[17]

As a result of the Chief Hill-Breeding fracas, Colonel Purington concluded it was necessary to station troops in the region to give the Indians confidence to return to their farms and finish their planting. "It will take some time to get the Indians back," he reported. "It seems the policy of people in the vicinity to keep the Indians away so that their lands can be used for grazing, etc."[18]

Accordingly, early in 1895 Capt. James O. Mackay and Troop A, Third Cavalry, were sent to establish a camp on Panther Creek. They remained there through the spring and were in the region in June when a young Cheyenne named Cosah Red Lodge was shot, stabbed, and beaten to near death by a white mob at Arapaho. An elderly white woman who had been raped had identified him as the culprit. Red Lodge was arrested by the sheriff of County G, and agent Woodson arranged for counsel through Richard Davis, an educated Cheyenne.

Not having a jail in Arapaho, the sheriff took Red Lodge with him to watch a local baseball game. A detachment of troops under Lieutenant Hedekin was also present to act in support of the sheriff. However, the officer left with his entire command to escort a ration train and was not on hand when an angry group of cowboys and town folks gathered with the intent of doing the Cheyenne harm.[19] Red Lodge did not speak English, but in true warrior fashion, he jumped from the buggy and defiantly motioned to his chest and head for the crowd to shoot him. Cowboys rode forth and tried to lasso him before he crumpled from a shot in the abdomen. The crowd then surged forward to beat and stab Red Lodge repeatedly, leaving him for dead when their fury was spent. A farmer from Seger's Colony, however, found that the boy was still alive and took him to a doctor in town. Eventually it was established that Red Lodge had not committed the rape, the woman admitting she had mistakenly identified him instead of another Cheyenne named Little Man.[20]

Fort Reno troops were also active during the summer of 1895 at removing sooners who had encroached into the Wichita Mountain region of the Kiowa/Comanche/Apache reservation.[21] During September, the Third Cavalry units were replaced at Fort Reno by Troop D, First Cavalry, from Fort Apache, Arizona, and Troop B, First Cavalry, from Fort Bayard, New Mexico.[22]

The peacetime routine of the Tenth Infantry and First Cavalry at Fort Reno was interspersed with summer maneuvers, baseball games, and autumn football contests with Fort Sill, Oklahoma City, and Arkansas City teams. The Fort Reno eleven visited Oklahoma City and, with stellar athlete Lt. Robert C. Van Vliet as quarterback, bested that team 22–0. The *Daily Oklahoman* observed that the Fort Reno "heavyweights," who averaged 160 pounds to the man, were simply too much for the Oklahoma City boys, who averaged 140 pounds.[23]

During the fall of that year, a party of Cheyennes and Arapahos led by Chief Powder Face tracked a pair of white horse thieves to Woodward. There they were joined by Marshal Eugene Hall and a posse of deputies. The trail of the thieves was followed on into the Panhandle. When the Kansas border was reached, however, the Indians were sent back, and the posse continued on to Coolidge, Kansas, where the two men were captured. The Indians had shown such great tracking ability that they were looked to when Al Jennings's gang robbed the Rock Island train at Chickasha.[24]

A significant element of Fort Reno history received its first formal attention in June 1896 when the Reno post of the Grand Army of the Republic arranged jointly with the Fort Reno garrison to hold a devotional service at the post cemetery. Led by the post band, a procession marched from El Reno to the cemetery, where a volley was fired by Tenth Infantry troops, addresses and prayers were issued, and graves were strewn with baskets of flowers by ten wagonloads of Indian students from the Darlington and Caddo Springs schools and El Reno flower girls.[25]

At this time in history, El Reno held a strong commercial relationship with the Cheyenne/Arapaho agency. In addition to government expenditures on food and clothing for the four thousand tribal members, considerable federal money was spent on the Indian schools and farming operations. But the most lucrative benefit to El Reno merchants were the semiannual annuity disbursements, a large portion of which found its way into their cash boxes through trade.

Some $50,000 annuity in silver dollars was issued to the

Cheyennes and Arapahos at Darlington during two weeks of July 1896. At this time, El Reno was filled with tribespeople who came en masse to view the windows of stores that were dressed in gaudy displays. The trading store at Darlington was also busy settling accounts with Indian customers who had run up charges during the past months. During the Christmas holidays, a party of nearly a hundred Kiowas under Chief Lone Wolf pitched their tepees at El Reno while on a shopping sojourn.[26]

A striking indication of the changing times occurred with the arrival at Cantonment of some forty Utes and Pueblo Indians who came to visit the Cheyennes and Arapahos during the fall of 1896. The visitors had made the twenty-four-day trip from the Rocky Mountains on horseback. For generations, these tribes had fought and killed one another regularly. Now the Utes and Pueblos went home, richer by some two hundred ponies, and the Darlington agency Indians looked to repaying their visit.[27]

In order to preserve order during disbursement of funds to Cherokee freedmen in February 1897, First Cavalry troops were ordered to eastern Oklahoma. These were first stationed at Hayden (west of Vinita) but later took up quarters on the parade ground of old Fort Gibson under Capt. Jacob G. Galbraith until August. The Fort Reno troops remained on duty there for the balance of the year.[28] When Chandler was struck by a March 30 tornado that killed twenty people, Colonel Pearson shipped thirty-five tents to the town.[29]

At the time of the Cheyenne/Arapaho land allotment in 1892, five sections around Cantonment had been reserved by the government. The Mennonites' school was replaced in 1898 with an Indian industrial school. It was attended largely by Cheyenne and Arapaho children.

During that same year, troops at Fort Reno found themselves thrust into an international conflict when the United States and Spain went to war. Not only did the Tenth Infantry serve with high honor, but so did other units that had previously been garrisoned at Fort Reno in earlier times. Among the ranking American officers of the Spanish-American war were men whose names had been involved in the history of Fort Reno and Indian Territory. These included Generals Nelson A. Miles, John J. Coppinger, James F. Wade, Henry W. Lawton, Wesley Merritt, and John M. Schofield.

On April 26 the *El Reno Democrat* reported that Fort Reno's

Tenth Infantry, having received orders from the War Department to proceed at once to Mobile, Alabama, had marched down El Reno's Bickford Avenue the night before. They were led by their bugle corps and regimental band to the lively tune of "Yankee Doodle." The soldiers were in full field uniform and carried their muskets, canteens, and bedrolls. Several hundred people cheered them loudly at the train station and visited with them in the cars after they had boarded the special Rock Island train.

The Tenth Infantry was followed the next evening by troops of the First Cavalry, who were destined for Chickamauga Park, Tennessee. Together with their wagons, harness, and other fixtures, the two units filled 448 cars. Fort Reno was left almost deserted, only two men of each company being left behind under 1st Lt. John H. Shollenberger to guard the post and oversee government property.[30]

There were so few men and so many women and children left at the base, some were calling it "Widowville."[31] A troop of Seventh Cavalry, however, was soon transferred there from Fort Sill under the command of Lt. Selah R. H. Tompkins.

In addition to the mustering of regular troops, a nationwide call was made for volunteers. This led to formation of the First U.S. Volunteer Cavalry, the famed Rough Riders, many of whom were recruits from Oklahoma and Indian Territories.[32] After being mobilized at San Antonio, Texas, in May, the unit was soon sent off by rail-car to Tampa, Florida. From there eight dismounted troops of the unit sailed for Cuba as a part of an American expeditionary force under Gen. William R. Shafter.

On July 1, 1898, units of the First, Third, Ninth, and Tenth Cavalry, all of which had served in Indian Territory, joined the Rough Riders in storming San Juan Heights. It was the white Rough Riders who received the main adulation of the nation, but the buffalo soldiers of the Ninth and Tenth Cavalry had fought every bit as bravely. Lt. John J. "Black Jack" Pershing, who drew his nickname from his service with the Tenth Cavalry, expressed the views of other white officers, saying: "We officers of the Tenth Cavalry could have taken our black heroes in our arms. They had again fought their way into our affections, as they here had fought their way into the hearts of the American people."[33]

A second call to enlist a regiment of infantry resulted in the formation of the First U.S. Volunteer Infantry. Because of War Department delays, it was the middle of July before some five hundred recruits of the Oklahoma infantry battalion mobilized at Fort Reno.[34] A sixteen-coach Sunday excursion train of the Choctaw line carried large crowds, among them territorial governor Cassius M. Barnes, from El Reno to Fort Reno to witness the volunteers going through their drills.

A reporter took note of their campsite east of the fort and the

Buffalo soldiers fought with great bravery during the U.S. Indian wars. *Harper's Weekly,* August 21, 1886.

"nice white tents with their innumerable flags."[35] The boys, he wrote, were feeling good at having received their new camping outfits, much preferring these quarters to the old barracks. Volunteer John Alley later recalled the experience differently:

> These five companies were soon established in camp on the sun-baked prairie slopes immediately east of Fort Reno. There we did "squads east and west" in the blistering July and August heat, wearing army blue woolens. But woolen uniforms, worn during strenuous drill exercises during Oklahoma's hottest season, were not the worst of the discomforts we suffered. We were crowded into small wall tents, without floors, other than the bare ground. No sleeping cots were furnished. Each soldier had a "bedsack" which he filled with straw and placed on the ground inside the tent. The balance of the bed equipment was a blanket —no pillow, no sheets. Our meals were prepared in an open kitchen over which was stretched a canvas, without walls or fly screens. Our latrines were open ditches screened only by piles of brush. Thus, flies circulated freely from the kitchen to the latrine and back again.[36]

The volunteers remained at Fort Reno until September, when they were sent off to Camp Hamilton at Lexington, Kentucky, believing they would see service in either Cuba or Puerto Rico. Instead they were eventually transferred to Camp Churchman at Albany, Georgia, where they were mustered out in February 1899.[37]

Regular troops returned to Fort Reno during the fall of 1898 along with twelve companies of Tenth Infantry and two troops of Sixth Cavalry that arrived in early 1899.[38] In June 1900, Troop A of the Eighth Cavalry replaced Troop D of the Sixth Cavalry, which was sent off to the Philippines to join the command of Gen. Henry W. Lawton.[39] Lawton had played a commanding role in Cuba. He served as a U.S. commissioner in the surrender and as military governor of Santiago. In the Philippines, he led American forces that took Santa Cruz, San Rafael, and San Isidoro before he was killed by a sniper while directing an attack at San Mateo. He is buried in Arlington National Cemetery.

In January 1901 Fort Reno's Troop A, Eighth Cavalry, was called upon to help put down a disturbance among traditional elements of the Creek Indians. This incident of Oklahoma history resulted from the determined opposition of a Creek full-blood faction to resist the forced allotment of Creek lands to tribal members. Led by elderly Chitto Harjo, or Crazy Snake, the group sought to make a final stand for what they conceived to be their treaty rights. Defying the authority of Chief Pleasant Porter and the United States, they established a new Creek government based on old tribal laws. Harjo's followers began intimidating tribal members, particularly mixed-bloods, through public whippings and threats.[40]

In response the government ordered Fort Reno troops to the Creek country. Troop A, Eighth Cavalry, under 1st Lt. Henry B. Dixon boarded a special train of the Choctaw Railroad with their horses and equipment, going into camp near Henryetta.[41] Joined by a posse under the U.S. marshal and Indian police, the troops conducted a systematic search for those who had enrolled as members of the Crazy Snake government. Chitto Harjo and ninety-four of his Crazy Snake rebels were taken prisoner; sixty-seven of those were jailed at Muskogee and tried in federal court there. They eventually accepted allotments as a price for their freedom.[42]

Alexander Posey, the famous Creek poet, saw the heroic in Harjo's desperate effort to defend his tribal rights:

> Down with him! chain him! bind him fast!
> Slam the iron door and turn the key!
> The one true Creek, perhaps the last!
> To dare declare "You have wronged me!"
> A traitor, outlaw—what you will,
> He is the noble red man still.
> Condemn him and his kind to shame!
> I bow to him, exalt his name![43]

With the arrival of the twentieth century, question arose as to the continued existence of Fort Reno as an active military post. Rumors floated about that the fort was to be abandoned. Maj. Richard T. Yeatman, commanding, reported to Department of Missouri headquarters that the six sets of enlisted men's quarters were in dilapidated condition with rotten windowsills and woodwork. The buildings, Yeatman claimed, were so close together that a fire would destroy half the post. Closets were wholly inadequate and baths obsolete and unsanitary to the point of threatening the health of the troops. [44]

Still another threat to soldierly health was revealed in the report on a private in the Eighth Cavalry who was discharged on a certificate of disability because of gonorrheal rheumatism. The report wryly noted that the disease was "Not contracted in line of duty."[45]

Fort Reno was still garrisoned by units of the Twenty-fifth Infantry and Thirtieth Infantry on October 2, 1905, when Gen. Frank Baldwin reviewed troops there during an inspection tour of army posts. Baldwin, who had fought in the Red River War of 1874, was given an official salute and honored at a reception in the residence of Maj. Joseph M. T. Partello, commanding.[46]

When Maj. William R. Abercrombie of the Thirtieth Infantry arrived in November to take command of the post, replacing Major Partello, the *El Reno American* hopefully reported that Fort Reno would now become a regimental post. Inside information had it that Reno would be the headquarters for the Twenty-second Infantry, soon to be moved there from the Philippines, and the Second Cavalry. Local citizens were further encouraged when the government installed a large steel tank, a pump, and three miles of pipe to run water from Caddo Springs to the post.[47]

The paper pointed to the site as one of the healthiest in the nation. No fort had a better rifle range, the *American* claimed, and its officer quarters were roomy and in good repair. "The driveways are shaded by beautiful elm and maple trees. The post is equipped with a fine hospital building."[48]

During July 1906, a young officer whose name would one day carry worldwide importance served briefly as acting commander at Fort Reno. He was 2d Lt. George C. Marshall of the Thirtieth Infantry.[49]

The immediate welfare of Fort Reno would be affected by a serious racial disturbance elsewhere within the U.S. Army, and its three-decade existence as an active military post was destined soon to end. During the fall of 1906, the army quietly shipped three companies of the First Battalion of the Twenty-fifth Infantry Regiment from Fort Brown at Brownsville, Texas, to Fort Reno. A racial fracas had erupted there on August 13 after white residents at Brownsville had initiated trouble with some black soldiers. Shots were fired into the homes of some white citizens, and one person was killed. The black troops were held responsible, but the army did not know precisely whom to charge.[50]

When soldiers of the Twenty-fifth Regiment refused to name any of their comrades as being the perpetrators, President Theodore Roosevelt ordered the entire First Battalion to be discharged without honor, making them ineligible for either military or civil service in the future. This severe punishment was mollified by Congress in 1909.[51]

In November, Maj. Charles J. T. Clarke, Twenty-sixth Infantry, who had been at Reno previously as post adjutant with the Tenth Infantry, replaced Maj. Charles W. Penrose as commandant at Fort Reno. In compliance with the president's harsh orders, Clarke began discharging soldiers of the Twenty-fifth Infantry at the rate of twenty-five a day. The army issued back pay and travel pay to the discharged soldiers, providing transportation to wherever they wished to go. By the end of the month, the three companies of Twenty-fifth Infantry were completely depleted. They were replaced at Fort Reno by troops of the Third Battalion, Twenty-fifth Infantry from Fort McIntosh at Laredo, Texas, while new recruits were enlisted to fill the vacated ranks of the First Battalion.[52]

Fort Reno troops were kept engaged with practice marches through the surrounding countryside. Officers carefully mapped the march areas, noting the line of approach from Fort Reno to the camp of the potential enemy. During the exercises, the troops were given instruction in pitching and striking conical, wall, and shelter tents and laying out a camp.[53]

In January 1907 the army announced that a squad of 150 recruits from Columbus, Ohio, would arrive at Fort Reno, where they would be drilled prior to assignments at other western posts. Plans were under way for Fort Reno to be turned into an army remount station for testing and training some 1,500 to 2,000 horses and mules for military use.[54] Before this took place, however, companies of the Oklahoma National Guard arrived at Fort Reno in September 1907, joining two companies of Nineteenth Infantry regulars for training exercises. The guard established its camp on the high ground east of the fort proper. On the evening of October 2, a disastrous prairie fire driven by a strong north wind swept through the camp, destroying military and personal equipment of both the guard and regular troops. Many of the guardsmen were taken to El Reno, where they were served sandwiches and coffee and provided quarters. Others entrained for their homes.[55]

During the spring of 1907, Secretary of War William Howard Taft toured the western military posts for the purpose of establishing a chain of brigade posts and at the same time eliminating others. There was a choice to be made between saving Fort Reno or Fort Sill. General Merritt much preferred Fort Reno, contending that the buildings at Fort Sill were beyond repair. Lt. Hugh Scott, however, argued effectively that a well had been sunk to 1,200 feet at Fort Reno at a cost of $15,000, and it had produced such bad water as to curl your teeth.[56]

The El Reno Commercial Club discussed the matter and decided to take action. In November 1907 it passed a resolution protesting the closing of Fort Reno and forwarded it to the War Department.[57] Scott's argument, however, persuaded Taft in Fort Sill's favor. As a result Fort Reno lost out and became one of the more than one hundred military posts to be closed. Realizing that its interests had been preempted, the El Reno Commercial Club looked wishfully to the use of the 26,000 acres embodied by Reno and Darlington for the capital of the new state of Oklahoma that had been formed out of Oklahoma and Indian Territories.[58]

Fort Reno's end as an active military base occurred on the evening of February 24, 1908. Soldiers of the Second Battalion of the Nineteenth Infantry gave a farewell salute as they passed through the gates of the fort and marched on to El Reno's Rock Island station. There they boarded a special train that would take them north to Fort McKenzie, Wyoming. A small detail of enlisted men remained behind to care for government property until it could be removed.[59] Surrounded by the vacant buildings and silent streets, an ancient figure of the post's history witnessed the departure. This was Ben Clark, who had been designated as caretaker of the now deserted fort.[60]

At that time, Commanding General of the Army Albert L. Meyer had noted Clark's service of more than fifty years: "It is believed that his service deserves recognition in the way of continued employment by the War Department as long as he lives."[61] The old scout was pro-

Ben Clark remained at Fort Reno as the last remnant of the old frontier. *Courtesy National Archives.*

vided a horse and equipment with which to ride the reservation daily and drive off any stray animals grazing there.

Col. E. P. Pendleton knew the frontiersman very well while serving at Fort Reno. "Altho he must have been often in an unrefined environment," Pendleton observed, "he never seemed affected by it. In all my acquaintance with him, he was always what I would call a natural born gentleman."[62]

Clark, with his Indian wife, Moka, and three children, had been the longest resident of the post. Seven other children rested in the post cemetery, and Moka was buried there in 1913. Clark continued to reside at Fort Reno until July 24, 1914, when after suffering a stroke, the archetypical frontiersman stood tall before a mirror and shot himself with his pistol. His death was the finale, the last breath of the old Indian frontier that had once swirled around the one-time cavalry post and Indian agency of the North Canadian valley. An era had ended.

New Duties, Old Memories

With the advent of Oklahoma statehood a new day began for Fort Reno. The colorful events of the past faded quietly into buried records and distant recall, but the old fort would continue to serve the needs of a post-frontier America in other capacities during the years ahead. On May 11, 1908, Congress established Fort Reno as a Remount Depot where horses and mules were trained for military use, a purpose it would address through World War I, World War II, and the Korean conflict.

Having been created for other purposes, the fort required certain improvements, one being to fence in the entire post and its pastures. This was a major project that took two years to complete.[1] Some 850 animals were shipped in when the remount operation was initiated that year under the command of Capt. Letcher Hardeman of the Eleventh Cavalry.

Sixteen 160-acre pastures were established, each enclosed with fences and equipped with a windmill, pump, and shelter shed. Other acreage was placed under cultivation to produce corn, oats, and hay for feeding the station's livestock. Former barracks were turned into stables.[2]

By 1909 forty-three Montana cowboys were breaking and training mounts, but there was no roping and throwing of the horse or use of spurs, as in the old Western broncho-busting style. Instead, each animal wore a curbless bridle. Each was taught to accept mounting from either side and carry his rider, then to walk, trot, and gallop. The horses received veterinarian care at an animal hospital, which was housed in one of three new barns. Hardeman personally broke and trained a horse named Dick for use by President Taft. Other mounts were destined for West Point.[3]

Gerald E. Griffin, Third Field Artillery veterinarian, paid a visit to the post in November 1915 for the purpose of becoming acquainted with the methods employed there in preparing young horses for the military. He was met at the post Rock Island station by Hardeman, "a tall robust, soldierly looking man," who himself drove an old express wagon pulled by a pair of mules.[4] Hardeman, Griffin found, was not only his own driver but also the quartermaster, adviser, fatherly friend, boss, well-informed horse handler, farmer, and motivating force of the Fort Reno Remount Depot. Hardeman was assisted by Lt. William P. Ennis, 1st Field Artillery.

In the course of his stay, Griffin was escorted to the trained horse pasture, the Virginia horse pasture, the Missouri horse pasture, the Montana horse pasture, and the colt pasture, which included some foals of Wyoming origin. "The service has been bettered by the establishment of these depots," Griffin concluded. "They have been instrumental in arousing an interest in horses, riding, and training that is a source of wonder and of glad surprise to everybody in our army."[5]

Fort Reno functioned at full capacity throughout World War I, its veterinarians traveling throughout Oklahoma and neighboring states to inspect and purchase animals. The breeding of animals was not begun until 1918.[6]

Through its era as a remount station, Fort Reno experienced a number of commanding officers. Two commanders, who were at the post longer than others, were particularly memorable. Maj. Henry J. Weeks, who headed the post from 1927 to 1931, brought national attention to Fort Reno as a peacetime center of polo activity in addition to training horses for cavalry and artillery work. Polo tournaments at Fort Reno were accompanied by horse shows, gymkhana, Indian fairs, horse and foot races, jackrabbit chases by greyhounds, parachute jumps, and concerts by the Fort Sill artillery band.

Weeks, a member of the All-American football team while at West Point, arrived at Fort Reno in 1924. He soon initiated an annual horse show and polo tournament at the post. A club composed of polo and horseback riding enthusiasts from Fort Reno and El Reno participated in the event, with competition among teams from Fort Sill, the University of Oklahoma, and Tulsa, as well as from Texas and other out-of-state locations.

In 1928 Capt. C. A. Wilkinson, a highly regarded poloist who had twice helped defeat the British team, was transferred to Fort Reno for the purpose of establishing a training program for polo players and ponies in preparation for a contest against England at Meadowbrook Club in Washington, D.C., the following year. Twenty officers were placed on orders to try out for the army polo team.[7]

During a meet held at Fort Reno in September 1929, the post was visited by world-famed humorist and native son Will Rogers, who arrived by airplane from Claremore.[8] "Fort Reno is sure a pretty place," Rogers, himself a polo enthusiast, told a Fort Reno gathering, "and I would like to buy it for a ranch. I heard about Fort Reno all my life but didn't know you had such a pretty place. Talking about the army, I don't know whether it can fight or not, but it sure can play polo."[9]

In 1930, Fort Reno consisted of 110 buildings that included stables, barracks, officers' quarters, and other facilities. More than eight hundred horses were on hand, one hundred of which were trained as polo ponies. The military personnel consisted of 115 men, while 50 civilians were employed at the post. Of Fort Reno's 10,000 acres of land, some 8,000 were in grass and 2,000 in forage and grain crops. Expert buyers scoured the nation and foreign countries for the best stock that could be purchased.[10]

During 1930 the federal government transferred 1,000 acres of the Fort Reno remount reservation to the Department of Justice for location of the U.S. Southwestern Reformatory. More of the Fort Reno reservation was added later, bringing the total to 2,500 acres. First offenders against federal laws, short-term prisoners, and convicts under thirty-five years of age are housed in what is now known as the Federal Corrections Center.[11]

In 1933 the principal mission of the depot under Col. James E. Skelley was described as being "to receive, care for and train, and issue to troops, horses and mules, for the various using arms of the War Department."[12]

Another notable Fort Reno commandant was Maj. Edward M. Daniels (1936–40), whose principal legacy was a marked improvement in facilities through the use of WPA labor. But as the war in Europe escalated, the pre–World War II U.S. Army was still essentially unmechanized and looked to the military potential of horses and mules. In 1938 Daniels spoke to a reporter about the role that Fort Reno played in providing trained animals. The post, he said, was the second largest in acreage of the existing three remount stations, but it provided more animals than the other two—one in Virginia and one in Nebraska— combined, furnishing 1,500 animals to the cavalry and artillery the previous year.

"Life in Fort Reno," the reporter noted, "is like living in a little big city. The population is small: 104 enlisted men, six officers, and 50 civilian employees, with 45 families and 70 children among the enlisted men. The fort has its own hospital, movie theater, utilities, water plant, and fire department. Supplies are bought from the government commissary."[13]

Each man at Fort Reno was required to work eight hours a day. There were no daily drills, but occasional military inspections were held. Entertainment at the post included card playing, swimming, tennis, polo, and hunting. Major Daniels himself owned twenty hounds that he used for running coyotes.

Daniels, who later became head of the U.S. Remount Service, knew that during the depression years of the 1930s the strapped, peacetime army could not provide funds to make needed repairs on the deteriorating fort. However, he saw opportunity in the potential of using WPA labor to repair old buildings and construct new ones. An old barracks building was converted into a hospital, new water and sewer systems were installed, streets were paved, and many other buildings were restored. New construction included a barracks building, clubhouse, headquarters building, veterinary hospital, three colt nurseries, and a dairy plant. The enterprising officer managed to obtain some $622,000 of construction for the post.[14]

One of the interesting family stories of Fort Reno was the three generations of Gallaghers who served there. The father of farm supervisor Sgt. Michael J. Gallagher, John O. Gallagher, had been a soldier at Reno prior to 1900, departing with the forces of the Spanish-American War. Sgt. Gallagher's son, James R., was a corporal at Reno in 1938. He later rose to the rank of lieutenant colonel during World War II.

A *Tulsa World* article told the Gallagher story: Sgt. John O. Gallagher came to Fort Reno with his family by train in 1894, and son Mike hauled water from Caddo Springs, where it was procured from a wooden-handle pump, and made trips as a civilian teamster driv-

The old post guardhouse, where Payne and his men were once held, still faces the Fort Reno parade grounds. *Author photo.*

ing a wagon and four-mule team to points in Kansas and Texas. As a corporal at the remount station, Sgt. Gallagher drew twenty-four dollars a month. Of his fifty-two years at Fort Reno, more than thirty-two of them had been as a soldier in the army.[15]

Major Daniels made note of twenty-five boxes of old records then stored at the fort. He liked to tell of one official order, written in longhand, that commanded the garrison to stop shooting buffalo from the windows of the barracks.

In 1939 Fort Reno was described as a Quartermaster's Intermediate Depot, pasturing some two thousand horses with twenty stallions that had been sires to winners of such prestigious races as the Kentucky Derby and Preakness.[16] Possibly the most famous stallion was Black Jack, the mount that was led with an empty saddle and stirrups reversed in the 1963 funeral of President John F. Kennedy.[17]

During World War II, the Fort Reno Remount Depot once again became actively involved in furnishing horses and mules for military use. More than three hundred men were stationed in temporary tent quarters at Reno during the war. Thousands of animals arrived at the post in boxcars for training and treatment.

The army eventually decided that mules, which served as pack animals in the mountains of Italy and jungles of the South Pacific, were more valuable to a modern army than horses. Accordingly, during 1943 Fort Reno dispensed some three thousand horses by selling them at auction.[18] The days of the post as a remount station were coming to an end, and even the importation of prize German horses that had been captured during the war could not overcome the effects of an altered military need.

World War II provided a unique chapter in Fort Reno history when the site was chosen for a German prisoner-of-war camp. Construction of the prisoner compound began in March 1943, and the first group of Hitler's *Afrika Korps* arrived in May. With them came a 130-man detachment of U.S. 435th Military Police. The German prisoners, wearing their own uniforms, worked as agricultural and industrial laborers during their confinement. Following the end of the war, the prisoners were returned to Germany, the last of them being released in May 1946.[19]

Remembrance of the prisoners and the World War II period of Fort Reno history is to be found in the seventy prisoner-of-war graves located at the rear of the Fort Reno Cemetery. Only one of those interred there was an inmate of the Fort Reno camp. Other bodies were brought there after the war from camps throughout the United States. Eight Italian wartime prisoners are also buried at Fort Reno.[20]

Bill Davenport, a Kentuckian who served as first sergeant at the post during World War II under Col. Frank L. Carr, recalls helping to bury some of those prisoners. During the war the remount station was still breeding horses and mules for military use, the Rock Island Railroad was running onto the base to pick up or deliver boxcar loads of animals, officers were practicing and playing polo on the post polo field, and soldiers on leave rode the interurban trolley from El Reno to Oklahoma City.[21]

Fort Reno would add three troops of the 252d Remount Corps to its garrison after the war. The old enlisted men's barracks had been remodeled to accommodate them, and a new chapel that the German prisoners built, the first for the post, was dedicated in May 1944. Col. Paul H. Morris, who took command at the fort in 1943, died following an operation at Walter Reed Hospital and was buried at Arlington

German prisoners of war incarcerated at Fort Reno during World War II constructed the post chapel. *Author photo.*

National Cemetery. During the forties, the post functioned in shipping mules to Greece to help defeat the communist guerilla movement. Later the fort would conduct the same service for Turkey, which was also caught up in Communist turmoil.[22]

In 1946 the post acquired racing grandstands made available by the closing of Fort Walters, Texas, and for a time the post entertained itself with horse races under the direction of post adjutant Maj. William A. Ranck.[23] At the same time, however, twenty-seven surplus buildings were sold at auction.[24]

A new debate over the future of Fort Reno had begun. One suggestion was to transfer it to the Veteran's Administration for a hospital. In February 1946, Commissioner of Indian Affairs William Brophy recommended giving Fort Reno back to the Cheyenne and Arapaho tribes. The following year, those tribes moved to gain possession of the Fort Reno land under the Treaty of Medicine Lodge in 1867. Hearings were held on the matter in Washington during June and July 1949, when testimony was taken from tribal members.[25]

The Indian claim was denied, however, and the U.S. Congress

chose instead to transfer the Fort Reno reservation to the U.S. Department of Agriculture. In July 1948 that department and Oklahoma State University (then Oklahoma A&M College) cooperated in establishing a Live Stock Research Station on the premises of Fort Reno. A year later OSU animal science professor Dwight Stephens was hired as superintendent, a job that he held for twenty-four years before retiring in 1974. Under his guidance a cadre of agricultural scientists, professors, and assistants conducted experiments in livestock management and farming, and many projects evolved that have proved beneficial to American agriculture.[26]

Dr. Jack Whenry, who was born and raised at Fort Reno during the 1930s and wrote a book in which a fictional character represented himself, recalled with great nostalgia his early life at the post, where his father was a soldier. He remembered the trains that carried loads of horses and mules in and out of the fort; the springtime polo matches as cavalry officers practiced their skills and trained their animals; visiting Indian chiefs in their colorful war bonnets; the old buildings of the post that were falling into disrepair; and officers' row, where house signs bespoke the name and military rank of each occupant.[27]

Additionally, Whenry recalled the adventures of his Huckleberry Finn days of boyhood at the post: fishing and swimming in the North Canadian River, carrying water to haying crews, earning spending money by walking the lathered polo ponies after a workout, and wintertime hunting and trapping experiences, the polecat aromas of which sometimes brought him temporary dismissal from school.

A portion of Fort Reno's history as a cavalry post is recorded on the tombstones in the post's cemetery. The neat, well-kept burial ground is enclosed by a low stone wall and shaded with a sprinkling of cedar trees. In the two hundred or so graves of the cemetery rest the remains of Fort Reno soldiers from the year 1874 to 1948, their family members, as well as Indian scouts and post employees.[28]

Of special interest are the graves of Ben Clark; his wife, Moka; and seven of their children; Arapaho scout Chalk and Cpl. Patrick Lynch, who were killed in the chase after Dull Knife; Mrs. Mary Elliott, who was murdered by a drunken soldier in 1884; Col. Alexander Hamilton Jones, one-time commandant of Fort Reno; Col. William P. Walters, who died while participating in a polo match at San Antonio in 1926; longtime frontiersman Tim O'Connell; quartermaster/settler Hermann

Hauser; and Hauser's little son Emil, who was killed in the Mennonite school fire of 1882.

Darlington has experienced considerable change during the twentieth century. An 1886 list of buildings at Darlington had itemized twenty-six structures. They were, by year of erection, as follows: an eight-room agent's residence, physician's residence, farmer's residence, and clerk's residence built in 1871; a two-room log residence, 1873; carpenter's residence and agency barn, 1873; physician's office and blacksmith's residence, 1874; carriage house/stable, 1875; two-story, thirty-three-room Arapaho school, 1876; issue clerk's residence and cattle corral, 1878; three-story, twenty-two-room Cheyenne school, 1879; three-story, 111-room brick warehouse, brick spring house, and gristmill, 1880; brick laundry, 1882; brick Mennonite mission and brick blacksmith/carpenter shop, 1883; guardhouse, two additional carriage houses/stables and second laundry house in 1885; and implement house and second farmer's house in 1886.[29]

For a number of years following 1900, the property that constituted the Cheyenne/Arapaho agency sat vacant, its buildings deteriorating and its grounds and pathways becoming overgrown with weeds. In 1910 the U.S. government sold the buildings and 676 acres of land to the Masonic Lodge of Oklahoma for $78,000. Among the existing structures at the time, three were brick: the large commissary building, which the Masons converted into an industrial school; a large girls' dormitory; and one cottage. The rest of the buildings, some forty years old, were frame structures and in bad shape. Water and sewer systems, roofs, walls, and plumbing were in disrepair.[30]

Sixty-five orphaned youngsters were brought to the location from Atoka on April 30, 1910, by Presbyterian minister Rev. T. C. Christianson, the orphanage's first superintendent.[31] They were quartered in the old wooden dormitories once used by Indian children even as the facilities were being reconstructed. The Masons spent all summer and fall making repairs and installing generators for electricity, a refrigerating plant, a water system, and new sewers. Seventeen houses were wired and streetlights installed. By November, seventy-four boys and girls occupied two large dormitories, and eleven elderly men and women resided in the nearby cottages. A grade school was maintained by four teachers.

There was still much to be done, however, including fencing the entire farm. Also lacking was a chapel. This need was satisfied in 1914 when the Masonic Order of the Eastern Star erected a Spanish-style brick chapel, which in addition to church services was used on occasion to show motion pictures.

That same year, a three-story brick dormitory was erected. Chores were expected to be performed by the children in the home; boys were required to milk three cows a day, in addition to other duties. When the Masonic board of control was unable to attend their annual meeting at the home because of impassible roads, the idea developed to change the location of the Masonic home. It was closed in 1922, some seventy-five children being transferred to a new site in Guthrie.[32]

In 1923 the state assumed ownership of the former agency and erected a hospital for drug addicts at the site. In the fall of 1924, a reporter had himself admitted to the institution as a patient in order to report on its operation. His articles contended that many of the inmates were there simply to receive daily doses of morphine or paregoric. Gov. Jack Walton and the Oklahoma Legislature were persuaded that the state could not afford to continue operation of the facility. A bill was passed closing the Darlington operation and transferring the patients to the Western Hospital for the Insane at Fort Supply.[33]

During the spring of 1925, M. M. Watson paid a nostalgic visit to the former Indian agency. As a young man he had often visited the agency as a stagecoach driver and as a teamster who sat astride a "wheeler" of an eight-mule team drawing three freight wagons on the Chisholm Trail. Eventually he became a state representative. On this occasion he was a legislator who had come to inspect the state home for drug addicts.[34]

It took Watson a few moments to get his bearings at the time-altered site. But gradually he began to recall the Indian lodges that dotted the Canadian valley as far as the eye could see, blanketed women smoking their old clay pipes, newborn babes peeking forth from their cradle boards, and tribal warriors dancing to the beat of drums.

Likewise, Mrs. Hattie Maurer, daughter of trader Neal Evans, recalled her childhood at Fort Reno—days she spent with her family picking wild daisies in the field, hearing the intermittent bugle calls that sounded across the North Canadian valley, viewing the colorful military dress parades, and enjoying evenings of entertainment with games, dances, and card parties.[35]

During the years 1926–32, Darlington found a new tenant in Wiley "Babe" Jones, who leased the area for the purpose of a horse farm. Jones purchased horses and resold them to Fort Reno to be trained for use by cavalry and artillery units. He also trained mounts as polo ponies to be used in matches at Fort Reno and elsewhere. Many of the animals were sold to polo clubs around the nation and in foreign countries.

With the old buildings untended and rapidly deteriorating, in 1933 the state legislature transferred the property to the Department of Wildlife Conservation.[36] The State Fish and Game Department began a program of raising bobwhite quail and other game birds, a program that was expanded when the Fourteenth Legislature deeded 125 acres of the property to the Game and Fish Department. W. A. Gaines served as superintendent for sixteen years. He was followed by George Wint, who instituted the first mass production of bobwhite quail through incubating eggs by artificial illumination, a procedure soon taken up by many national hatcheries. On Wint's retirement in 1973, Clarence Rex Brothers took over as foreman of the Darlington Game Farm until the state discontinued the program.[37]

During its twentieth-century existence, the physical features of the original Darlington agency were drastically altered. Most of the old wooden agency buildings were demolished, and though a few, including the stock barns, remain, the original plan of the Cheyenne/Arapaho agency is virtually undiscernible. The dominant buildings are the vacated Masonic Lodge and the Eastern Star chapel. In 1998 the state legislature transferred most of the Darlington property to Redlands College, assigning a strip of land along the north bank of the North Canadian River to the Oklahoma Historical Society.

On July 1, 1903, the Arapaho school at Darlington and the Cheyenne school at Caddo Springs were unified under the single superintendency of Maj. George W. H. Staunch. In 1906, Charles E. Shell became superintendent, and two years later the two schools were consolidated at Caddo Springs. In order to distinguish the school from the agency, the new Cheyenne/Arapaho school was renamed

Concho, the title being taken from the Spanish word for "shell," *concha*. In 1909, the original agency at Darlington was abandoned and the Cheyenne/Arapaho agency was moved to Caddo Springs, where it operated as the administrative center for tribal affairs, supervising Indian Trust lands in Canadian and three adjoining counties.[38]

The Concho school provided education for Indian children, including those from many other regions, at both the elementary and high school level. Operating under the platoon plan, the school provided boys training in dairying, farming, shop work, and sporting activities such as football, basketball, baseball, and track. The girls were instructed in various homemaking skills in addition to practice in music and athletics.

In late April 1911, the three-story frame building that housed some sixty-five boys and two large classrooms, in addition to school administrators and employees, burned to the ground.[39]

This and the competition of other Indian schools caused the Concho enrollment to dwindle. The Concho high school was closed in 1953, its students being transferred to El Reno; and in 1985 the entire school was moved to Anadarko. Today the Concho site is the administrative headquarters for the Cheyenne/Arapaho tribal government.[40]

Even today Fort Reno and the Darlington agency are moving toward fulfilling new purposes and serving new destinies. It appears this dual complex will continue to illuminate the historic past of Native American life, military service, frontier commerce, missionary dedication, and early settlement.

APPENDIX

FORT RENO MILITARY UNITS

1875—4th Cav., 2 cos.; 5th Inf., 2 cos.
1876—4th Cav., 2 cos.; 5th Inf., 2 cos., to Dec. 1876
1877—4th Cav., 2 cos.; 23d Inf., 2 cos., Jan.–May 1877
                16th Inf., 2 cos., June–Dec. 1877
1878—4th Cav., 2 cos.; 16th Inf., 2 cos.
1879—4th Cav., 2 cos.; 16th Inf., 2 cos.
1880—4th Cav., 2 cos.; 24th Inf., 2 cos.
                23d Inf., 1 co., Apr.–Dec. 1880
1881—4th Cav., 2 cos. to Nov. 1881, when replaced by 9th Cav.
        9th Cav., 2 cos.; 24th Inf., 1 co.; 2 cos., Oct. 1881
        23d Inf., 2 cos.
1882—9th Cav., 2 cos.; 23d Inf., 1 co.
                24th Inf., 2 cos., to May 1882
                20th Inf., 2 cos., May–Dec. 1882
1883—9th Cav., 2 cos.; 24th Inf., 1 co.
                20th Inf., 2 cos.
1884—9th Cav., 2 cos.; 24th Inf., 1 co.
                20th Inf., 2 cos.
1885—9th Cav., 2 cos., to June 1885
        5th Cav., 3 cos., replaced 9th Cav. in June 1885, enlarged to 4 cos. in Oct. 1885
        7th Cav., 1 co.
        24th Inf., 1 co.; 3 cos. as of Aug. 1885
        20th Inf., 2 cos., replaced by 18th Inf. as of July 1885
        18th Inf., 3 cos., Aug.–Sept. 1885
1886—5th Cav., 4 cos.; 24th Inf., 3 cos.; Indian scouts, 1 co.
1887—5th Cav., 4 cos.; 24th Inf., 2 cos.; Indian scouts, 1 co.
                13th Inf., 2 cos., replaced 24th Inf. as of Mar. 1887
1888—5th Cav., 4 cos.; 13th Inf., 2 cos.; Indian scouts, 1 co.
1889—5th Cav., 4 cos.; 13th Inf., 1 co.; Indian scouts, 1 co.
1890—5th Cav., 6 cos.; 13th Inf., 1 co.; Indian scouts, 1 co.
1891—5th Cav., 6 cos.; 13th Inf., 1 co.; 15 Indian scouts
1892—5th Cav., 6 cos., 13th Inf., 1 co.; 7 Indian scouts
1893—5th Cav., 6 cos., replaced by 3d Cav. as of June 1893
                13th Inf., 1 co.; 2 Indian scouts
      3d Cav., 7 cos., reduced to 4 cos. in Nov. 1893
1894—3rd Cav., 2 cos.; 13th Inf., 6 cos. to Oct. 1894
                10th Inf., 4 cos., as of Oct. 1894

1895—3d Cav., 2 cos., to Oct. 1895
    1st Cav., 4 cos., replaced 3d Cav. Oct. 1895
        10th Inf., 4 cos.
1896—1st Cav., 2 cos.; 10th Inf., 4 cos.
1897—1st Cav., 2 cos.; 10th Inf., 4 cos.
1898—1st Cav., 2 cos.; 10th Inf., 4 cos.—both to Mar. 1898.
    Spanish war created drastic reduction in garrison, leaving post under detachment of 10th Inf. caretakers.
1899—6th Cav., 2 cos.
1900—6th Cav., 1 co., to June 1900
    8th Cav., 1 co., as of June 1900
1901—8th Cav., 1 co., increased to 4 cos. during year.
1902—8th Cav. to May 1902—Cavalry presence ends at Fort Reno.
    22d Inf., 5 cos.; 25th Inf., 5 cos. as of Oct. 1892
1903—30th Inf., 2 cos.; 25th Inf., 4 cos.
1904—30th Inf., 2 cos.; 25th Inf., 4 cos.
1905—30th Inf., 2 cos.; 25th Inf., 4 cos.
1906—30th Inf., 2 cos.; 25th Inf., 4 cos.
1907—19th Inf., 1 battalion
1908—Post closed in Apr. 1908, caretaker detachment only
    9th Cav. and 25th Inf. were Afro-American units
    Post band operated 1887–97
    (Note—the above reflects a reading of the Fort Reno post returns. It does not agree entirely with a list included in a 1918 "History of Fort Reno, Okla.," Entry 2386, RG92, NARS, Fort Worth, Texas.)

FORT RENO COMMANDERS

(Per post returns 1876 to 1907)

*   General rank (*—Brig. Gen., **—Maj. Gen., ***—Lt. Gen., ****—Gen.)
#   Commanding General U.S. Army
MOH Medal of Honor
!   Brevet promotion for gallant and meritorious service
KIA   Killed in Action
WP   West Point

    ! Jeremiah P. Schindel (PA, 6th Inf.), first officer to command troops at the Cheyenne/Arapaho Agency
    **!!!!! Thomas Newton Neill (PA, WP, 6th Cav.), CO at the site of Fort Reno in 1874
    !!!! Wirt Davis (VA, 4th Cav.), CO at the site of Fort Reno in 1875
    !! Clarence Mauck (IN, 4th Cav.), first CO of Fort Reno, Feb. 1876 to Apr. 1876
    *!!! John Kemp Mizner (NY, WP, 4th Cav.), CO, July 1876 to Apr. 1880
    !! Henry Brevoort Bristol (MI, 5th Inf.), acting CO, June–July 1876
    **!!! John Joseph Coppinger (Ireland, 23d Inf.), acting CO, May–June 1877
    !! Joshua Stroud Fletcher (PA, 16th Inf.), acting CO, June–July 1877
    !!!!MOH Eugene Beauharnois Beaumont (PA, WP, 4th Cav.), acting CO,

Jan.–Feb. 1880
    *!!!!! George Morton Randall (PA, 23d Inf.), CO, Apr. 1880–Nov. 1882
    !! William Henry Clapp (OH, 16th Inf.), acting CO, Sept.–Nov. 1880
    Alfred Collins Markley (PA, 24th Inf.), acting CO, Oct.–Nov. 1881
    !! Frank Tracy Bennett (OH, 9th Cav.) acting CO, Aug.–Dec. 1882
    *! Henry Carroll (NY, 9th Cav.), acting CO, Dec. 1882–Feb. 1883
    ! Thomas Bull Dewees (PA, 9th Cav.), CO, Feb. 1883–May 1885
    *! Frederick Mortimer Crandal (PA, WP, 24th Inf.), acting CO, Jan.–Feb.
1885, May–June 1885
    Charles Oscar Bradley (NH, 20th Inf.), acting CO, Mar.–Apr. 1885
    *! Edwin Vose Sumner, the younger (PA, 5th Cav.), CO, June 1885–Aug. 1887
    *!!!! James Franklin Wade (OH, 5th Cav.), CO, Aug. 1887–June 1893
    !!!! Robert Hugh Montgomery (PA, 5th Cav.), acting CO, Sept. 1888
    Benjamin H. Rogers (RI, 13th Inf.), acting CO, Sept. 1888
    ! Gerald Russell (Ireland, 5th Cav.), acting CO, Apr.–May 1889, Apr. 1890
    Robert London (NC, WP, 5th Cav.), acting CO, Sept. 1889
    * Albert Emmett Woodson (KY, 5th Cav.), acting CO, Nov. 1890
    *MOH!!!!! Louis Henry Carpenter (NJ, 5th Cav.), acting CO, Aug.–Sept. 1892
    Philip Howard Ellis (MD, 13th Inf.), acting CO, June 1893
    *MOH!!!! Anson Mills (IN, WP, 3d Cav.), acting CO, June–July 1893
    *!! Edward P. Pearson (PA, 10th Inf.), CO, Oct. 1894–Apr. 1898
    *!!! George Augustus Purington (OH, 3d Cav.), acting CO, Aug. 1893
    ! Augustus Hudson Bainbridge (NY, 10th Inf.), acting CO, Sept. 1895,
July–Aug. 1896
    ! Gregory Barrett (MD, 10th Inf.), acting CO, Sept. 1896
    ! Richard Isaac Eskridge (MO, 10th Inf.), acting CO, July 1897
    John Henry Shollenberger (PA, WP, 10th Inf.), acting CO, Apr.–Sept. 1898
    Eli Alva Helmick (IN, WP, 10th Inf.), acting CO, Oct.–Dec. 1898
    ! Augustus Perry Blocksom (OH, WP, 6th Cav.), acting CO, Jan.–Apr. 1899,
Oct. 1899–Jan. 1900
    Thomas Michael Corcoran (MA, WP, 6th Cav.), CO, Mar. 1899–Feb. 1900
    George Smith Anderson (NJ, WP, 6th Cav.), acting CO, Apr.–June 1899
    Henry Benjamin Dixon (IA, WP, 8th Cav.) CO, June 1900–Apr. 1901
    David Alexander Lindsay (PA, 1st Inf.), acting CO, Jan.–Apr., 1901
    Walter Lawrence Reed (AZ, 10th Inf.), acting CO, Mar. 1901
    William Stanton (NY, 8th Cav.), CO, July 1901–June 1902
    * Louis Henry Rucker (IL, 8th Cav.), acting CO, Mar. 1902
    Richard Thompson Yeatman (OH, WP, 22d Inf.), acting CO, May 1902
    MOH Marion Perry Maus (MD, WP, 22d Inf.), acting CO, Aug. 1903
    Joseph M. T. Partello (OH, 23d Inf.), CO, Sept. 1903–Dec. 1905
    ! Hobart Whiteman Bailey (IN, 25th Inf.), CO or acting CO,
Mar. 1904–Jan. 1905
    William Ralph Abercrombie (MN, 30th Inf.), CO, Jan. 1906–Sept. 1906
    Charles Wilkinson Penrose (MI, 25th Inf.), acting CO, Oct.–Dec. 1906,
May 1907
    Edward Colby Carey (NM, WP, 3d Inf.), acting CO, Jan.–Mar. 1907
    Charles Bertody Stone Jr. (CA, 16th Inf.), acting CO, Apr. 1907
    James Buick Goe (OH, WP, 19th Inf.), CO, June–Oct. 1907

James Justice (TX, WP, 19th Inf.), acting CO, Nov.–Dec. 1907

Other temporary Fort Reno CO's include John B. Johnson, PA (Oct. 1893); Philip H. Ellis, MD (Oct. 1893); Charles G. Starr, IL, WP (Sept. 1902); Frank H. Albright, OH, WP (Nov. 1905); Edward S. Walton, LA (Feb. 1906); ____ Clarke (1906); #George C. Marshall, PA (July 1906); J. B. Corbly (Aug. 1906)

OTHER FORT RENO MEDAL OF HONOR WINNERS

!MOH Matthias Walter Day (OH, WP, 9th Cav.)
MOH William Preble Hall (MO, WP, 9th Cav.)
MOH Hugh Joslyn McGrath (WI, WP, 4th Cav.)
!MOH Wilber Elliott Wilder (MI, WP, 4th Cav.)

GENERALS ASSOCIATED WITH FORT RENO

****# Philip Henry Sheridan (OH, WP)
**!! Edward Hatch of Maine (IA)
***#!!MOH Nelson Appleton Miles (MA)
*! William Auman (PA)
* Theodore Anderson Baldwin (NJ)
*! Theodore Harvey Barrett (NY)
**!!!! John Wynn Davidson (VA, WP)
*!! Edward Mortimer (Jack) Hayes (NY)
**MOH!KIA Henry Ware Lawton (OH)
* Theodore Jonathon Wint (PA)
*** Hobart R. Gay

REMOUNT DEPOT COMMANDING OFFICERS

Capt. Letcher Hardeman, 1908–11; Capt. William P. Ennis, 1911; Capt. Leon B. Kroemer, 1912; Capt. William S. Valentine, 1912–15; Col. James N. Munro, 1915–17*; Maj. Alexander H. Jones, 1918–24; Maj. Henry J. Weeks, 1924–31; Col. James E. Shelley, 1931–36; Col. Edward M. Daniels, 1936–40; Col. Harry A. Fudge, 1943; Col. Paul H. Morris, 1943–44; Lt. Col. Crist C. Jones, 1944; Col. Frank L. Carr, 1946; Col. Ralph E. Ireland, 1946–47; Col. Carl M. Raguse, 1947; Maj. Leo Cooksey, 1947; Col. Norris M. L'Abbe, 1949; Maj. C. D. Ramsel, 1951; Maj. Fred Burke, 1951; Col. T. C. Wenzlaff, 1952; Col. Michael H. Zwicker, 1954.

* A history prepared under Maj. A. J. Jones in 1924 lists Munro as commanding June 6, 1915, through 1917, and Capt. William H. Clopton Jr., Nov. 1, 1915, to May 9, 1917. History of Fort Reno, Okla., RG92, Entry No. 2386, NARS, Fort Worth, Texas.

NOTES

ABBREVIATIONS

AGO	Adjutant General's Office
C/A	Cheyenne and Arapaho
CofIA	Commissioner of Indian Affairs
Dept./Mo.	Military Department of the Missouri
Dept./Tex.	Military Department of Texas
Div./Mo.	Military Division of the Missouri
NA	National Archives
OHS/AM	Oklahoma Historical Society, Division Archives and Manuscripts
OHS/LIB	Oklahoma Historical Society, Library
OIA	Office of Indian Affairs
OU/WHC	University of Oklahoma, Western History Collection
UCO/OC	University of Central Oklahoma, Oklahoma Collection

CHAPTER 1: AGENCY ON THE NORTH CANADIAN

1. Born in Fayette County, Pennsylvania, on December 3, 1804, Darlington married at the age of twenty-five and with his new wife, Martha, moved to Salem, Ohio. Two children, William and Anna, were produced by this marriage. (Darlington file, Thoburn Collection, OHS/AM.)

At Salem he became co-owner of a factory producing woolen goods. When a raging fire destroyed the plant, its machinery, and most of the raw wool, Darlington was wiped out financially. In an effort to start over again, the Darlingtons moved to Muscatine, Iowa Territory, where he served as county clerk. But, after five austere and lonely years away from their friends and family in Ohio, tragedy struck again.

Following a sudden three-day illness with scarlet fever, Martha died. Darlington, too, became deathly sick and barely survived. In 1849 he married again, this time to Mary Hall, who was a minister in the Quaker Society of Friends. A daughter named Sallie was born to this marriage before Mary also died in 1860. Still another wife, Lois Cook, whom he married in 1863, died within a few years. (Darlington, the Indian's Friend, Darlington file, Thoburn Collection, OHS/AM.)

2. Hoag to Parker, June 11, 1869, LR, OIA, Central Suptcy., NA.
3. Hazen to Sherman, June 30, 1869, LR, OIA, Central Suptcy., NA.
4. Hazen to Hoag, July 24, 1869, LR, OIA, Upper Arkansas Agency, NA.
5. Bonney to Elderkin, August 7, 1869, Camp Supply Letter Book, 16.
6. Carriker, *Fort Supply*, 35. A Quaker party that passed by Round Pond Creek in November noted the two unfinished, sod-covered log houses that had been left

by Darlington. Since the cabins had housed livestock for a time, the Quakers declined to use them for shelter. A large party of Osage Indians was camped across the creek from the site. The tribesmen, "many of them sturdy, rough-looking customers," crowded around the Quakers with a number of papers dating from 1812 to 1869, which they indicated they wished to have interpreted. The Quakers found this difficult to do, having to communicate by sign language; but in the interest of safety they supplied the Osages with some of their molasses, sugar, and coffee. *Friends' Review* 23 (January 15, 1870): 325.

7. Pepoon report, July 22, 1869, LR, OIA, Upper Arkansas Agency, NA.

8. Hoag to Parker, July 30, 1869, ibid.

9. Kappler, *Indian Treaties,* 839–41.

10. *Friends' Review* 23 (November 6, 1869): 161–63; Stanley Ltr., *Emporia News,* August 20, 1869.

11. *Friends' Review* 23 (November 6, 1869): 160–61; Annual Report, CofIA, 1869, 52–55. On August 21, Lt. Myron J. Amick was ordered to go to Pond Creek with scout Ben Clark and seventeen soldiers to protect the stores there until such time as they could be picked up. Ben Clark file, Camp Supply order, August 21, 1869, OU/WHC.

12. Darlington to Hoag, August 20, 1869, LR, OIA, Upper Arkansas Agency, NA; Hoag to Parker, September 3, 1869, ibid.; Darlington to Hoag, September 4, 1869, ibid.

13. Roe, *Army Letters from an Officer's Wife,* 73–74.

14. Darlington to Hoag, August 27, 1869, LR, OIA, Upper Arkansas Agency, NA; Hoag to Parker, November 5, 1869, ibid. See also Buntin, "Difficulties," 37–45.

15. Darlington Ltr., September 1, 1869, Issues file, C/A Agency, OHS/AM.

16. Darlington to Hoag, September 3, 1869, Issues file, C/A Agency, OHS/AM.

17. Bonney to Elderkin, September 8, 1869, Camp Supply Letterbook; Darlington to Hoag, September 17, 1869, LR, OIA, Upper Arkansas Agency, NA.

18. Bonney to Elderkin, September 19, 1869, Camp Supply Letterbook, 58.

19. Bonney to Morgan, October 1, 1869, Camp Supply Letterbook, 67.

20. Darlington to Hoag, November 6, 11, 1869, LR, OIA, Upper Arkansas Agency, NA.

21. Darlington to Hoag, March 1, 1871, C/A Letterbook, Gilcrease.

22. Orders, Camp Supply, March 29, 1870, LR, OIA, Upper Arkansas Agency, NA. During the spring of 1868, Rankin and a group surveying the Creek lands had been surrounded by a band of hostile Kiowas, Comanches, and Cheyennes while on the North Canadian. Rankin's attempt to pacify them with presents failed, and they were saved only when Jesse Chisholm came forth and remonstrated with the Indians for interfering with the men. Wortham to Taylor, June 27, 1868, LR, OIA, Creek Agency, NA. Despite his dismissal, Rankin was soon back at Camp Supply, his wagons loaded with trade goods. A detailed account of his 1871 trading visit to a Cheyenne camp appears in the March 9, 10, and 11, 1872, *Kansas Daily Tribune.*

23. Ibid., April 12, 1870.

24. Ibid., April 13, 1870. Neighbors removed the Comanches and other Texas Indians to the Indian Territory in 1859. He was killed from ambush by a Texas renegade soon afterward.

25. Ibid.

26. "Account of Meeting between Quakers and Indians, April 22, 1870," LR, OIA, Central Suptcy., NA.

27. Carriker, *Fort Supply*, 45–46.

28. Ridings, *The Chisholm Trail*, 148–49.

29. Darlington to Hoag, February 9, 1871, C/A Letterbook, Gilcrease.

30. Report to Nicholson, July 17, 1871, Agents and Agency file, C/A Agency, OHS/AM.

31. Darlington to Hoag, January 15, 1872, Agents and Agency file, C/A Agency, OHS/AM.

32. Darlington to Hoag, July 15, 1871, Employees file, C/A Agency, OHS/AM; Nicholson, "Tour of Indian Agencies," 347; Berthrong, *Southern Cheyennes*, 352. Smith had served as official U.S. interpreter at the Treaty of Fort Laramie in 1851, Treaty of Fort Wise in 1861, Treaty of Little Arkansas in 1865, and Treaty of Medicine Lodge in 1767. See Hoig, *Western Odyssey of John Simpson Smith*. Guerrier, the son of a French trader and a Cheyenne woman, had a long association with the tribes. He had been at Sand Creek when the Cheyennes were attacked by Chivington in 1864 and served as a guide for Custer on numerous occasions. He is the namesake of Geary, Oklahoma.

33. Collins, "Edwin Williams, Engineer," 331–47. Evidently Rankin installed a sawmill before that of Williams. The trader wrote to Hoag well before Darlington moved to the site of the new agency, saying: "The saw mill brought to this place by me has been set up and put in running order and is now sawing lumber for the purpose of building a store house for storing Indian goods . . . the ground is frozen . . . shall have men framing a house in a few days." Rankin to Hoag, LR, OIA, Upper Arkansas Agency, January 28, 1870. The existence of Rankin's sawmill finds support in a letter written by S. N. Wood from Fort Sill on January 31, 1871. Wood writes: "There is a saw mill on the North Fork and another here, but none on the Washita" (*Kansas Daily Tribune*, February 10, 1871).

34. Collins, "Edwin Williams, Engineer," 346.

35. Darlington to Hoag, Upper Arkansas Agency, January 23, 27, 1871.

36. Davidson to AAG, Dept./Mo., March 15, 1871, LR, OIA, Upper Arkansas Agency, NA.

37. Darlington to Hoag, April 4, 1871, C/A Letterbook, Gilcrease.

38. Darlington to Hoag, April 1, 6, 16, 1871, LR, OIA, Central Suptcy., NA.

39. Schindel to Davidson, March 22, 1871, ibid.

40. *Kansas Daily Tribune*, March 9, 1871.

41. Darlington to Hoag, April 25, 29, 1871, C/A Letterbook, Gilcrease; Seger, *Early Days*, 4. Still another visitor to the territory in early 1871 added to the description: "On the North Fork of the Canadian we stopped at the Cheyenne and Arapaho Agency and found some old friends and acquaintances; also several "big chiefs" of the Cheyenne and Arapaho tribes. Most the tribes, however, were on a buffalo hunt. Agent Darlington seems to be succeeding well with these Indians. Jesse Townsend and wife have started a school here, and much interest and a desire to learn is manifested by the young Indians" (*Kansas Daily Tribune*, February 16, 1871).

42. McConnell, *Five Years a Cavalryman*, 249.

43. Darlington to Hoag, May 4, 1871, LR, Central Agency, OIA, NA.

44. Darlington to Hoag, July 15, 1871, Agents and Agency file, C/A Agency, OHS/AM.
45. *Emporia News,* December 1, 1871.
46. *History of Canadian County,* 12.
47. *Friends' Review* 25 (June 29, 1872): 707.

CHAPTER 2: CATTLE, COMMERCE, AND CONFLICT

1. *Kansas Daily Tribune,* April 22, 1871.
2. McCoy, *Historic Sketches,* 148–49, 190, 201. Generally overlooked in accounts of Chisholm Trail activity were the Texas mustangs that were driven over the trail to Kansas markets. A report in May 1882 listed eleven herds of cattle, for a total of 8,986 head for the year to that date. But also there were seventeen drovers who had brought up some 5,500 head of mustangs. *Cheyenne Transporter,* May 10, 1882.
3. *Kansas Daily Tribune,* September 17, 1869.
4. Seger, *Early Days,* 5. With the arrival of Miles came new staff members. Joshua Trueblood and his wife, Matilda, were hired as teachers, and Trueblood's widowed sister as matron. Joseph Hoag was brought on as head farmer for the agency; Tom George as government carpenter; William Darlington, son of the former agent, as engineer and sawmill operator; and John H. Seger as a general handyman. Ibid, 7–9.
5. Miles to Hoag, June 4, 1872, LR, OIA, Central Suptcy., NA.
6. The agency at that time was still known as the "Upper Arkansas Agency." Alvord pointed out that this was no longer appropriate and the name should be the "Cheyenne and Arapaho Agency." Alvord, *Report of Special Commissioners,* 6.
7. Ibid., 6–9.
8. Miles to Hoag, January 1, 1873, C/A Letterbook, Gilcrease.
9. *Emporia News,* September 27, 1871; *Kansas Daily Tribune,* October 19, 1873.
10. Berthrong, *Ordeal,* 373. Another contractor was Theodore H. Barrett. Womack, *Norman,* 11; *Emporia News,* September 29, 1871.
11. Reports, March 6, 18, 19, 1873, LR, Dept./Mo., RG393, NA. Berthrong, 375, citing Miles to Hoag, March 15, 1873, LR, OIA, Central Suptcy, NA; Brooke to AAG, Dept./Mo., March 15, April 4, 1873, Ltrs. Sent, Fort Supply.
12. Ibid., February 13, 1873.
13. Ibid., March 27, 1873.
14. This was the Lee and Reynolds ranche for a time. When freighter Oliver Nelson passed it in 1880, it was run by a man named Chapin. Nelson described it as a twelve-by-fourteen log house with a dirt roof and dirt floor, one door facing west and one-sash windows to the north and south. The station featured a pole corral and a grass-covered shed for a stable. Nelson, *Cowman's Southwest,* 49.
15. *Caldwell Commercial,* May 27, 1880, lists the distances from Caldwell to Pole Cat as twelve miles; to Pond Creek, fourteen; to Skeleton twenty-one; to Buffalo Springs, sixteen; to Haines ranche, eight; to Little Turkey Creek, four; to Red Fork, four; to Kingfisher, ten; to the Cheyenne agency, twenty-one; to Fort Reno, two. Laban S. Records in *Cherokee Outlet Cowboy,* 200–208, provides a good description of stage coach travel on the route.
16. Barker, *Fort Reno,* 14.

17. *Caldwell Commercial*, May 1, 1873.

18. *Wichita Eagle*, April 10, 1891.

19. Ibid., July 10, 1873.

20. Miles to Hoag, June 13, 1873, OIA, Central Suptcy., NA.

21. Miles to Hoag, December 7, 9, 1873, ibid.

22. Berthrong, *Ordeal*, 373.

23. Nelson, *Cowman's Southwest*, 189.

24. *History of Canadian County*, 12; Darlington Agency File, Thoburn Collection, OHS/AM.

25. Rister, "Significance of Destruction of the Buffalo," *Southwest Historical Quarterly* 33 (July 1929): 43, 47; *Emporia News*, November 28, 1872.

CHAPTER 3: BIRTH OF FORT RENO

1. *Kansas Daily Tribune*, October 19, 1873.

2. Pratt, *Battlefield and Classroom*, 104 n. 2.

3. J. Holloway Ltr., July 21, 1874, June 3, 1875, El Reno Carnegie Library.

4. Ibid.; Collins, "Edwin Williams, Engineer," 342–43; *Kansas Daily Tribune*, July 6, 1876.

5. *Kansas Daily Tribune*, August 9, 1874.

6. Berthrong, *Southern Cheyennes*, 386–87.

7. These included Sarah Darlington Covington, Amach Covington, William Malaley. Darlington file, Thoburn Collection, OHS/AM.

8. Miles to Smith, July 7, 1874, *The Friend*, August 8, 1874, 403.

9. B. K. Wetherell letter, July 4, 1874, to Enoch Hoag, Kiowa Depredations file, Indian Archives, OHS; Annual Report, CofIA, 1874, 234. Miles to Smith, *Kansas Daily Tribune*, July 8, 1874.

10. Ibid.

11. Wire, Pope to Murdock, et al., July 10, 1874, *Wichita Eagle*, July 16, 1874.

12. Barker, *Burials in the Fort Reno Cemetery*, preface, citing Fort Reno Record of Events.

13. *Emporia News*, July 3, 1874.

14. Ibid., July 24, 1874.

15. Ibid., July 31, 1874.

16. Berthrong, *Southern Cheyennes*, 389.

17. *Emporia News*, October 2, 1874.

18. Wright, "Fort Reno," 4, citing *Annual Report, Sec. of War, 1874*, 70–71. Neill, a native of Pennsylvania, graduated from West Point in 1843, winning five brevet promotions to the rank of major general of Pennsylvania volunteers. Heitman, *Historical Register*, 1:742.

19. *Kansas Daily Tribune*, July 18, 1874.

20. Davidson to AAG, Dept./Tex., August 27, 1874, LR, OIA, Wichita Agency, NA; report of T. Connell, *Leavenworth Times*, September 8, 1874.

21. *Kansas Daily Tribune*, November 13, 29, 1874.

22. *Leavenworth Times*, September 8, 1874.

23. Berthrong, *Southern Cheyennes*, 390; *Annual Report, Sec. of War, 1874*, 26–29.

240 NOTES TO PAGES 29–37

24. Miles to Pope, September 17, 1874, Div./Mo., Special File, NA; *Leavenworth Times,* September 22, 1874.

25. Rucker, "Amos Chapman—Hero of Buffalo Wallow," *Daily Oklahoman,* April 14, 1929. Chapman was awarded a medal by the army for his heroic effort in trying to save a dying soldier at Buffalo Wallow. He died in 1925 and was buried four miles east of Seiling, Oklahoma.

26. Mackenzie to AAG, Dept./Tex., October 12, 29, November 9, 1874, LR, AGO (Main Series), Roll 159, NA.

27. *Leavenworth Times,* November 25, 1874.

28. Darlington report, March 5, 1875, *Leavenworth Times,* March 14, 1875.

29. Neill to AAG, Dept./Mo., October 2, 4, 1874, LR, AGO (Main Series), Roll 159, NA; *Kansas Daily Tribune,* October 7, 1874.

30. *Leavenworth Times,* October 16, 1874.

31. Neill to AAG, Dept./Mo., October 27, 1874, cited by *El Reno Times,* July 23, 1957.

32. *Leavenworth Times,* October 16, 1874.

33. *Kansas Daily Tribune,* November 29, 1874; Berthrong, *Southern Cheyennes,* 394; Miles to Smith, October 28, LR, OIA, Upper Arkansas Agency, NA.

34. Berthrong, *Southern Cheyennes,* 393.

35. Sheridan to AAG, November 17, 1874, Ltrs. Sent, Dept./Mo., NA; *Leavenworth Times,* November 25, 1874; Baldwin, *Memoirs,* 5; Haywood, *Trails South,* 53.

36. *Leavenworth Times,* December 27, 1874.

37. Neill to AAG, Dept./Mo., March 7, 1875, LR, Dept./Mo., NA.

38. Ibid.; Berthrong, *Southern Cheyennes,* 400; Darlington Agency file, Thoburn Papers, OHS/AM.

39. *Leavenworth Times,* March 11, May 19, July 23, 1875.

40. Most authorities say it was Black Horse who was killed. Acting agent J. A. Covington, however, states that another Cheyenne was the victim. Covington to Smith, April 7, April 10, 1875, LR, OIA, Berthrong Collection, OU/WHC. See also *Wichita Eagle,* April 15, 1875; Annual Report, CofIA, 1875, 269; *Annual Report, Sec. of War, 1875,* 87–88.

41. Neill to Williams, April 7, 1875, LR, Dept./Mo., NA.

42. *Wichita Eagle,* April 15, 1875; Wright, "Fort Reno," 7, citing *Annual Report, Sec. of War, 1875,* 86–87; Annual Report, CofIA, 1875, 269.

43. Barker, *Burials in the Fort Reno Cemetery,* 4.

44. Covington to Smith, April 4, 1875, Berthrong Collection, Folder 38, OU/WHC.

45. Peery, "The Indians' Friend," 861.

46. Ibid., 589, 861.

47. Henley report, April 24, 1875; *Leavenworth Times,* April 25, 1975.

48. Miles to Smith, April 22, 1875, LR, Cheyenne agency, OIA, NA, Berthrong Collection, Box 5, Folder 37.

49. *Leavenworth Times,* March 14, April 15, 1875.

50. Ibid., May 9, 1875; Pratt, *Battlefield and Classroom,* 107–8, 138–40.

CHAPTER 4: AN INTERIM OF TRANQUILITY

1. Miles said that Wint came to his office and asked him to help select a site. Fort Reno file, C/A Agency, OHS/AM.

2. Collins, "Edwin Williams," 346.

3. *El Reno Democrat,* December 19, 1912.

4. Miles letter, undated, Fort Reno file, C/A Agency, OHS/AM.

5. Hensley, "A Little Metal Check," Neil Evans file, Fort Sill Museum.

6. *Outline Descriptions of the Posts in the Division of the Missouri,* U.S. Army. Mil. Div. of the Missouri, 1876.

7. Post Returns, Fort Reno, February 1876, OHS/LIB. A native of Indiana, Mauck had won brevet commendations during the Civil War for action during the Battle of Stone River, Tennessee, and with Sherman's Atlanta campaign. Heitman, *Historical Register,* 1:697.

8. Wright, "Fort Reno," 16–17.

9. Ibid., 25.

10. *Army and Navy Journal* 14 (November 18, 1876): 229.

11. *Kansas Daily Tribune,* November 23, 1876.

12. Mothershead, "Journal of Ado Hunnius," 456.

13. Ibid., 458. Hunnius does not mention Bull Foot Station. When freighter Oliver Nelson passed by in 1880, he found it burned to the ground. Hennessey's grave was lined with sandstone rocks turned on edge. Nelson, *Cowman's Southwest,* 37.

14. Mothershead, "Journal of Ado Hunnius," 460.

15. McConnell, *Five Years a Cavalryman,* 249.

16. Mothershead, "Journal of Ado Hunnius," 461–62.

17. Ibid., 462.

18. Berthrong, *Ordeal,* 78–79.

19. *Cheyenne Transporter,* November, 26, 1880, January 25, 1881; Rex Brothers, manuscript (personal copy), 7, citing "A History of Concho" by Mrs. Ruth P. Eichor's group of C/A Indian School, 1937.

20. *Arkansas City Traveler,* May 10, 1876.

21. *Wichita Eagle,* April 6, 1876.

22. *Arkansas City Traveler,* July 5, 1876.

23. *Wichita Eagle,* January 6, 1876.

24. *Arkansas City Traveler,* February 2, 1876.

25. Ibid., June 21, 1876.

26. Ibid., April 11, 1877; May 21, 1879.

27. Mizner to Remington, July 29, 1876, Fort Supply papers, UCO/OC; Berthrong, *Ordeal,* 25.

28. *Arkansas City Traveler,* 33.

29. *Wichita Eagle,* November 9, 1876.

30. *Arkansas City Traveler,* November, 15, 1876.

31. *Friends' Review,* December 9, 1876, 262–63.

32. *Kansas Daily Tribune,* January 19, 1877.

33. Ibid., January 19, 1877.

34. Ibid.

35. *Wichita Eagle,* August 2, 1877.
36. *Arkansas City Traveler,* February 21, 1877.
37. Ibid., May 9, 30, 1877.
38. Berthrong, *Ordeal,* 61.

Chapter 5: Cousins from the North

1. Berthrong, *Ordeal,* 25–26.
2. *Wichita Eagle,* August 31, 1876.
3. Post Returns, Fort Reno, January 1877, OHS/LIB; Grinnell, *Fighting Cheyennes,* 365.
4. U.S. Senate, *Report on Removal,* 54, 111; Covington, "Causes of the Dull Knife Raid," 15.
5. Mizner to AAG, Dept./Mo., August 8, 1878, *Annual Report, Sec. of War, 1878,* 51; U.S. Senate, *Report on Removal,* 55.
6. Berthrong, *Ordeal,* 37.
7. U.S. Senate, *Report on Removal,* 58.
8. Ibid., 58; Annual Report, CofIA, 1877, 85.
9. Miles to Mizner, September 20, 1878, *Annual Report, Sec. of War, 1878,* 49.
10. Stubbs to Miles, July 12, 1877, LR, OIA, C/A Agency, NA; Mizner to AAG, Dept./Mo., September 19, 1878, LR, AGO (Main Series), NA; Morrison, *Military Posts and Camps in Oklahoma,* 148–49.
11. Gunther to Adj., Fort Reno, December 4, 1877, LR, OIA, C/A Agency, NA.
12. Covington to Hoyt, January 6, 1878, LR, OIA, C/A Agency, NA.
13. Mizner to AAG, Dept./Mo., September 19, 1878, *Annual Report, Sec. of War, 1878,* 46–47.
14. Lawton report, September 27, 1877, LR, OIA, C/A Agency, NA. Lawton was present when rations were being issued, and the Indians contended that they were getting more rations when he was looking on. Supplement to Sheridan Report of 1878, Papers Relating to Military Operations.
15. Covington, "Causes of the Dull Knife Raid," 19, citing U.S. Senate, *Report on Removal,* 83; Berthrong, *Ordeal,* 30–31, citing Lawton to Adj., 4th Cav., Fort Sill, IT, September 13, 1877 (Copy), LR, C/A Agency, NA.
16. U.S. Senate, *Report on Removal,* 59.
17. Berthrong, *Ordeal,* 32, citing McCusker to Hoyt, October 31, 1877, LR, C/A Agency, NA.
18. Annual Report, CofIA, 1877, 83; *Cheyenne Transporter,* May 10, 1881.
19. Annual Report, CofIA, 1878, 57.
20. March 3, 1878.
21. *Dodge City Times,* February 16, 1878.
22. *Wichita Eagle,* April 25, 1878.
23. Annual Report, CofIA, 1877, 85; Wright, "The Pursuit of Dull Knife," 142; Annual Report, CofIA, 1878, 55.
24. *Army and Navy Journal* 15 (April 27, 1878).
25. Miles to Nicholson, September 21, 1878, *Friend,* November 2, 1878, 90.
26. Annual Report, CofIA, 1879, 58.
27. U.S. Senate, *Report on Removal,* 60–61.

28. Ibid., 111; Mizner to AAG, Dept./Mo., September 5, 1878, *Annual Report, Sec. of War, 1878; Army and Navy Journal* 16 (October 12, 1878): 150. Rendlebrock, Wirt Davis, and Sebastian Gunther, serving together in the Fourth Cavalry during the Civil War, each received brevet promotion recommendations for their pursuit of the rebels under Hood during the battle of Nashville, Tennessee. *Rebellion Records* 49, pt. 1, 400–401.

29. U.S. Senate, *Report on Removal*, 113, 148; *Annual Report, Sec. of War, 1878*, 44–45.

30. Ibid., 106–7.

31. Ibid., 62; Annual Report, CofIA, 1878, 54–57.

32. Mizner to AAG, Dept./Mo., September 18, 1878, *Annual Report, Sec. of War, 1878*, 44–45.

33. "Proceedings of Board of Officers," January 21, 1869, LR, AGO (Main Series), NA.

34. Miles to Hoyt, September 10, 1878, Ltrs., Recd., OIA, C/A Agency, NA. In withdrawing from the other Northern Cheyennes, American Horse lost nearly all of his property.

35. U.S. Senate, *Report on Removal*, 112; SO 118, Fort Reno, September 5, 1878.

36. *Leavenworth Times,* September 12, 1875. Ben Clark was told by an old Northern Cheyenne woman, who with her teenage son had been left behind at the South Platte, that a few Southern Cheyennes were among the Northern Cheyenne party. Clark to Whipple, October 16, 1878, Papers Relating to Military Operations, LR, AGO (Main Series), NA.

37. U.S. Senate, *Report on Removal*, 135, 145; Annual Report, CofIA, 1877, 40.

CHAPTER 6: PURSUIT OF THE NORTHERN CHEYENNES

1. Fort Reno letter, September 11, 1878, *Leavenworth Times,* September 12, 1878. E. A. Bode in *A Dose of Frontier Soldiering*, 34–35, states that he and a detail of sixteen infantrymen from Fort Sill constructed a telegraph line from that fort to Fort Reno in June 1878.

2. *Cherokee Advocate,* October 19, 1878.

3. Pope to Sheridan, September 12, 1878, LR, AGO (Main Series), NA.

4. Rendlebrock to Hatch, December 12, 1878, LR, Dept./Mo., NA. A Fort Reno dispatch states that news of the Turkey Springs fight was brought back to Fort Reno by a Cheyenne scout named Yellow Bear. Yellow Bear was an Arapaho chief. *Leavenworth Times,* September 25, 1878.

5. Rendlebrock to Hatch, December 12, 1878, LR, Dept./Mo., NA.

6. Ibid. In a newspaper interview he said that one of his officers counted 130 warriors. *New York Herald,* October 21, 1878.

7. Ives, "Battle of Turkey Springs," 60.

8. Colcord, *Autobiography*, 73–74.

9. Gunther's testimony, U.S. Senate, *Report on Removal*, 148. The most accurate report places the battle site near Turkey Springs at the head of present Anderson Creek, some forty to fifty miles northeast of Camp Supply. This would be some twelve miles west of present Alva and nine miles north of Freedom on the ranch of Mr. and Mrs. DeWayne Hodgson. A roadside marker was erected on

244   NOTES TO PAGES 66–72

State Highway 64 by the Oklahoma Historical Society in 1978 with the able
research assistance of the Cherokee Strip Volunteer League of Alva. A fenced sandstone marker for the cowboy salt haulers stands a few miles to the northwest.

10. Grinnell, *Fighting Cheyennes,* 404.

11. Gunther's testimony, U.S. Senate, *Report on Removal,* 148; Miles to Hoyt,
September 19, 1878, LR, OIA, C/A Agency, NA.

12. Gunther to Hatch, November 22, 1878, LR, Dept./Mo., NA. The name of
the Company H private is not clear on the Fort Reno returns for October 1878. It
appears to read "Strnad," but his tombstone at Fort Reno reads "Straud." A grave
marker also exists in the Fort Reno cemetery for Lynch. It is not known if their
bodies were recovered and reburied at Fort Reno or if their tombstones are merely
memorials.

13. Wood to Hatch, November 22, 1878, LR, Dept./Mo., NA.

14. Chalk remained in the post hospital at Camp Supply for some time, eventually returning to Fort Reno, where he died in 1881 and was buried in the post
cemetery.

15. Wilder's testimony, U.S. Senate, *Report on Removal,* 128. See also
Berthrong, *Ordeal,* 34, citing LR, C/A Agency, Miles to Hayt, September 19, 1878,
P. H. Sheridan to Crook, September 19, 1978 (telegrams); Carriker, *Fort Supply,*
123–24, citing *Army and Navy Journal* 16 (October 12, 1878): 150; Hambright to CO,
Fort Elliott, September 16, 18, 1878, Fort Supply LS, Vol. 29.

16. Wilder's testimony, U.S. Senate, *Report on Removal,* 128–29.

17. *Leavenworth Times,* September 21, 26, 1878.

18. Morse to Keefe, September 27, 1878, Campbell Collection, OU/WHC;
McNeal, *When Kansas Was Young,* 88; Statement of Col. W. E. Iliff in "Heat
Was One Cause of Comanches' [Cheyennes'] Flight North," *Daily Oklahoman,*
July 21, 1929.

19. Wilder's testimony, U.S. Senate, *Report on Removal,* 129.

20. Rendlebrock interview, *New York Herald,* October 21, 1878.

21. Morse to Keefe, September 27, 1878, Campbell Collection, OU/WHC.

22. *Leavenworth Times,* October 1, 1878; Carriker, *Fort Supply,* 120–28; Wright,
"Fort Reno," 41–59. In 1862 Lewis won a brevet promotion at Apache Canyon, New
Mexico, and another for his action in the Battle of Peralta, New Mexico. Colton,
Civil War in the Western Territories, 48, 78; Heitman, *Historical Register,* 1:630.

23. Lewis to AAG, Dept./Mo., September, 15, 1878, Papers Relating to Military
Operations, LR, AGO (Main Series), NA; *Leavenworth Times,* September 20, 1878.
This letter, which also appeared in other newspapers, was stoutly refuted by Miles,
who insisted that the Northern Cheyennes were getting their beef issues regularly.
Mizner supported this, but said the problem was that some families got much
poorer cows than others. U.S. Senate, *Report on Removal,* 59, 124–25.

24. According to the Cheyennes, this stream was so named long before the
whites arrived. It was here that a Cheyenne woman who had committed adultery
was given up to all of the band by the Dog Soldiers as punishment. Afterward, the
tribe would wait until they arrived at the stream to chastise any woman guilty of
infidelity. Creel, Cheyenne Grammar and Ethnology, Book A, Gilcrease.

25. Peters, *Indian Battles and Skirmishes,* 81.

26. Clark to Whipple, October 16, 1878, Papers Relating to Military Operations,
LR, AGO (Main Series), NA.

27. U.S. Senate, *Report on Removal,* 139; Berthrong, *Ordeal,* 37.

28. Carroll, *Papers of the Order of Indian Wars,* 91.

29. *Leavenworth Times,* December 19, 1878; Collins, *The Indians' Last Fight,* 316–19.

30. Special Order 79, Hqs., Div./Mo., September 30, 1878, LR, C/A Agency, NA; Journal of Lieut. Creel, Gilcrease.

31. *Calumet Chieftain,* July 28, 1932.

32. *New York Herald,* October 21, 1878.

33. Ibid.

34. Wright, "Fort Reno," 60–62.

35. Chalfant, *Cheyennes and Horse Soldiers,* 290. While Gunther was in escort of a band of Northern Cheyennes on a futile buffalo hunt during 1878, an old warrior recounted the Solomon River fight, drawing in the sand a map of the rivers, tributaries, forts, Sumner's march, and the battle action.

36. Wright, "Fort Reno," 60–61, citing Camp Supply Post Returns, December 1878, February, March, April 1879 and *Army and Navy Journal* 16 (April 12, 1879): 884.

37. U.S. Senate, *Report on Removal,* 58–59, 112, 127.

38. *Army and Navy Journal* 12 (October 26, 1878): 185.

39. Covington, "Causes of the Dull Knife Raid," 21.

40. Grinnell, *Fighting Cheyennes,* 418–27. See also Report of Lieutenant Colonel Van Voast, October 29, 1878, Campbell Collection, OU/WHC.

41. *New York Times,* October 27, 1878, March 29, 31, 1879.

42. Berthrong, *Ordeal,* 40–41; *Wichita Eagle,* July 3, 1879; *Wichita Beacon,* October 22, 1879. The Cheyennes were first sent to Dodge City, where their photo was taken on the steps of the Ford County courthouse. Appearing in the picture is interpreter George Reynolds, son of stage entrepreneur P. G. Reynolds and nephew of Kansas/Oklahoma Territory newspaperman Milton W. Reynolds. Haywood, *Trails South,* 168.

CHAPTER 7: FORT RENO AND THE OKLAHOMA BOOM

1. *Wichita Eagle,* October 3, 1878.

2. Report of Lieutenant Colonel Van Voast, October 29, 1878, Campbell Collection, OU/WHC.

3. Powers, "The Kansas Indian Claims Commission of 1879," 202, 205, 210.

4. Kime, "Indian Territory Journals" (manuscript pending publication at OU Press).

5. Carriker, *Fort Supply,* 130, citing Fort Supply post returns, January 1879; Keeling, "My Experiences," 70. Gen. Jefferson Columbus Davis of Indiana, a much-decorated Union general, is not to be confused with Jefferson Davis, U.S. secretary of war and president of the Confederate States.

6. Pope to Sheridan, December 26, 1878, LR, AGO (Main Series), NA.

7. Keeling, "My Experiences," 70; Carriker, *Fort Supply,* 130; Carter, *Dian Takes to the Indians,* 51.

8. *Friends' Review* 33 (October 4, 1879).

9. *Cheyenne Transporter*, September 10, 1881; Heitman, *Historical Register*, 1:815.

10. *Cheyenne Transporter*, March 10, October 25, December 10, 1881; February 25, 1882. Henry Keeling said that the poles of the telegraph line were sections of iron pipe that became rusted and broke off. Settlers would later run into the stumps with their plows. Keeling, "My Experiences," 73.

11. Keeling, "My Experiences," 61.

12. Ibid., 61.

13. Ibid., 67.

14. See U.S. Senate, *Report on Removal*.

15. McKeever to Clark, September 5, 1881; Berthrong, *Ordeal*, 43.

16. Sweeney to Post Adjutant, Fort Reno, May 21, 1879, and Coppinger letter, May 28, 1879, Box 427H, Papers Relating to Intrusion by Unauthorized Persons into I.T., RG393, NA.

17. Sherman to Sheridan, May 7, 1879; Platt to AAG, Ft. Leavenworth, May 7, 1879, "Files Relating to Military Operations in the Indian Territory," M-1495, Roll 10, NA.

18. President's Proclamation, *Wichita Eagle*, February 19, 1880.

19. Gale report, May 17, 1880, LR, AGO (Main Series), NA; *Caldwell Post*, May 20, 1880; *Caldwell Commercial*, May 27, 1880.

20. Whipple to AGO, July 16, 1880, LR, AGO (Main Series), NA.

21. Gale report, April 13, 1880, ibid.

22. *Wichita Eagle*, July 22, 1880.

23. *Cheyenne Transporter*, November 26, 1880.

24. December 24, 1880.

25. Hoig, *David L. Payne*, 105.

26. *Cheyenne Transporter*, January 10, 1881, citing the *Commercial*.

27. Kime, "Indian Territory Journals."

28. *Cheyenne Transporter*, August 22, 1880; Dyer, *Fort Reno*, 192.

29. Hancock, "William Box Hancock," 365. Hancock was down and out when he arrived at Fort Reno, having lost all his food while crossing the flooded Canadian. Randall willingly supplied him food without charge, saying that "a frontier post always supplied people who were in trouble."

30. Keeling, "My Experiences," 67–68.

31. *Cheyenne Transporter*, June 25, 1882.

32. *Army and Navy Journal* 18 (January 23, 1881): 499.

33. *Army and Navy Journal* 18 (March 26, 1881): 699.

34. *Cheyenne Transporter*, March 1, 1881.

35. Ibid., May 25, 1881. Oliver Nelson in his book *Cowman's Southwest*, 252–53, relates an incident in 1885 when a stage driver was dared by an English passenger to cross the flooded Wolf Creek at the Buzzard's Roost (Little Wolf Creek) station just east of present Gage, Oklahoma. The stage was swamped, it and the horses were washed downriver, and the Englishman drowned.

36. Shirk, "Military Duty," 122–23.

37. *Cheyenne Transporter*, June 25, 1881. Pendleton, who served under Major Randall, said that the commanding officer and Wild Hog were good friends, the latter being "very serviceable" to Randall during the trouble with Mad Wolf. Shirk, "Military Duty," 123.

38. Mizner to AAG, Dept./Mo., June 25, 1879, LR, Dept./Mo., NA.

39. Berthrong, *Ordeal,* 38.

40. Ibid., 42.

41. Ben Clark papers, OU/WHC; Berthrong, *Ordeal,* 46–47, 70–71. The remainder of the Northern Cheyennes would follow in July 1883.

42. *Cheyenne Transporter,* November 10, 1881.

43. Ibid., December 26, 1881; Annual Report, CofIA, 1883, 30.

44. Hoig, *David L. Payne,* 115.

45. Pope to Sheridan, May 23, 1882, LR, AGO (Main Series), NA.

46. *Cheyenne Transporter,* July 10, 1882.

47. Ibid.

48. Ibid.

49. Pope to Sheridan, May 23, 1882, LR, AGO (Main Series), NA; ibid., Chandler letter, July 24, 1882.

CHAPTER 8: A FADING FRONTIER

1. *Cheyenne Transporter,* October 25, 1882.

2. Ibid., June 25, 1882.

3. Fort Reno Post Returns, October 1881–December 1882; Heitman, *Historical Register,* 1:211, 286, 689.

4. Ibid.; Wright, "Fort Reno," 72–73.

5. Stevens to AAG, August 4, 1883, LR, OIA, C/A Agency, NA.

6. *Cheyenne Transporter,* June 10, 1882.

7. Ibid., May 10, 1882.

8. Major Drumm, a native of Ohio, located his "U" brand on some 150,000 acres near present Cherokee, Oklahoma. L. Records, *Cherokee Outlet Cowboy,* 301.

9. *Cheyenne Transporter,* May 10, September 11, December 26, 1882; March 12, 1883.

10. *Arkansas City Traveler,* January 17, 1883; McCallum, *The Wire That Fenced the West,* 168–70.

11. *Cheyenne Transporter,* February 26, 1883.

12. Ibid., June 27; *Arkansas City Traveler,* September 19, 1883.

13. *Cheyenne Transporter,* March 25, 1882; *Wichita Eagle,* March 30, 1882.

14. *Cheyenne Transporter,* September 26, 1882; Barker, *Fort Reno,* 18–19; *Arkansas City Traveler,* August 22, 1883.

15. Nelson, *Cowman's Southwest,* 188–89.

16. *Cheyenne Transporter,* April 10, 1882; *Wichita Eagle,* March 30, April 13, 1882.

17. *Cheyenne Transporter,* May 10, 1882.

18. Hofsommer, "The Railroads in Oklahoma," 3.

19. Ibid.; *Cheyenne Transporter,* September 11, November 25, 1882.

20. *Topeka Commonwealth,* April 27, 1887; *Arkansas City Weekly Republican-Traveler,* April 29, 1887.

21. *Arkansas City Traveler,* December 5, 1883; Hoig, "Rail Line That Opened the Unassigned Lands," 19–30.

22. Berthrong, *Ordeal,* 80–81, 85.

23. Miles to Smith, January 1, 1876, LR, OIA, Central Suptcy., NA.

24. Berthrong, *Ordeal*, 85.

25. *Cheyenne Transporter*, February 10, 1883.

26. Ibid., October 13, 1883.

27. Ibid., December 24, 1880.

28. Veenendaal, "Herman F. C. Ten Kate, Jr.," 37–38. Ten Kate was miffed that when he headed on to Anadarko, Fort Reno commander Thomas Bull Dewees refused to supply him a horse and a guide even though he carried a letter of recommendation from the commander of the U.S. Army, Gen. William T. Sherman.

29. *Arkansas City Traveler*, January 23, 1884; *Cheyenne Transporter*, February 13, 1884.

30. Miles to Smith, January 1, 1876, LR, OIA, Central Suptcy., NA; Berthrong, *Ordeal*, 78.

31. *Cheyenne Transporter*, December 13, 1883.

32. Ibid., April 25, 1881.

33. Ibid., May 25, 1881; January 11, July 12, 1883; January 13, December 13, 1884.

34. Berthrong, *Ordeal*, 110.

35. Heitman, *Historical Register*, 1:370–71.

36. Welge, "Colonial Experience," 13; *Cheyenne Transporter*, January 28, 1884.

37. Berthrong, *Ordeal*, 99. The Miles's three children, Sue, Eva, and Whit, had attended school at Lawrence for a time. In September 1882, young Whit rode to Caldwell on horseback, entrained to Wichita, and then rode his father's new horse all the way back to Darlington. Sue Miles later attended school at Bethany College in Topeka. *Cheyenne Transporter*, May 25, September 11, 1882.

38. *Cheyenne Transporter*, May 10, 1882.

39. Berthrong, *Ordeal*, 85–86.

40. Kroeker, "The Mennonites of Oklahoma," 17.

41. *Cheyenne Transporter*, April 27, 1882.

42. Ibid., February 25, 1882.

43. "Rev. H. R. Voth, Mennonite," File Drawer D-8, Carnegie Library, El Reno.

44. *Cheyenne Transporter*, February 25, December 26, 1882.

45. Ibid., June 25, December 26, 1882, February 10, 1883; Cassal, "Missionary Tour," 404 n. 14; Berthrong, *Ordeal*, 87–88.

46. *Cheyenne Transporter*, June 25, 1882.

47. Ibid., September 11, 1882.

48. Ibid., April 25, 1881; Berthrong, *Ordeal*, 85.

49. *Cheyenne Transporter*, June 25, 1881.

50. Ibid., April 13, 1883; June 30, 1885.

51. Rickey, *Forty Miles*, 194–95; *Annual Report, Sec. of War, 1884*, 54.

52. *Cheyenne Transporter*, April 13, 1884.

CHAPTER 9: PUNISHING PAYNE

1. *Cheyenne Transporter*, September 11, 1882.

2. Ibid.

3. Hoig, *David L. Payne*, 124–25; Correspondence Bearing Signature of Payne File, Athey Collection, OHS/AM; *Caldwell Commercial*, September 28, 1882.

4. Osburn, "A Tribute," 15–16.

5. *Caldwell Commercial,* February 16, 1882; Osburn, "A Tribute," 16.

6. *Cheyenne Transporter,* September 11, 1882.

7. Payne to Bennett, September 8, 1882, Correspondence Bearing Signature of Payne File, Athey Collection, OHS/AM.

8. *Caldwell Commercial,* October 5, 1882.

9. Ibid., September 18, October 5, December 14, 1882.

10. Ibid., September 28, 1882; telegrams, August 28, August 31, 1882, LR, AGO (Main Series), NA.

11. *Wichita Eagle,* April 12, 1883; *Wichita Beacon,* February 14, 1883; Payne's diary, Athey Collection, OHS/AM; *Cheyenne Transporter,* February 10, 1883.

12. *Wichita Eagle,* April 12, 1883. Payne told Carroll that he had no authority, that the colony was under the command of a committee of five. Report of Captain Carroll, March 3, 1883, LR, AGO (Main Series), NA.

13. February 26, 1883.

14. H. M. Maidt affidavit, Barde Collection, OHS/AM.

15. *Cheyenne Transporter,* March 27, 1883.

16. *Oklahoma War Chief,* April 26, 1884.

17. Ibid., May 10, August 6, 1884; *Arkansas City Traveler,* May 21, 1884.

18. *Oklahoma War Chief,* April 26, May 10, 1884; Report of Captain Carroll, April 28, 1884; report of Captain G. B. Russell, May 26, 1884; J. S. Anderson to Senator Plumb, May 27, 1884; LR, AGO (Main Series), NA.

19. Report of Lt. W. W. Day, May 8, 1884, LR, AGO (Main Series), NA; *Oklahoma War Chief,* May 10, 1884.

20. Hatch reports, June 22, 26, 1884, LR, AGO (Main Series), NA; *Oklahoma Chief,* July 31, 1884; *Caldwell Journal,* August 14, 1884; *Wichita Eagle,* July 11, 1884.

21. Rister, *Land Hunger,* 162.

22. Moore report, August 9, 1884; Cusack report, August 10, 1884; LR, AGO (Main Series), NA; *Caldwell Journal,* August 7, 1884.

23. Hoig, *David L. Payne,* 198–206.

24. Payne's dairy, Mosely account, Athey Collection, OHS/AM.

25. Ibid.

26. Day report, January 1, 1885, LR, AGO (Main Series), NA.

27. Hatch report, February 7, 1885, LR, AGO (Main Series), NA; *Arkansas City Traveler,* January 14, 1885.

28. February 4, 1885. Hatch, who had won brigadier and major general brevets during the Civil War and had commanded a Ninth Cavalry unit in the Texas Panhandle at Mobeetie, died suddenly during reveille at Fort Robinson eleven days before the opening of the Oklahoma lands to settlement. *Leavenworth Times,* April 12, 1889.

29. *Army and Navy Journal* 22 (February 7, 1885): 549.

CHAPTER 10: THE DOG SOLDIERS AND THE STOCKMEN

1. Colcord, *Autobiography,* 104–6.

2. Ibid.

3. *Cheyenne Transporter,* March 13, 1884.

4. Gibbon to Post Adjutant, Fort Reno, May 9, 1884, LR, AGO (Main Series), NA.

5. *Cheyenne Transporter*, May 10, 1884; Keeling, "My Experiences," 73.

6. Telegram, Haury to Dyer, 7 P.M., May 4, 1884, LR, OIA (Main Series), NA.

7. Gibbon to Post Adjutant, Fort Reno, May 9, 1884, LR, AGO (Main Series), NA.

8. Dyer claimed that the Indians had been willing to settle with Horton for fifteen to twenty-five ponies, but when Chapman arrived from Fort Supply they demanded half of the herd. Dyer to Price, May 20, 1884, U.S. Senate, *Investigation of Conditions*, 524–26.

9. Berthrong, *Ordeal*, 100–101; Nelson, *Cowman's Southwest*, 190–91.

10. *Cheyenne Transporter*, August 30, 1884.

11. Sheridan's report, July 24, 1885, LR, AGO (Main Series), NA.

12. Berthrong, *Ordeal* 104; *Wichita Eagle*, July 10, 1885.

13. Berthrong, *Ordeal*, 106.

14. *Cheyenne Transporter*, May 15, 1885.

15. Ibid., June 30, 1885.

16. *Wichita Eagle*, July 17, 1885.

17. Berthrong, *Ordeal*, 106.

18. *Leavenworth Times*, July 11, 1885.

19. Ibid., July 16, 1885; *Wichita (Weekly) Eagle*, July 17, 1885.

20. *Leavenworth Times*, July 10, 1885.

21. *Wichita Eagle*, July 10, 1885; Berthrong, *Ordeal*, 107.

22. Carriker, *Fort Supply*, 165 n. 21.

23. *New York Tribune*, July 9, 1885.

24. Nelson, *Cowman's Southwest*, 246.

25. *Army and Navy Journal* 22 (July 18, 1885): 1030.

26. Ibid.

27. *St. Louis Post-Dispatch*, July 15, 1885; *Wichita (Weekly) Eagle*, July 10, 1885; Wright, "Fort Reno," 99; Carriker, *Fort Supply*, 165; Brief of Paper Relating to Disturbances among the Cheyenne and Arapaho Indians, LR, AGO (Main Series), NA.

28. Wright, "Fort Reno," 99.

29. *Wichita (Weekly) Eagle*, July 10, 1885.

30. *Leavenworth Times*, July 7, 14, 1885.

31. *Wichita Eagle*, July 31, 1885.

32. Ibid.

33. *Army and Navy Journal* 22 (July 25, 1885): 1050.

34. Berthrong, *Ordeal*, 108.

35. *Wichita (Weekly) Eagle*, July 5, 1885.

36. Ibid., July 31, 1885.

37. Sheridan report, July 24, 1885, LR, AGO, NA.

38. *Wichita Eagle*, July 31, 1885.

39. Ibid.

40. Ibid.

41. Brief of Papers Relating to Disturbances among the Cheyenne and Arapaho Indians, LR, AGO (Main Series), NA.

42. *Leavenworth Times*, July 22, 1885.

43. Ibid., July 23, 1885; *Wichita (Weekly) Eagle,* July 24, 1885.

44. *Wichita (Weekly) Eagle,* July 31, 1885.

45. *Cheyenne Transporter,* August 15, 1885.

46. Berthrong, *Ordeal,* 115.

47. Heitman, *Historical Register,* 1:624.

48. Telegram, J. M. Lee to CofIA, November 6, 1885, C/A Letterbook: 8:454–57; 9:168–71, 345; 10:26, 42–44, OHS/AM.

49. *Cheyenne Transporter,* November 2, 1885.

50. Rex Brothers, manuscript (personal copy), 5.

51. *Army and Navy Journal* 22 (November 7, 1885): 283.

52. *Cheyenne Transporter,* November 12, 1885.

53. *Arkansas City Traveler,* October 14, 1885.

CHAPTER 11: PRELUDE TO SETTLEMENT

1. Dyer, *Fort Reno,* 51.

2. *Wichita Eagle,* November 29, 1885.

3. *Cheyenne Transporter,* July 15, 30, 1885; February 20, March 4, 1886.

4. Dyer, *Fort Reno,* 31.

5. Ibid., 42.

6. Ibid., 45.

7. Ibid., 50.

8. *Cheyenne Transporter,* January 15, 1885.

9. *Wichita Eagle,* May 8, 1885.

10. May 25, 1885.

11. *Cheyenne Transporter,* June 30, 1885.

12. Ibid., April 15, 1885.

13. Ibid., May 15, 1885.

14. Ibid., June 30, July 15, 1885; *Leavenworth Times,* July 14, 1885; *Kansas Cowboy,* July 18, 1885.

15. Cassal, "Missionary Tour," 403.

16. *Cheyenne Transporter,* June 20, 1884; October 13, November 15, 1884.

17. Ibid., May 25, 1885.

18. Cassal, "Missionary Tour," 410.

19. Ibid., 413.

20. Berthrong, *Ordeal,* 122; *Cheyenne Transporter,* Aug. 25, 1882, Mar. 27, 1883, May 15, 1885.

21. *Cheyenne Transporter,* August 25, 1880.

22. Ibid., September 25, October 25, 1880, January 25, 1881.

23. Ibid., March 25, April 10, December 11, 26, 1882; Berthrong, *Ordeal,* 61–62, 121; Annual Report, CofIA, 1876, 86–87; Seger, *Early Days,* 108.

24. Seger, *Early Days,* 103–4.

25. Seger was joined there in July 1886 by his wife and family. *Cheyenne Transporter,* July 12, 1886.

26. Seger, *Early Days,* 120; Berthrong, *Ordeal,* 121.

27. Berthrong, *Ordeal,* 128–29.

28. Carter, *Dian Takes to the Indians,* 32–33.

29. Nelson, *Cowman's Southwest,* 218–19.

30. *Arkansas City Traveler,* January 27, 1886.

31. Ibid., 49.

32. *Cheyenne Transporter,* March 15, 1886.

33. Ibid., July 12, 1886.

34. Ibid.

Chapter 12: Monitoring the White Deluge

1. CO, Fort Reno, to AAG, Dept./Mo., November 30, 1887, LR, Fort Reno, NA.

2. Brandt manuscript, citing records of AGO.

3. Ibid.

4. Letter from officer in Sumner's command, *Arkansas City Traveler,* November 18, 1885.

5. Hoig, "The Rail Line That Opened the Unassigned Lands," 19–30.

6. Wade letter, December 24, 1887, cited by Dept./Interior report, January 17, 1888, LR, Fort Reno, NA.

7. Report of courts-martial, August 1887, LR, Fort Reno, NA.

8. Martin to CO, Fort Reno, August 20, 1887, LR, Fort Reno, NA; Mrs. A. Machacek to Asst. Surg., Fort Reno, October 30, 1887, LR, Fort Reno, NA.

9. Report of an Inspection, October 12, 1887, LR, Fort Reno, NA.

10. AAG, Dept./Mo. to CO, Fort Reno, August 16, 1888, LR, Fort Reno, NA.

11. Macomb report, April 7, 1888, LR, Fort Reno, NA.

12. Letters, October 21, 30, November 6, 29, 1886, LR, Dept./Mo., NA; *Arkansas City Traveler,* September 22, 1885.

13. Letters, February 12, 19, 1887, LR, Dept./Mo., Vol. 53, NA. Sommers's daughter Eva would be the first child born at the site of present Oklahoma City. *Purcell Register,* March 3, 1888.

14. *Purcell Register,* April 29, 1887.

15. Macomb to Post Adjutant, Fort Reno, March 26, April 7, 1888, LR, Fort Reno, NA.

16. Letter, February 14, 1887, LR, Dept./Mo., Vol. 53, NA.

17. Brandt manuscript, citing report of the AGO.

18. Report of General Merritt, September 12, 1889, *Annual Report, Sec. of War, 1889,* 163.

19. Woodson to Post Adjutant, Fort Reno, January 31, 1889, LR, Fort Reno, NA.

20. Ibid.; Woodson to Post Adjutant, Fort Reno, February 26, 1889, LR, Fort Reno, NA.

21. *Wichita Eagle,* January 11, 1889.

22. Ibid.

23. Ibid.

24. Carson letters, March 16, 20, April 5, 10, 1889, LR, Fort Reno, NA; *Kansas City Gazette,* March 20, 1889; Arnold Papers, Harn Collection, OHS/AM.

25. Kelton to Crook, April 16, 1889, U.S. Senate, *Correspondence,* 7.

26. Merritt Report, September 12, 1889, *Annual Report, Sec. of War, 1889,* 164.

Merritt claimed that "on April 22 there was in the field in Oklahoma a force equal to a regiment of cavalry and more than a regiment of infantry."

27. Telegram, Merritt to Crook, April 20, 1889, U.S. Senate, *Correspondence*, 11.

28. Photo, Officers at Fort Reno, 1889, Carnegie Library, El Reno. These officers included Capt. Edward S. Godfrey, Capt. James F. Bell, Capt. John B. Babcock, Maj. Frank Baldwin, Maj. James W. Forsyth, Maj. John M. Bacon, Colonel Wade, Maj. Caleb H. Carlton, 1st Lt. Hugh L. Scott, and Maj. Edward B. Williston. This Fort Reno photo may have been taken as a result of a letter from D. W. Tainker of Wichita requesting permission to come to Fort Reno with a photographic outfit following a visit to Camp Supply. Tainker to CO, Fort Reno, January 5, 1889, LR, Fort Reno, Box 2, NA.

29. *New York Tribune*, April 20, 1889; *Arkansas City Republican-Traveler*, April 25, 1889.

30. *Daily Inter-Ocean*, April 23, 1889.

31. *New York Tribune*, April 20, 1889.

32. Stetler, "Rivers a Problem to Homesteaders," 136.

33. Merritt to AAG, Dept./Mo., May 2, 1889, LR, AGO (Main Series), NA; Hoig, *Oklahoma Land Rush*, 86, 91–92.

Chapter 13: They Came Running

1. Remington, "Artist Wanderings," 537–38.

2. *Arkansas City Republican-Traveler*, April 25, 1889.

3. Ben Clark file, OU/WHC.

4. Service records, Ben Clark file, OU/WHC.

5. *Oklahoma Democrat*, December 26, 1891.

6. Ben Clark file, OU/WHC.

7. Remington's Oklahoma sketches appear in the April 6, 1889, issue of *Harper's Illustrated Weekly* and the August 1889 issue of *Century Magazine*.

8. Zogbaum sketches appear with his article "Life at an Indian Agency," *Harper's Illustrated Weekly*, June 4, 1890. Other drawings that he made during his tour through the Indian Territory appear in *Harper's Illustrated Weekly*, April 18, July 6, 1889, and January 4, 1890.

9. Ibid.

10. *St. Louis Republic*, April 23, 1889.

11. *Daily Inter-Ocean*, April 23, 1889.

12. *Arkansas City Republican-Traveler*, April 25, 1889.

13. *Caldwell Journal*, May 2, 1889.

14. *Chicago Tribune*, April 23, 1889; *New York Herald*, April 23, 1889.

15. Penn, "Roughing It in the '80s."

16. Hoig, *Oklahoma Land Rush*, 180–81.

17. Carter, *Dian Takes to the Indians*, 60–61.

18. Chapman, "Founding of El Reno," 108; *Oklahoma Democrat*, February 13, 1892.

19. Jane Beecham interview, Indian-Pioneer Papers, 66:169–77.

20. Brandt manuscript, 20–21.

21. *New York Times*, April 23, 1889.

22. Pickler Report, *Senate Ex. Doc. 33*, 51st Cong., 1st sess., 9.

23. Martin C. Lawrence and Thomas J. Moore affidavits, Harn Papers, OHS/AM.

24. Stiles to Post Adj., December 20, 1889, U.S. Senate, *Reports on the Settlement of Oklahoma*, 51.

25. Stiles to Sanger, November 7, 1889, U.S. Senate, *Correspondence*, 33.

26. *Oklahoma Democrat*, December 12, 1891.

27. Snyder to Sanger, October 26, 1889, U.S. Senate, *Correspondence*, 37.

28. Stiles to Post Adjutant, December 20, 1889, U.S. Senate, *Correspondence*, 51.

29. Telegram, Tilford to CO, Fort Sill, April 18, 1889, Letters and Telegrams from Fort Sill, supplied on request by NA.

30. Cornelius and Pickler to Noble, U.S. Senate, *Reports on the Settlement of Oklahoma*, 2.

31. Pickler Report, U.S. Senate, *Reports on the Settlement of Oklahoma*, 26–30.

32. Merritt to AAG, Div./Mo., U.S. Senate, *Correspondence*, 13.

33. *Oklahoma Gazette*, May 23, 1889; Berthrong, *Ordeal*, 148–49.

34. Carriker, *Fort Supply*, 188.

35. Gibson, *Oklahoma*, 180.

36. *Wichita Eagle*, July 12, 1890.

37. Berthrong, *Ordeal*, 165–66.

38. Ibid., 167–69.

39. July 23, October 15, 1891

40. Berthrong, *Ordeal*, 170.

41. Ibid., 181.

CHAPTER 14: THE CHEYENNE/ARAPAHO OPENING

1. Carriker, *Fort Supply*, 194.

2. *New York Times*, April 19, 1892; Berthrong, *Ordeal*, 182–83.

3. *New York Times*, April 18, 1892.

4. *Arkansas City Republican-Traveler*, April 21, 1892.

5. Ibid.

6. *Oklahoma Democrat*, April 2, 1892; R. Records, "Recollections," 20–21.

7. *New York Times*, April 16, 1892.

8. Ibid., April 18, 1892.

9. Ibid., April 19, 1892.

10. Ibid., April 20, 1892.

11. Ibid., April 14, 20, 1892.

12. R. Records, "Recollections," 20.

13. *New York Times*, April 18, 1892.

14. Ibid., April 18, 1892.

15. Ibid., April 16, 1892.

16. Ibid., April 19, 1892; Hofsommer, *Railroads in Oklahoma*, 149.

17. *Wichita Eagle*, April 22, 1892.

18. *New York Times*, April 14, 1892.

19. Ibid., April 19, 1892.

20. Ibid.

21. Ibid., April 18, 1892.
22. Ulysses B. Roberts interview, Indian-Pioneer Papers, 69:18.
23. April 21, 1892.
24. *New York Times,* April 20, 1892.
25. L. Records, *Cherokee Outlet Cowboy,* 310.
26. Annual Report, CofIA, 1892, 374–75. Earlier the Iowa and Kickapoo reservations had been designated as County "A," while the Potawatomi and Sac and Fox lands had been designated as County "B." The designated county seats were Watonga for "C," Taloga for "D," Ioland for "E," Cheyenne for "F," Arapaho for "G," and Cloud Chief for "H."
27. Annual Report, CofIA, 1892, 373–75.
28. Berthrong, *Ordeal,* 185.
29. Ibid., 376.
30. Annual Report, CofIA, 1892, 372–73.
31. These were the Santa Fe lines from Arkansas City to the Oklahoma Lands; a Santa Fe line cutting across the northwest from New Kiowa, Kansas, to the Texas Panhandle; and the Rock Island line from Caldwell, Kansas, to El Reno.
32. Carriker, *Fort Supply,* 201.
33. June 24, 1893.

CHAPTER 15: THIS LAND IS OUR LAND

1. *Arkansas City Weekly Republican-Traveler,* September 21, 1893.
2. Carriker, *Fort Supply,* 204.
3. *Oklahoma State Capital,* September 11, 1893.
4. *Kingfisher Free Press,* September 7, 1893; *Wichita Eagle,* August 25, 1893; Carriker, *Fort Supply,* 204–5; *Guthrie Daily Leader,* September 12, 1893.
5. *Wichita Eagle,* September 15, 1893; U.S. Senate, *Opening,* 11.
6. U.S. Senate, *Opening,* 4.
7. *Oklahoma State Capital,* September 14, 1893.
8. Carriker, *Fort Supply,* 209–10.
9. U.S. Senate, *Opening,* 8.
10. Ibid., 4.
11. *Arkansas City Republican-Traveler,* September 14, 1893.
12. *Wichita Eagle,* September 15, 22, 1893.
13. Rucker, "Bullets Curbed Greed," *Daily Oklahoman,* September 22, 1929.
14. *Wichita Eagle,* September 22, 1893; *New York Times,* September 17, 1893, made similar estimates.
15. September 17, 1893.
16. *New York Times,* September 17, 1893.
17. Ibid.
18. *Wichita Eagle,* September 22, 1893.
19. *Arkansas City Republican-Traveler,* September 21, 1893; *Wichita Eagle,* September 22, 1893; U.S. Senate, *Opening,* 5.
20. *Arkansas City Republican-Traveler,* September 22, 1893; Carriker, *Fort Supply,* 213.
21. September 22, 1893.

22. *Wichita Eagle*, September 22, 1893.
23. U.S. Senate, *Opening*, 7; Newsom, *Cherokee Strip*, 49–50.
24. *Wichita Eagle*, September 22, 1893.
25. Carriker, *Fort Supply*, 213–14.
26. *Wichita Eagle*, September 22, 1893.
27. Ibid.
28. U.S. Senate, *Opening*, 8.
29. Rucker, "Bullets Curbed Greed," *Daily Oklahoman*, September 22, 1929.
30. Ibid.,
31. Baldwin, *Memoirs*, 36–37.

CHAPTER 16: ONE LAST WAR

1. August 8, 1891.
2. Morrison, *Military Posts and Camps in Oklahoma*, 154.
3. *Norman Transcript*, April 14, 1893; *Indian Citizen*, April 6, 1893; *Kingfisher Times*, April 20, 1893; *Indian Methodist*, May 4, 1893.
4. *Brief Description of Oklahoma*, 13–14.
5. Creel, *Cheyenne Grammar and Ethnology*, Book A.
6. *El Reno Democrat*, October 4, 1894.
7. *El Reno Eagle*, November 22, 1894.
8. Berthrong, *Ordeal*, 137–38, 145, 175–79, 226. Ora May Smith Dever, whose father came to work at Darlington in 1892, described Woodson as an austere and stern man who commanded strict military discipline at the agency. He owned a fine home with house servants and a coachman and kept several deer in a parklike enclosure. Ora May Smith Dever interview, Indian-Pioneer Papers, 65:447–52.
9. Berthrong, *Ordeal*, 185–86; Carriker, *Fort Supply*, 215–16.
10. Berthrong, *Ordeal*, 188.
11. Turington to AAG, Dept./Mo., April 4, 1894, Ltrs. Sent, Fort Reno, NA.
12. *Daily Oklahoma State Capital*, April 12, 1894.
13. In a 1937 interview, E. H. Cook claimed that the troops arrived just in time to prevent a battle; Indian-Pioneer Papers, 20:399–401.
14. *Daily Oklahoma State Capital*, April 13, 1894; Berthrong, *Ordeal*, 187–88.
15. Purington to AG, Dept./Mo., August 26, 1894, Ltrs. Sent, Fort Reno, NA.
16. *Daily Oklahoman*, April 4, 1894.
17. *Guthrie Daily Leader*, April 5, 8, 1894; *Daily Oklahoma State Capital*, April 6, 1894; *Daily Oklahoman*, April 4, 5, 6, 7, 1894; *El Reno Democrat*, April 5, 1894. The truth of these reports is subject to question in that the names of the supposed victims, white or Indian, were never brought to public attention. An item of historical curiosity, however, did surface in this immediate area in 1904 when the *Arapaho Bee*, May 13, 1904, reported that seven skeletons had been unearthed at the town of Foss by workmen excavating for a building. There being no Indian artifacts present, it was surmised that these were men of Gen. George A. Custer's Seventh Cavalry killed during his attack on Black Kettle's village in 1868. Custer's nineteen or twenty dead, however, were buried farther to the north on the bank of the Washita River west of Strong City.
18. Turington to AAG, Dept./Mo., April 9, 1894, Ltrs. Sent, Fort Reno, NA.

19. Post Adj. to Mackay, Fort Reno, June 18, 1895, LR, Fort Reno, NA.

20. Berthrong, *Ordeal*, 188–89.

21. *Industrial Head Light*, March 21, 1895.

22. *Cavalry Journal* 31 (April 1922): 173.

23. *Industrial Headlight*, December 13, 1895; *El Reno News*, January 8, 1897; December 31, 1897; *El Reno Democrat*, January 7, 1898; *El Reno Globe*, November 20, 1896.

24. *Kansas City Star*, October 5, 1895.

25. *El Reno Eagle*, June 5, 1896.

26. *El Reno Weekly Globe*, March 6, July 24, December 25, 1896.

27. Ibid., November 20, 1896.

28. *Cavalry Journal* 31 (April 1922): 173; *Muskogee Phoenix*, April 22, 1897.

29. *El Reno News*, April 9, 1897.

30. Pearson to AG, Dept./Mo., April 7, 1898, LS, Fort Reno, RG393, NA; April 21, 1898; *El Reno News*, April 22, 1898.

31. *El Reno Globe*, June 3, 1898.

32. *El Reno News*, May 6, 1898.

33. Trask, *War with Spain*, 247.

34. *El Reno News*, July 22, 1898.

35. Ibid., August 5, 1898.

36. Alley, "Oklahoma in the Spanish-American War," 47.

37. *El Reno Times*, September 23, 1898; Alley, "Oklahoma in the Spanish-American War," 47.

38. *El Reno Globe*, January 6, 1899; *El Reno News*, January 6, 1899.

39. *El Reno News*, June 21, 1900.

40. Gibson, *Oklahoma*, 195–96.

41. *Daily Oklahoman*, January 25, 1901.

42. Morton, "Government of the Creek Indians, the Snake Rebellion," 192–93.

43. Morrison, *Military Posts and Camps in Oklahoma*, 156.

44. Yeatman to AG, Dept./Mo., May 14, 1902, Ltrs. Sent, Fort Reno, NA.

45. Report to Surgeon, February 14, 1902, Ltrs. Sent, Fort Reno, NA.

46. *El Reno Globe*, September 29, 1905.

47. *El Reno American*, November 16, 1905; January 18, 1906; *El Reno Democrat*, March 8, 1906.

48. *El Reno American*, November 22, 1906.

49. Fort Reno Post Returns, July 1906; Report, July 9, 1906, Fort Reno correspondence, Box 10, NA.

50. Derrick, "Fort Reno," 119–20; Barker, *Fort Reno*, 49–50, citing *El Reno American*, August 30, November 4, 8, 1906.

51. Fowler, *Black Infantry in the West*, 147.

52. Barker, *Fort Reno*, 50–51 citing *El Reno American*, November 22, 29, December 13, 1906.

53. Wolfe report with map, September 13, 1903, Harris reports with maps, March 22, April 9, 23, 1906, LR, Fort Reno, NA. One report in 1906 indicated that the steel bridge still existed over the North Canadian at Darlington.

54. *El Reno Democrat*, January 23, 1907.

55. Ibid., October 3, 1907; *Okarche Times*, October 4, 1907.

56. Scott, *Some Memories*, 140–41.

57. *El Reno American,* September 26, November 4, 1907.

58. Moorhead, "Passing of Historic Forts," 677, 680; *El Reno American,* September 26, October 31, 1907.

59. Walton to AAG, Dept./Tex., February 6, 1908, Fort Reno correspondence, Box 10, NA.

60. *Daily Oklahoman,* February 25, 1908; *El Reno Democrat,* February 27, 1908.

61. Ben Clark file, OU/WHC.

62. Shirk, "Military Duty," 124.

EPILOGUE: NEW DUTIES, OLD MEMORIES

1. Stout, "U.S. Army Remount Depots," 122.

2. Morrison, *Military Posts and Camps in Oklahoma,* 157.

3. *Daily Oklahoman,* August 8, 1909; Griffin, "The Fort Reno Remount Depot," 1125.

4. Griffin, "The Fort Reno Remount Depot," 1115.

5. Ibid., 1126.

6. *Daily Oklahoman,* February 9, 1930.

7. Bob Harris, "Men and Horses at Fort Reno," *Daily Oklahoman,* April 1, 1928.

8. *Daily Oklahoman,* Sept. 20, 21, 22, 24, 1929.

9. Ibid., Feb. 9, 1930; *El Reno American,* Aug. 22, 1935.

10. *Daily Oklahoman,* Feb. 9, 1930.

11. Morrison, *Military Posts and Camps in Oklahoma,* 157; *Oklahoma: A Guide to the Sooner State,* 250.

12. Potts, "Fort Reno—the Remount Depot," Entry 2386, RG92, NARA SW Region, Fort Worth, Tex.

13. *Sunday Oklahoman,* January 9, 1938.

14. *History of Canadian County,* 22.

15. July 31, 1966.

16. Murray/Ledsham, WPA Writers' Project article, OHS Vertical file, Fort Reno.

17. *History of Canadian County,* 16.

18. Ibid., 22.

19. Wilson, "The Afrika Korps in Oklahoma," 360–69.

20. Barker, Burial in the Fort Reno Cemetery, 25, 30.

21. Personal Interview with Bill Davenport, Laramie, Wyo.

22. *El Reno Tribune,* May 28, 1944, June 6, 1976; *El Reno American,* May 3, 1943; Apr. 27, July 20, 1944; Aug. 28, 1947; Aug. 9, Sept. 20, 1951; *Daily Oklahoman,* Mar. 30, 1952.

23. *El Reno American,* Apr. 18, 1946; *El Reno Tribune,* May 7, 1946. The late Bill Ranck was a personal friend of the author, who as a boy went with him to feed stock at his Gage, Oklahoma, ranch where one pleasure was cracking a long leather bullwhip. Bill occasionally told of horse-purchasing trips to Central and South American countries.

24. *El Reno American,* May 2, 1946.

25. *El Reno Tribune,* February 20, 1946; February 27, 1947; *El Reno American,* April 27, 1945.

26. Kruse, "Mr. Fort Reno, Dwight Stephens," *Orbit Magazine, Daily Oklahoman,* March 24, 1974; *History of Canadian County,* 22; Ruth, *Oklahoma: A Guide to the Sooner State,* 253.

27. Whenry, *Tom Reno and the Chief.*

28. *History of Canadian County,* 276.

29. Statement giving Number and Description of Buildings, Building file, Cheyenne/Arapaho Agency, OHS/AM.

30. Article dated November 16, 1910, unidentified newspaper clipping, Darlington File, Thoburn Papers, OHS/AM. The Masonic refuge at Darlington was described in a *Daily Oklahoma,* September 17, 1822, article:

> In the old location at Darlington five miles west of El Reno, the home was located on a beautiful farm of 676 acres. Here, there were about twenty buildings grouped conveniently about a shaded square in which had been placed several pieces of playground equipment. At the north side of the square, facing the south, are the school buildings, and the boys' and girls' dormitories. On the east side is the chapel. On the west side of the square are a number of small cottages where the aged Masons and their wives, who are able to care for their own room and who preferred to be alone, were allowed to live.

31. "Oklahoma's Masonic Orphans Are 'Moving to Town,'" *Daily Oklahoman,* September 17, 1922. Succeeding superintendents were Alfred G. Guy, H. W. Sullins, Wiloliam M. Roberson, and A. J. Weir.

32. *History of Canadian County,* 15.

33. Ibid.

34. *Daily Oklahoman,* April 18, 1925.

35. Morris, *Oklahoma Yesterday, Today, Tomorrow,* 230, citing *Daily Oklahoman,* February 9, 1930.

36. *History of Canadian County,* 16.

37. Paper by W. D. Welge, "Darlington Indian Agency: A Brief History, 1870–1996," OHS.

38. *History of Canadian County,* 17.

39. *The Carrier Pigeon,* March 1, 1911.

40. *History of Canadian County,* 17.

BIBLIOGRAPHY

ARCHIVAL MATERIALS

Barker Texas History Center, Austin, Texas
    John Ford Memoirs
El Reno Carnegie Library, El Reno, Oklahoma
    Document Cases No. 1 and No. 2
    File Drawers D-6, D-7, D-8
        "Darlington Indian Agency," paper by Martha Hake, 1965
        Fort Reno from the National Archives, Doc. Case No. 1
    Fort Reno Remount Depot Daily Bulletin
        "History of the Mennonite General Conference," by H. P. Krehibel, 1898
        J. Holloway correspondence
        Map of Fort Reno and Darlington areas
        "The Mennonites of Oklahoma to 1907," thesis by Marvin Elroy Kroeker, University of Oklahoma, 1954
        "The Quaker Agents of Darlington," paper by Sandra W. LeVan, 1971
        "John Homer Seger," paper by Autumn Seger Webster
        "Rev. H. R. Voth," paper by Martha Dyck and Edna Voth
Fort Sill Museum, Lawton, Oklahoma
    John H. Brandt manuscript
    Neil Evans file
    Fort Reno Vertical file
    Journal of the U.S. Cavalry Association
Gilcrease Institute, Tulsa, Oklahoma
    Cheyenne/Arapaho Letterbook, 1871–73
    Lt. Herber M. Creel Papers
        Cheyenne Grammar and Ethnology, Book A
        Ethnology Notebook, Book D
        Journal, Fort Reno, I.T., 1871
National Archives, Washington, D.C.
    Photo Archives, Cabinet 25
        Oklahoma file
        Tenth Cavalry file
    Record Group 393
        Department of the Missouri, Ltrs. Recd.
        Fort Reno Ltrs. Recd.
        Fort Reno Ltrs. Sent
National Archives Southwest Region, Fort Worth, Texas
    History of Fort Reno, Entry 2386, RG92

Oklahoma Historical Society, Oklahoma City, Oklahoma
    Archives/Manuscripts Division
        Athey Collection
        Barde Collection
        Cheyenne/Arapaho Agency
            Agents and Agency file
            Employees file
            Fort Reno file
            Issues file
            Letterbooks
        Harn Collection
            Arnold papers
        Indian-Pioneer Papers
        Kiowa Depredations file
        Manuscript file, Herbert E. Collins Material
        Sec. X, Fort Reno, file
        Thoburn Collection
            Darlington file: *The Indians' Friend, A Memorial to Brinton Darlington*
            Vertical files
    Library
        Darlington vertical file
        Fort Reno Medical Records
        Fort Reno Post Returns
        Fort Reno vertical file
University of Central Oklahoma, Edmond, Oklahoma
    Oklahoma Collection
        Fort Supply Records
        Vertical file
University of Oklahoma Western History Collection, Norman, Oklahoma
    Berthrong Collection
        Fort Supply, Ltrs. Sent, 1869–74
    Walter S. Campbell Papers
        Ben Clark file
        Camp Supply Letterbook
        Report of Lt. Colonel Van Voast
    Ben Clark file
    Oklahoma Art Exhibit, Books 2 and 3
    Oklahoma Image, Book 1
    J. S. Shuck Collection

BOOKS AND ARTICLES

Alley, John. "Oklahoma in the Spanish-American War." *Chronicles of Oklahoma* 20 (March 1942): 43–50.
Baldwin, Alice Blackwood. *Memoirs of the Late Frank D. Baldwin, Major General, U.S.A.* Los Angeles: Wetzel Publishing Co., 1929.

Barker, Carolyn. *Burials in the Fort Reno Cemetery, 1874–1948*. Author, 1996.

———. *Fort Reno Remount Station*. Author, 1998.

———. *Fort Reno Research Station*. Author, 1998.

———. *Fort Reno, the Military Post*. Author, 1993.

Bass, Althea. *The Arapaho Way: A Memoir of an Indian Boyhood*. New York: Clarkson N. Potter, 1966.

Battles and War Leaders of the Civil War. 4 vols. New York: Century Co., 1894.

Berthrong, Donald C. *The Cheyenne and Arapaho Ordeal, Reservation and Agency Life in the Indian Territory, 1875–1907*. Norman: University of Oklahoma Press, 1976.

———. *The Southern Cheyennes*. Norman: University of Oklahoma Press, 1963.

Bode, E. A. *A Dose of Frontier Soldiering: The Memoirs of Corporal E. A. Bode*. Ed. Thomas T. Smith. Lincoln: University of Nebraska Press, 1994.

Brief Description of Oklahoma, El Reno, and Canadian County. El Reno: El Reno Commercial Club, 1893.

Brill, Charles J. "Cheyenne Defiance." *Daily Oklahoman*, March 29, 1936.

Buntin, Martha. "Difficulties Encountered in Issuing Cheyenne and Arapaho Subsistence, 1861–70." *Chronicles of Oklahoma* 13 (March 1935): 37–45.

———. "The Murder on Turkey Creek." *Chronicles of Oklahoma* 12 (September 1974): 258–63.

———. "The Removal of the Wichitas from Butler County, Kansas, to the Present Agency." *Panhandle-Plains Historical Review* 4 (1931): 62–72.

Campbell, C. E. "Down among the Red Men." *Kansas State Historical Collections*, 17 (1926–28): 623–91.

Carriker, Robert C. *Fort Supply, Indian Territory, Frontier Outpost on the Plains*. Norman: University of Oklahoma Press, 1970.

Carroll, John M. Introduction. *The Papers of the Order of Indian Wars*. Fort Collins, Colo.: Old Army Press, 1975.

Carter, Joseph LeRoy. *Dian Takes to the Indians*. Author, 1979.

Cashin, Henry V., et al. *Under Fire with the Tenth U.S. Cavalry*. New York: Arno Press and the New York Times, 1969.

Cassal, Rev. Hilary. "Missionary Tour in the Chickasaw Nation and Western Indian Territory." *Chronicles of Oklahoma* 34 (winter 1956–57): 397–416.

Chalfant, William Y. *Cheyennes and Horse Soldiers: The 1857 Expedition and the Battle of Solomon's Fork*. Norman: University of Oklahoma Press, 1989.

Chapman, Berlin B. "Establishment of Wichita Reservation." *Chronicles of Oklahoma* 11 (December 1933): 1044–53.

———. "Founding of El Reno." *Chronicles of Oklahoma* 24 (spring 1956).

Colcord, Charles Francis. *Autobiography*. Privately printed, 1970.

Collins, Dennis. *The Indians' Last Fight or the Dull Knife Raid*. New York: AMS Press, 1972. Reprint of 1915 edition.

Collins, Hubert E. "Edwin Williams, Engineer." *Chronicles of Oklahoma* 10 (spring 1932): 331–47.

Colton, Ray C. *The Civil War in the Western Territories*. Norman: University of Oklahoma Press, 1959.

Covington, James Warren. "Causes of the Dull Knife Raid." *Chronicles of Oklahoma* 26 (spring 1948): 13–22.

Derrick, W. Edwin. "Fort Reno: Defender of the Southern Plains." *Early Military Forts and Posts in Oklahoma.* Ed. Odie Faulk, Kenny A. Franks, and Paul F. Lambert. Oklahoma City: Oklahoma Historical Society, 1978.

Drass, Richard R., and Christopher L. Turner. *An Archeological Reconnaissance of the Wolf Creek Drainage Basin, Ellis County, Oklahoma.* Oklahoma Archeological Survey, *Archeological Resource Survey Report No. 35,* University of Oklahoma, 1989.

Dyer, Mrs. D. B. *Fort Reno or "Picturesque Cheyenne and Arapahoe Army Life," before the Opening of Oklahoma.* New York: G. W. Dillingham, 1896.

"Fort Reno." *Daily Oklahoman,* August 14, 1949.

Fort Reno Tombstone Tales. El Reno: Fort Reno Visitor Center, 1999.

Fowler, Arlen L. *The Black Infantry in the West, 1869–1891.* Foreword by William H. Leckie. Norman: University of Oklahoma Press, 1996.

Gibson, Arrell Morgan. *Oklahoma: A History of Five Centuries.* Norman: University of Oklahoma Press, 1981.

Griffin, Gerald E. "The Fort Reno Remount Depot." *Journal of the U.S. Cavalry Association* 21 (May 1911): 1115–27.

Grinnell, George Bird. *The Fighting Cheyennes.* Norman: University of Oklahoma Press, 1958.

Haley, James L. *The Buffalo War.* Garden City, N.Y.: Doubleday & Co., 1976.

Hammond, George P., and Agapito Rey, eds. and trans. *Don Juan de Oñate, Colonizer of New Mexico, 1595–1628.* 2 vols. Albuquerque: University of New Mexico Press, 1953.

Hancock, Richard H. "William Box Hancock, Trail Driver and Cattlemen." *Chronicles of Oklahoma* 76 (winter 1998–99): 356–73.

Harris, Bob. "Men and Horses at Fort Reno." *Daily Oklahoman,* April 1, 1928.

Hart, Herbert M. *Old Forts of the Southwest.* Seattle: Superior Publishing Co., 1944.

Haywood, C. Robert. *Trails South: The Wagon-Road Economy in the Dodge City-Panhandle Region.* Norman: University of Oklahoma Press, 1986.

Heitman, Francis B. *Historical Register and Dictionary of the United States Army.* 2 vols. Washington: GPO, 1903.

History of Canadian County. El Reno: Canadian County Historical Society, 1991.

Hofsommer, Donovan L. "The Railroads in Oklahoma." In *Railroads in Oklahoma,* ed. Donovan L. Hofsommer. Oklahoma City: Oklahoma Historical Society, 1977.

———, ed. *Railroads in Oklahoma.* Oklahoma City: Oklahoma Historical Society, 1977.

Hoig, Stan. *David L. Payne: The Oklahoma Boomer.* Oklahoma City: Western Heritage Books, 1980.

———. "The Rail Line That Opened the Unassigned Lands." In *Railroads in Oklahoma,* ed. Donovan L. Hofsommer. Oklahoma City: Oklahoma Historical Society, 1977.

———. *The Western Odyssey of John Simpson Smith.* Glendale, Calif.: Arthur H. Clark Co., 1974.

Iliff, W. E. "Heat Was One Cause of Comanches' [Cheyennes'] Flight North." *Daily Oklahoman,* July 21, 1929.

Ives, Nell. "Battle of Turkey Springs." *True West* (August 1980): 60–61.

Jackson, Helen Hunt. *A Century of Dishonor*. Williamstown, Mass.: Corner House
    Publishers, 1973.
James, Gen. Thomas. *Three Years among the Mexicans and the Indians*. Chicago:
    Rio Grande Press, 1962.
Kappler, Charles J., ed. *Indian Treaties*. New York: Interland, 1972.
Keeling, Henry C. "My Experiences with the Cheyenne Indians." Ed. Joseph
    Thoburn. *Chronicles of Oklahoma* 3 (April 1924): 59–73.
Kime, Wayne R. "The Indian Territory Journals of Colonel Richard Irving
    Dodge." In press.
Kruse, Loren. "Mr. Fort Reno, Dwight Stephens." *Orbit Magazine, Daily
    Oklahoman*, March 24, 1974.
Leckie, William H. *The Buffalo Soldiers*. Norman: University of Oklahoma Press,
    1967.
Leckie, William H., and Shirley A. Leckie. *Unlikely Warriors: General Benjamin
    Grierson and His Family*. Norman: University of Oklahoma Press, 1984.
Litton, Gaston. *History of Oklahoma*. 4 vols. New York: Lewis Historical Publishing
    Co., 1957.
McCallum, Henry D., and Frances T. *The Wire That Fenced the West*. Norman:
    University of Oklahoma Press, 1965.
McConnell, H. H. *Five Years a Cavalryman*. Foreword by William H. Leckie.
    Norman: University of Oklahoma Press, 1996.
McCoy, Joseph G. *Historic Sketches of the Cattle Trade of the West and Southwest*.
    Ed. Ralph P. Bieber. Lincoln: University of Nebraska Press, 1985.
McNeal, T. A. *When Kansas Was Young*. New York: Macmillan Co., 1922.
Merserve, John Bartlett. "The Plea of Crazy Snake." *Chronicles of Oklahoma* 11
    (September 1933): 899–911.
Montaignes, François Des. *The Plains, Being No Less than a Collection of Veracious
    Memoranda Taken during the Expedition of Exploration in the Year 1845*. Ed.
    and intro., Nancy Apert Mower and Don Russell. Norman: University of
    Oklahoma Press, 1972.
Moorhead, F. G. "The Passing of Historic Forts." *World To-Day* 13 (July 1907):
    677–84.
Morris, Lerona Rosamond. *Oklahoma Yesterday, Today, Tomorrow*. Guthrie:
    Co-Operative Publishing Co., 1930.
Morrison, William B. *Military Posts and Camps in Oklahoma*. Oklahoma City:
    Harlow Publishing Corp., 1936.
Morton, Ohland. "Government of the Creek Indians: The Snake Revolution."
    Chronicles of Oklahoma 8 (June 1930): 189–225.
Mothershead, Harmon. "The Journal of Ado Hunnius, Indian Territory, 1876."
    Chronicles of Oklahoma 51 (winter 1973–74): 451–72.
Nelson, Oliver. *The Cowman's Southwest*. Ed. by Angie Debo. Glendale, Calif.:
    Arthur H. Clark Co., 1953.
Newcomb, W. W., and T. N. Campbell. "Southern Plains Ethnohistory: A Re-
    examination of the Escanjaques, Ahijados, and Cuitoas." Ed. Don G. Wycoff
    and Jack L. Hoffman. *Oklahoma Anthropological Society Memoir 3* (1982). The
    Cross Timbers Heritage Association, Contributions, 1:29–43.
Newsom, D. Earl. *The Cherokee Strip: Its History and Grand Opening*. Stillwater:
    New Forums Press, 1992.

Nicholson, William. "A Tour of Indian Agencies in Kansas and the Indian Territory in 1870." *Kansas Historical Quarterly* 3 (August–November 1934): 289–326, 343–84.

Nye, W. S. *Carbine and Lance: The Story of Old Fort Sill.* Norman: University of Oklahoma Press, 1937.

"Oklahoma's Masonic Orphans Are 'Moving to Town.'" *Daily Oklahoman,* September 17, 1922.

Osburn, William H. "A Tribute to Captain D. L. Payne by His Private Secretary, W. H. Osburn, Also Colony Secretary during the Fourth Raid." *Chronicles of Oklahoma* 7 (September 1929): 266–77; 8 (December 1929): 375–87; 9 (March 1930): 13–34.

Peery, Dan W. "The Indians' Friend, John H. Seger." *Chronicles of Oklahoma* 10 (December 1932): 570–91; 11 (June 1933): 843–68.

Penn, Julius A. "Roughing It in the '80's." *Daily Oklahoman,* April 22, 1909.

Peters, Joseph P., comp. *Indian Battles and Skirmishes on the American Frontier, 1790–1898.* New York: University Microfilms and Argonaut Press, 1966.

Powell, Peter J. *Sweet Medicine.* Norman: University of Oklahoma Press, 1969.

Powers, Ramon E. "The Kansas Indian Claims Commission of 1869." *Kansas History* 7 (March 1984): 199–211.

Pratt, Richard Henry. *Battlefield and Classroom: Four Decades with the American Indian, 1867–1904.* Ed. Robert M. Utley. New Haven: Yale University Press, 1966.

———. "Some Indian Experiences." *Journal of the U.S. Cavalry Association* 16 (October 1905): 200–217.

Prucha, Francis Paul. *The Great Father: The United States Government and the American Indian.* 2 vols. Lincoln: University of Nebraska Press, 1984.

Records, Laban S. *Cherokee Outlet Cowboy, Recollections of Laban S. Records.* Ed. Ellen Jayne Maris Wheeler. Norman: University of Oklahoma Press, 1995.

Records, Ralph H. "Recollections of April 9, 1892." *Chronicles of Oklahoma* 21 (March 1943): 16–27.

Remington, Frederick. "Artist Wanderings." *Century* 34 (December 27, 1890): 1004–6.

Rickey, Don, Jr. *Forty Miles a Day on Beans and Hay.* Norman: University of Oklahoma Press, 1963.

Ridings, Sam P. *The Chisholm Trail.* Guthrie, Okla.: Co-Operative Publishing, 1936.

Rister, Carl Coke. *Land Hunger.* Norman: University of Oklahoma Press, 1942.

———. "Significance of Destruction of the Buffalo." *Southwest Historical Quarterly* 33 (July 1929): 34–49.

Roe, Frances M. A. *Army Letters from an Officer's Wife, 1871–1888.* New York: D. Appleton, 1909.

Rucker, Alvin. "Amos Chapman—Hero of Buffalo Wallow." *Daily Oklahoman,* April 14, 1929.

———. "Bullets Curbed Greed at Cherokee Strip Opening." *Daily Oklahoman,* September 15, 22, 1929.

Ruth, Kent, comp. *Oklahoma: A Guide to the Sooner State.* Norman: University of Oklahoma Press, 1941.

Sandoz, Mari. *Cheyenne Autumn.* New York: McGraw-Hill, 1953.

Scott, Hugh Lenox. *Some Memories of a Soldier.* New York: Century Co., 1928.

Seger, John H. *Early Days among the Cheyenne and Arapahoe Indians.* Introduction by Stanley Vestal. Norman: University of Oklahoma Press, 1934.

Seymour, Flora Warren. *Indian Agents of the Old Frontier.* New York: Octagon Books, 1975.

Shirk, George. "Military Duty on the Western Frontier." *Chronicles of Oklahoma* 47 (spring 1969): 118–25.

Stetler, Eugene. "Rivers a Problem to Homesteaders." *Kingfisher Free Press, 75th Anniversary Issue,* April 3, 1964.

Stout, Joseph A. "United States Army Remount Depots: The Oklahoma Experience, 1908–1947." *Military Affairs* 50 (July 1986): 121–26.

Thwaites, Reuben Gold, ed. *James's Account of the S. H. Long Expedition, 1819–20. Early Western Travels.* Cleveland: Arthur H. Clark Co., 1905.

Trask, David F. *The War with Spain in 1898.* New York: Macmillan, 1981.

Veenendaal, Augustus J., Jr. "Herman F. C. Ten Kate, Jr.: An Adventurous Dutch Ethnologist in Indian Territory, 1883." *Chronicles of Oklahoma* 73 (spring 1995): 32–51.

Whenry, Jack L. *Tom Reno and the Chief.* El Reno: El Reno Junior College, 1984.

Wilson, Terry Paul. "The Afrika Korps in Oklahoma: Fort Reno's Prisoner of War Compound." *Chronicles of Oklahoma* 52 (fall 1974): 360–69.

Womack, John. *Norman: An Early History, 1820–1900.* Norman: Author, 1976.

Woods, H. Merel. *Fort Reno, the Protector.* El Reno: El Reno American, 1975.

Wright, Muriel. "A History of Fort Cobb." *Chronicles of Oklahoma* 34 (spring 1956): 52–63.

Wright, Peter M. "The Pursuit of Dull Knife from Fort Reno in 1878–1879." *Chronicles of Oklahoma* 46 (summer 1968): 141–54.

Zogbaum, Rufus. "Life at an Indian Agency." *Harper's Weekly* 34 (January 4, 1890): 8–11.

GOVERNMENT DOCUMENTS—PUBLISHED

Alvord, Henry E. *Report of Special Commissioners to Visit the Kiowas and Comanches, Arrapahoes and Cheyennes, Caddoes, Wichitas, and Affiliated Bands in the Indian Territory.* Washington: GPO, 1872.

Annual Reports of Commissioner of Indian Affairs, 1869–92.

Annual Reports of Secretary of War, 1874, 1889, 1884.

Compilation of the Official Records of the War of the Union and Confederate Armies, War of the Rebellion.

U.S. Army. *Outline Descriptions of the Posts in the Division of the Missouri, U.S. Army. Mil. Div. of the Missouri,* 1876.

U.S. Department of War. *Inventory of Federal Archives in the States.* Series IV, No. 35, Oklahoma. Oklahoma City: Historical Records Survey, 1938.

U.S. Senate. *Correspondence Regarding the Affairs at Guthrie and Oklahoma City, Indian Territory.* 51st Cong., 1st sess., 1889–1890. Sen. Ex. Doc. 72.

———. *Investigation of Conditions of Indians in the Indian Territory.* 40th Cong., 1st sess., 1885. S. Rept. 1278.

———. *Opening of the Cherokee Strip.* 53d Cong., 1st sess., 1893. House Ex. Doc. 27.

———. *Report on Removal of Northern Cheyennes from Sioux Reservation to the Indian Territory.* 46th Cong., 2d sess., 1879–80. Sen. Rept. 708.

———. *Reports on the Settlement of Oklahoma.* 51st Cong., 1st sess., 1889–1890. Sen. Ex. Doc. 33.

———. "Reports of Explorations and Surveys to Ascertain the Most Practicable and Economical Route for a Railroad from the Mississippi River to the Pacific Ocean," Amiel W. Whipple. 33d Cong., 2d sess., 1854–55. Sen. Ex. Doc 78.

GOVERNMENT DOCUMENTS—UNPUBLISHED

Adjutant General's Office, Ltrs. Recd., AGO (Main Series), 1871–80, NA (M666)
Files Relating to Military Operations in the Indian Territory, M-1495, Roll 10, NA
Letters and Telegrams from Fort Sill, 1889, NA
Letters Received by Office of Indian Affairs
    Cheyenne and Arapaho Agency
Office of Indian Affairs, Ltrs. Recd., NA (M234)
    Central Superintendency
    Cheyenne/Arapaho Agency
    Creek Agency
    Upper Arkansas Agency
    Wichita Agency
Papers Relating to Cheyenne/Arapaho Strip Land Opening, Interior Department Territorial Papers (M828, Roll 1).
Papers Relating to Military Operations against the Northern Cheyennes, 1878–79 (M666, Roll 428)
Papers Relating to the 1874–75 Campaign against Arapaho, Cheyenne, Comanche, and Kiowa Bands in Indian Territory (M666, Rolls 159–164)
Papers Relating to the Intrusion by Unauthorized Persons (Boomers) into Indian Territory, etc. (Box 427H or M666, Rolls 471–488)
Records of U.S. Army Continental Commands, NA (RG 393)
    Department of the Missouri, Ltrs. Recd.
    Fort Reno Ltrs. Recd.
    Fort Reno Ltrs. Sent (Bound Vols.)
U.S. Army Military Records, 1874–75, Oklahoma Collection, University of Central Oklahoma

PERIODICALS

Arapaho Bee
Arkansas City Republican-Traveler
Arkansas City Traveler
Army and Navy Journal
Caldwell Commercial
Caldwell Journal
Caldwell Post

Calumet Chieftain
Canadian County Courier
Carrier Pigeon (Darlington)
Cavalry Journal
Century Magazine
Cherokee Advocate
Cheyenne Transporter
Chicago Tribune
Daily Inter-Ocean
Daily Oklahoman
Daily Oklahoma State Capital (Guthrie)
Dodge City Times
El Reno American
El Reno Globe
El Reno (Weekly) Globe
El Reno Democrat
El Reno Eagle
El Reno Herald
El Reno News
El Reno Times
El Reno Tribune
El Reno Weekly Globe
Emporia News
The Friend
Friends' Review
Frisco Herald
Guthrie Daily Leader
Guthrie State Capital
Harper's Illustrated Weekly
Indian Citizen (Atoka)
Indian Methodist (Muskogee)
Industrial Head Light (El Reno)
Inter-Ocean (Chicago)
Kansas City Gazette
Kansas City Star
Kansas City Times
Kansas Cowboy (Dodge City)
Kansas Daily Tribune
Kingfisher Free Press
Kingfisher Times
Leavenworth Daily Conservative
Leavenworth Times
Muskogee Phoenix
New York Herald
New York Times
New York Tribune
Newsletter, Oklahoma Archeological Survey (Norman)
Norman Transcript

Okarche Times
Oklahoma Democrat (El Reno)
Oklahoma State Capital
Oklahoma War Chief
Purcell Register
St. Louis Post-Dispatch
St. Louis Republic
Sunday Oklahoman
Topeka Commercial
Topeka Commonwealth
Watonga Republican
Wichita Beacon
Wichita Eagle
Wichita (Weekly) Eagle
Yukon Sun

OTHER SOURCES

Brothers, Rex. Unpublished manuscript on Fort Reno and Darlington (personal copy).

Welge, William D. "Colonial Experience on Cobb Creek: A Modest Attempt of Indian Acculturation." Master's Thesis, University of Central Oklahoma, 1988.

Wright, Peter Melton. "Fort Reno, Indian Territory." Master's Thesis, University of Oklahoma, 1965.

INDEX

Wade, Col. James F., 153, 155–56, 165, 174–77, 182, 185, 188–89, 209, 253
Waite, Lt. Henry D., 170–71
Walk-a-bit (Arapaho), 18
Walker, Lt. Kirby, 193, 199
Walnut Creek, 113
Walter, George, 154
Walter Reed Hospital, 224
Walters, Col. William P.: grave, 226
Walton, Gov. Jack, 228
Wano, Pete (Potawatomi), 142–43
War Department, 1, 3, 27, 100, 117, 131, 203, 210–11, 216, 221; officials, 78
Washington, D.C., 8, 12, 21, 27, 81–82, 90, 92, 103, 109, 113, 115, 152, 154, 167, 171, 221, 225
Washita campaign, 165
Washita Cattle Company ranch, Ind. Terr., 146
Washita River, 8, 17, 32, 51, 54, 146–47, 149, 178, 256; Black Kettle attacked, 102
Waterbury, Capt. William M., 193
Watkins, William, 25
Watonga, Okla., 255
Watson, M. M., 228
Watts, Capt. Charles H., 174
Waynoka, Okla., 153, 192–93
Wedemeyer, Capt. William G., 78
Weekly Republican Traveler, 185
Weeks, Maj. Henry J., 220
Weir, A. J., 259
Wellington, Kans., 119
Wells-Fargo Express Company, 176
Well's store, 115
Wellston, Okla., 115
Wessells, Lt. Morris C., 80
Western Cattle Trail, 96
Western Hospital for the Insane, 228
Wharton station, Ind. Terr., 198
Wheaton, Capt. Charles, 80
Wheeler, Lt. Fred, 86
Whenry, Dr. Jack, 226
Whirlwind (Cheyenne), 24, 30, 81, 103, 126, 131, 169; war bonnet, 77
White Antelope (Cheyenne), 46, 140
White Bead Hill, 142
White Bear (Arapaho), 36
White Horse (Cheyenne), 31, 124, 126
White River, 63
White Shield (Cheyenne), 28, 103–4, 188
White Turtle (Cheyenne), 188
Wichita, Kans., 4, 15, 19, 21, 26–27, 39, 41, 46–47, 49, 52, 55–57, 77–78, 82, 85, 98, 115–16, 195, 248, 253; federal court, 118

Wichita agency, 11, 20–21, 23, 30–31, 46, 97; fight at, 28
Wichita Beacon, 93
Wichita/Caddo reservation, 204
Wichita Eagle, 47, 84, 131, 154, 157, 184, 196, 200
Wichita Indians, 6, 12
Wichita Mountains, 207
Wichita reservation, 4, 183–84, 189
Wicks, Rev. John B., 107
Wilcox, Maj. John A., 82
Wilder, Lt. Wilbur E., 56, 59, 63, 66–67, 81
Wild Hog (Northern Cheyenne), 55, 57, 59–60, 246; wife, 81
Wilkinson, Capt. C. A., 220
Williams, Ben, 22, 32, 36
Williams, Edwin F., 9–10, 237
Williams, Gilbert B., 181
Williams, John F., 9
Williams, U.S. Deputy Marshal W. B., 117
Williams, W. G. "Caddo Bill," 48, 174
Williston, Maj. Edward B., 253
Willow Springs, Ind. Terr., 156
Winfield, Kans., 129, 151, 161
Wint, Capt. Theodore J., 39
Wint, George, 229
Wister, Thomas, 6
Wolf Creek, 4, 17, 46, 54, 89, 97, 101, 246
Wolf Hair (Cheyenne), 204–5
Wood, Lt. Abram E., 61, 63, 67, 86; orders troops to fire, 66; promotion, 75
Wood, S. N., 237
Woodbury, Lt. Thomas C., 56
Woodson, Capt. Alfred E., 142, 150, 156, 162, 205, 256; arranges counsel for Cheyenne, 207; named Cheyenne/Arapaho agent, 204; puts up bail for Cheyenne, 206
Woodward, Okla., 101, 153, 159, 191, 193, 208
World War I, 219
World War II, 219, 221, 224–25
WPA, labor used at Fort Reno, 221–22
Wyoming, 51, 72, 167, 216, 220

Yeatman, Maj. Richard T., 213
Yellow Bear (Arapaho), 102, 243
YL ranch, Ind. Terr., 128
Young, Pvt. Clark, 35
Young Whirlwind (Cheyenne), 178

Zogbaum, Rufus, 165; sketch by, 152; visit to Darlington, 169–70